795
01
MC

Choice and the Politics of Allocation

Choice and the Politics of Allocation

A Developmental Theory

by David E. Apter

New Haven and London: Yale University Press

1971

Published with assistance from the
Kingsley Trust Association Publication Fund
established by the Scroll and Key Society of Yale College.

Library of Congress catalog card number: 70–151566
International standard book number: 0–300–01444–9

Designed by John O. C. McCrillis
and set in Garamond type.
Printed in the United States of America by
The Carl Purington Rollins Printing-Office of
the Yale University Press, New Haven, Connecticut.

Distributed in Great Britain, Europe, and Africa by
Yale University Press, Ltd., London; in Canada by
McGill-Queen's University Press, Montreal; in Mexico
by Centro Interamericano de Libros Académicos,
Mexico City; in Central and South America by Kaiman
& Polon, Inc., New York City; in Australasia by
Australia and New Zealand Book Co., Pty., Ltd.,
Artarmon, New South Wales; in India by UBS Publishers'
Distributors Pvt., Ltd., Delhi; in Japan by John
Weatherhill, Inc., Tokyo.

Published under the auspices of the Institute of International
Studies, University of California, Berkeley.

For

H. A.

and

P. G. S.

Contents

Figures

Acknowledgments

A book of this nature, with its tone and purposes, is too personal to blame on collaborators. My debts to friends and colleagues are enormous, even though in innumerable instances I do violence to their ideas. In an enterprise of this kind it is no good claiming shelter, not even the sort that comes with hospitality.

I must first thank the Warden and Fellows of All Souls College, Oxford University, for granting me a visiting fellowship during 1967–68 that allowed me to write up these thoughts in an exceptionally congenial and pleasant atmosphere. I am grateful, too, to the Guggenheim Foundation for a fellowship enabling me to accept the All Souls appointment. My friends and colleagues on the Politics of Modernization Project of the Institute of International Studies at the University of California were the specific sources of inspiration for many of these ideas. Some of our arguments and discussions have been transmuted into the words that appear on these pages. To Mario Barrera, Torquato Di Tella, Ernst Haas, José Nun, Magali Sarfatti, Carlos Strasser, and Ivan Vallier this book owes a great deal, although quite often they may not be able to agree with the form it has taken. I particularly acknowledge the help of Oscar Oszlak of the Instituto Torquato Di Tella in Buenos Aires and Berkeley, and William Ascher and Guillermo O'Donnell of Yale. They went over the manuscript in detail, proposed many changes in formulation, and pointed out a number of important inconsistencies as well as errors in logic and formulation. Finally, to Mrs. Gloria Mims and Mrs. Cleo Stoker I must record special debts. The former typed innumerable drafts of this book with unfailing cheerfulness and unflagging zeal. The latter protected me when the pressures of administrative duty became excessive.

D. E. A.

Yale University
December 1970

A Point of Departure

Let us consider two questions. One concerns empirical research and the character of findings in the social sciences. It can be phrased in the following form: How much is it necessary to know in order to explain? Answers will depend, among other things, on the nature of the research problem and on the size of the units or systems being examined. Broad macrosystems require a different data strategy from specialized microsystems. What represents irrelevant detail from one point of view may be the focus of new information from another. At each level, data are affected and a relevant universe is defined.

The other question is personal and intellectual. It concerns the character of "real" problems, problems moreover that seem to proliferate at every turn. We ask: What are the tasks of theory when confronted with such problems? The world has never before undergone such dramatic changes. They dwarf both in scope and in significance earlier historic revolutions, even those once seen as demarcating points of change. Today the whole world is *engagé*. The "participation revolution" is no ordinary revolution in the sense that it represents some particular event sufficiently powerful to serve as a promontory for changes elsewhere. Now all such events are part of a more general turmoil. No place is immune. No country is privileged. The revolution is total. And it undermines all previous definitions of it.

The first question, a professional one, is how to deal with the organization of research and the development of technique. Such a preoccupation produces a need for those who emphasize rules of logic, verification, and the possible formulation of laws. The second question, an intellectual one, involves a different emphasis and even a different language. It is symbolic, arrogant at times, emotive, hortatory, thrusting, and personal. It begins with a need to change the universe and bend professionalism to that end.

The professional emphasis without the intellectual one is pale and sterile or worse. The intellectual without the professional is idiosyncratic, presumptuous, and possibly autocratic because behind the drama of action may lurk punitive self-righteousness. The central object of this book is to try to bring together the professional and intellectual outlooks in a political synthesis. We hope to point a way toward a conceptual synthesis that, avoiding simplistic solutions to complex problems, nevertheless allows us to sustain an involvement in problems along with a professional modesty. Such an approach refuses to accept a view of society that sees the virtue of the damned as the sole criterion for politics. This view is as gloomy and negative as it is innocent, and although critically important it is too narrow. Social morality is not the special attribute of marginal persons; to regard society merely as hostage to them and their condition as the definition of injustice or inequity is by itself an insufficient basis for political theory. Yet because social morality is so important, such views continue to lie behind the two prevailing approaches in political theory, both of which in my opinion lead to inadequate conclusions.

One approach, a liberal notion, seeks improvement of the conditions of democracy by reforming political mechanisms so that they more adequately reflect public need. Marginal persons are poor or outside the scheme of things. Improve their lot and the goals of stability and harmony will be achieved. Such a liberal viewpoint pervades the American discipline of political science, including group-interest and pluralistic theories of politics, and has resulted in the redefinition in such terms of the significance of all events, from the Gracchi revolts in the Roman Republic to the American Revolution. The other approach, a radical one, is embodied in the proposition that proper recognition of the claims of a society's marginal persons will result in the continuous transformation of society itself. Although this is the view toward which I am inclined, I believe it is more a critique of what is wrong than a solution for what needs to be done. Continuous revolution, despite its liberating force at a given moment, also unleashes other forces that are less rewarding, such as opportunism, cynicism, and political manipulation—all made worse by the invocation of higher motives. Hence if revolutionaries are serious people they need to be serious about the consequences of revolutions as well as the making of them. Indeed, the field of combat in political theory is already littered with the pennants and armor of primitive radicals, many of whom shed their doctrines after only a few more or less bloody preliminary engagements. All the more urgent, then, is the need for a wider and more capable theory; that is, one able to capture normative truths without paying some exorbitant ideological price. Sought is some mode of reckoning between the liberal and radical normative points of departure so that a structural theory may come closer to the spectrum of working politics, where events have many meanings and purposes.

We will employ three levels of analysis. The first, using a combination of functional and dialectical methods, will establish normative and structural boundaries around choice. These in turn will be translated into a simple equilibrium political model. The terms of this model will be put into descriptive variables. The descriptive variables will examine the political model in modernizing and industrial societies with a view to determining certain behavioral processes which we will call "embourgeoisement" and "radicalization." Such responses will serve as reference points for a prescriptive or normative statement of the political model with a remedial purpose in mind.

We will attempt this by using two main criteria for the evaluation of political systems. One is appropriate for modernizing societies and the other for industrial ones. In the case of the former the primary "test" is the effect a government can have on the form of development that expands choice and distributes it through a population. In the case of industrial societies the criterion is equity, not development, and its consequences in terms of the relationship between allocation and participation. Marginals are thus critical indicators of political responsibilities because their condition defines the limits of public commitment. However, since equity is a broad concept made up of a multiplicity of norms, the greater the degree of participation the more anomalies are likely to result, penalizing government and diluting its moral imperatives. In this sense even a good government, capable of responding to the diversity of its members and their needs, may come to abdicate its responsibilities.

This does not mean that a developing society is more likely to be "radical" and an industrial society more "liberal." Indeed, as I think I can show, the opposite is more likely the case. But no matter what tendencies prevail in any given case, it is not an either-or matter. A particular mixture of radicalism and liberalism may define a normative and structural framework that will vary in content and form according to place and time.

That all real systems show a huge discrepancy between liberal or radical theory and its practice should not serve to dismay us but rather to encourage us in the search for still other ways of understanding. If the daily life of politics results in compromises and makes continuous change characteristic of even the most monolithic and totalitarian of societies, then we need categories that are neither liberal nor radical but that are capable of including both. To this end the immediate past has not served us well. Both intellectual and professional studies of recent events, nationalism, socialism, development, and so on, have been cast in liberal or radical terms that occasionally have failed to conceal a dramatist viewpoint. Some force representing progress is seen as working its way through history, uncertainly perhaps, and continuously thwarted by wicked men and evil institutions, but inexorably and in the end triumphantly. This view, compelling though it is, is a snare for the unsuspecting. Big events disguise many realities, but the "force of progress" is not one of them. What is required is a better set of theories whose modes of observation will be neither those of the primitive radical searching for political hope through revolution nor those of the liberal cynic, artful and benign, viewing political life as a series of good or bad theatrical performances.

An analytical theory works best when, by means of a few highly powerful a priori variables, it establishes certain hypotheses that may be applied empirically. Such hypotheses, if sufficiently sensitive, ought to draw attention to the general propositions contained in particular facts, with results that are cumulative and capable of wide empirical application by means of comparative or another form of analysis. Too much emphasis on abstraction cripples our ability to see the world with freshness and common sense and, most important, to interpret it in ordinary language. Too much emphasis on technique and empirical data without a relevant intellectual context (the current trend) reduces us to the level of a child who has been given a high-powered microscope and asked to describe what he sees. The specifications of an analytical theory needed for such matters as unit variation and boundaries of explanation are (1) an interrelated set of general variables capable of generating systematic hypotheses; (2) an intermediate set of analytical variables capable of empirical operationalization linking general systemic hypotheses with concrete units of observation; (3) a technique for handling large numbers of empirical variables in terms of measurement and covariation; (4) a set of criteria for validation of both logical models and empirical propositions; and (5) an established set of new empirical propositions that form a basis for new theories.

In this volume we cannot deal with all such matters but will attempt to be explicit about the first two. The point of departure is a division of the general dimension of structure into the normative and the structural. The normative level of theory is basically cultural and intellectual. It begins with the observer as ego, as the center of the universe. The concern is whether such a universe is benign or hostile, good or bad, conservative or destructive. These are preoccupations of the observer as participant and also as moral being, and the form of the discussion is dialectical. The structural level is professional. It can be, but is not necessarily, anti-intellectual. It starts with a unit of observation, and the emphasis is on discovering the relationship of this unit to other units or of the components of the unit to each other. A key problem with the structural approach is the matter of of control, for experimental control groups to apply to macrounits are lacking.

It should be noted that discussion of political parties is omitted. This is because as political mechanisms they represent units *for* analysis rather than *of* analysis. In any concrete research applying the theories discussed in this book, political parties, movements, coalitions, and factions represent actual strategies by means of which society, elites, and government relate to each other in the making of public policy. We have dealt with them in other books and do not wish to go over that ground again here. They will emerge as primary units for analysis in empirical research.

Our kind of approach has important implications for any student of human affairs, as we hope to show. The most important implication of the structural-normative combination is the need for the observer to synthesize the roles of intellectual and professional. In order to discover "meaning" in its totality, he must continuously move between these roles—between involvement and reflection, sectarianism and universalism. He can no more be a normative prig than a professional automaton. The more whole-hearted the participation and direct the involvement, the more intensely personal the experience of meaning. Indeed, in this sense, outrage is an excellent tool of research, although perhaps not a useful guide to action.

Where should such research lead? Eventually to an improved policy—to better political conduct. It was a relatively minor British author who gave expression many years ago to what now is surely a widely held view:

> Nothing is more rooted in my mind than the vast distinction between the individual and the class. Take a man by himself, and there is generally some reason to be found in him, some disposition for good. Mass him with his fellows in the social organism, and ten to one he becomes a blatant creature, without a thought of his own, ready for any evil to which contagion prompts him. It is because nations tend to stupidity and baseness that mankind moves so slowly; it is because individuals have a capacity for better things that it moves at all.[1]

1. See George Gissing, *The Private Papers of Henry Ryecroft* (New York: Modern Library, 1913), p. 40.

1. The Structural Theory and Its Boundaries

This theory is designed to suggest alternative ways of understanding and solving a central problem of contemporary politics, the relationship between development and order. If such a relationship is unmanageable, political life will be little more than a set of narrow escapes sandwiched between catastrophes. The theory implies that both terms of the relationship can be made subject to planning and control. To identify systems of order that do not penalize development and patterns of development that do not jeopardize order is the object of this inquiry.

Development and order are obviously complex; many factors, ecological, normative, and structural, impinge upon them. In most theories the extent of development and the maintenance or degree of order are seen as independent variables. This is an appropriate emphasis for studies of newly independent societies. Our immediate concern is with finding a suitable political framework for maximizing both these variables. We will define a suitable political system as one with appropriate relationships between legitimacy and participation, which will in turn draw our attention to normative and structural variables. For this purpose it is useful to regard norms and structures as independent, and development and order as dependent variables. We do this as a matter of strategy, fully aware that norms and structures are also in part determined by the level of development as well as the degree of order that obtain in a system. We wish to suggest which normative and structural mixtures will be likely to bring about a new stage in the process.

Our point of departure is choice, the scope of possible alternatives open to persons in society. Structurally, choices are manifested in roles, which represent social options. Choice is related to development and order in the following way. Development is the set of system changes corresponding and leading to the expansion of choice. Controlling individual relationships while people are choosing and demanding broader choice is the classic problem of order as defined by Hobbes. Development and order are interrelated. Disorder may make development more difficult to achieve, by affecting, for example, the rate of development whenever resources available for development are diverted into maintaining order. In turn, development may generate disorder. These and other seemingly paradoxical conditions that concern us arise from the emphasis on choice as a basic characteristic of human action.

How can order be maintained while choice expands? The ultimate answer is a rationalistic one. We need to identify and assess the differing priorities and concerns men set for themselves again and again as development continues, recognizing that whatever order is maintained hinders the rectification of certain perceived injustices. No political system and no political solutions are permanent. Sometimes the change is abrupt and catastrophic. Sometimes the change is slow and subtle. For years scholars of politics have tried to locate the best methods of rule, those that in the face of varied political pressures and changes seem best able to promote growth and stability, development and order. Their emphasis contrasts with the one commonly employed by economists and others whose concern is with the mechanisms of economic growth (with political aspects held residual, or, more likely, with a liberal political framework assumed), and it shows concern for the political means available for new social solutions, or ultimately the norms and structures that men can live by.

Choice is not, of course, a particularly novel point of departure. David Easton is concerned with normative aspects of choice when he emphasizes an essentially distributive notion of values in his definition of a political system. The concept of the "authoritative allocation of values" has relevance because it presupposes some restrictions on choice and some means to specify priorities or alternatives.

One difficulty with Easton's concept is that it fails to distinguish clearly between values in general, core or central values for society, and specific political values (what Almond called political culture). Obviously, what discrepancies might exist between them would generate conflicts over means and ends. Accordingly, we will distinguish between priority-setting norms for society as a whole, using the term "equity of allocation," and those governing the distribution of political power or political equity. These, when examined in the form of ideologies, can be evaluated in terms of the congruity between them, i.e. by analyzing their content. In turn, such evaluation will require an interpretive standard. We have used the terms consummatory and instrumental for this purpose in order to determine whether the norms in question are final or ultimate ends or variable and immediate. Hence, the following variables are built into the normative boundary of choice: (1) the content of specific ideologies, (2) the relations between core or central and political values, and (3) the distribution of end-states and ends, or consummatory and instrumental values.

Harold Lasswell's notion of "who gets what, when, how" is more structural. It emphasizes relations between actors, since choice is not limited by properties of objects and events but only by other persons; the mechanisms of allocation are the key concerns. Both men share an interest in the scope of choice, one stressing the normative, and the other the structural.

Preferring a more specific structural emphasis than Easton and a more specific normative emphasis than Lasswell, we want to combine both the normative and the structural to determine the social conditions of choice rather than which choices are made. This differs from concepts of choice employed by Kenneth Arrow, R. Duncan Luce and others more interested in individual choices and the motivational conditions under which they are made. In short, at this stage of analysis we are less concerned with what selections are made than with what alternatives are possible. We are interested in how the problem manifests itself at various degrees of development in order to determine the appropriate political mixture for the next stage. Indeed, in our view the difference between a structural and a behavioral theory of choice is that the former seeks to define the circumstances under which choices are possible, whereas the latter attempts to discover the reasons for the selection of particular options.

Our concept of structure represents the totality of distributions taking place in a society. Such distributions can be identified in many ways. For example, they can be observed from the standpoint of the economic marketplace or the political marketplace. Liberal economic theory deals with the former and pluralistic political theory with the latter. In our view, both are too limited. They disguise preferences for particular methods of distribution, the one favoring a free market, the other a system of voting and representative government. Neither is sufficiently general to encompass the problem of distribution as a whole.

Our solution to this is to regard distribution as an allocation problem with roles as claims on resources. The ranking of roles according to how much they can command—what we call stratification—answers the question of how allocation occurs. In turn, allocation can be divided into several variables: the discrete distribution of roles, the criteria of ranking and access, the relation between roles that are clustered in society as a whole, or classes, and those that have particular reference to political power, or strategic elites. These variables compose our second boundary around choice. The basic model is derived from both the normative and structural boundaries and the relationships between them.

The general formulation is a modification of structural components employed originally by Talcott Parsons and Edward Shils in their description of the theory of action.[1] However, as Neil Smelser points out, their point

1. See Talcott Parsons and Edward A. Shils, eds., *Toward a General Theory of Action* (Cambridge: Harvard University Press, 1951) p. 53.

of reference is the individual actor, precisely what we are excluding.[2] In this respect the model is closer to Smelser's formulation. We accept his distinction between values and norms, in which the former is more general than the latter, and we add to it the translation of norms into those dealing with equity, from our point of view the specific source of legitimacy. Although the model will rely on structural and normative factors and by and large exclude behavioral ones, we should be able to specify the behavioral factors needed for a total theory of choice.

If *behavior* is the independent variable, then the unit is the *individual,* action is seen as maximizing or "satisficing," the basic model is the rationalistic pursuit of self-interest in (a) the economic market and (b) the political market.

If *structure* is the independent variable, then the unit is the *role,* action is determined by functionality, which in turn is based on needs of the collectivity and distributed according to (a) requisite functions and structures and (b) nonrequisite functions and structures.

If *norms* are the independent variable, then the unit is the *collectivity,* action is determined dialectically, which in turn is based on changes or altered patterns of meaning resulting from (a) symbolization and (b) ideological conflict.

To summarize briefly, our theoretical components begin with action. The action that concerns us is choice. The first boundary around the action of choice we call norms. Norms represent the meanings of choice. The second boundary around choice is structure. Structure represents the relations of choice. The third boundary is behavior. Behavior is the motivation for choice. The first two boundaries limit the terms of the third, or, the third defines the limits of the first two.[3]

The procedure to be followed will be a bit cumbersome because first we want to deal with these matters abstractly. For every abstract term we will then employ a directly empirical surrogate. For the analysis of norms, for example, we will be concerned with social and political equity. For the analysis of structure, we will be concerned with patterns of allocation. Regularities in empirical relationships should have analytical counterparts in the relations of the theory. Specific hypotheses will be derived and descriptive categories used in identifying data. When this larger task is accomplished it should be possible to describe a normative

2. See Neil J. Smelser, *Theory of Collective Behavior* (New York: The Free Press of Glencoe, 1963), pp. 24–34.

3. See Peter Winch, *The Idea of a Social Science* (London: Routledge and Kegan Paul, 1958), for an analysis of the epistemological aspects of the relations between these three dimensions.

model capable of suggesting certain policy priorities. The theory itself relies primarily on distributional variables.

Before going further let us make clear what we mean by the terms *choice* and *development*. In our usage development refers to the expansion of choice opportunities, alternative modes of action available to a given population in any society. Choice is the range of role options open in a system at any given time. Behavior then refers to the capacity of individuals to perceive the alternatives and make efficacious decisions. It should be understood that if structure is primarily concerned with role alternatives and different arrangements of roles, then analytically the conditions of choice can be translated into social structures. With a structural theory the empirical task will be to determine the consequences of different distributions of roles at various degrees of development on the range of options open to individuals or groups.

As indicated norms refer to the prescriptive preferences prevailing in a system, that is, the principles of equity. Some of these will be very generalized and broadly accepted prescriptions of right or wrong that define the objects and meaning of role relationships. Such prescriptions may be embodied in religious beliefs or in political ideologies. The more general principles of equity we see as societal norms. Political norms deal with governmental decisions. Both are political in the sense that they define the manner of role relationships, but the compatibility of societal and political norms may vary considerably. If they vary greatly, legitimacy is likely to be threatened.

Norms, structures, and behavior are thus the three main components of choice. Theories of choice can be based on the combination of any two to determine the third. An analysis of normative and behavioral combinations allows us to infer structure because the analysis of norms and behaviors would result in the identification of roles. (This is essentially what anthropologists do when they study an ethnic group never before examined.) Similarly, the analysis of behavior and structure will allow the inference of norms. This has been a critical feature of the macrotheories of Emile Durkheim, Max Weber, Talcott Parsons, and psychologists who have concentrated on the articulation of normative prescriptions.

Insofar as development levels change and open up new ranges of choice, particular combinations of norms and structures affect the capacities of individuals to make choices. Which alternatives they choose—perhaps the most fascinating area of inquiry of all—can best be studied after the normative and structural factors are understood.

With these definitions in mind the first element of the structural theory can now be introduced. In any system the beliefs about how choices or claims on choices should be allocated as well as beliefs about what choices should be available constitute the normative boundary. This, in general terms, is a matter of values and more explicitly, of ideology. We can call this normative parameter a distribution of beliefs about allocation or, more explicitly, *equity of allocation*. The second element of the theory involves the way allocation occurs by means of the distribution of roles. We can refer to this simply as allocation. The social conditions of choice, then, are determined by the way people think allocation should occur and by the way it does occur. If these are in good fit, if there are not many discrepancies between them, then a condition of order prevails; and legitimacy and participation are in balance.

Historically speaking, such periods of good fit are temporary. This temporality, in effect, is what generates the political problem that we see as twofold. First, there is the problem of maintaining order itself, possible by sustaining a good balance between how people want choices to be distributed and how they are actually distributed. Second, there is the problem of development, or how to maximize the satisfactions that people may actually obtain by increasing the potential range of alternatives. Ideally both should be solved by increased output; but this is often not the case. Pressures to develop occur when it is not possible to realize equity of allocation because reallocation is politically impossible within given limits of resources. Development in turn will change beliefs about equitable allocation. Thus, development and order are in a continuously dynamic relationship that manifests itself in normative-structural imbalances.

Further, in our theory such imbalances will define a "field of political information." More specifically, political information includes knowledge of what people believe to be equitable allocation and what the pattern of role allocation actually is. Three main types of political information may be delineated. The first includes broad public reaction to social conditions, which we will call "populist." The second refers to more specific organized responses on the basis of what we will call "interests." The third, which involves technical knowledge and remedial knowledge about the ways and means of expanding choice or analyzing the obstacles that lie in its path, we call "professional." Populist information arises on a societal level, whereas interest and professional information inheres at lower levels. Government is the key functional unit able to utilize all three types of information in order to maximize both development and order in society. How specific governments make use of all three types of information will vary with the type of political system. This brings us to the second set of elements in the theory, the relationship between political norms and political allocation.

The political system constitutes its own relationship between political norms and structures. *Political norms* are those that translate general ideological predispositions at the societal level into specific statements of how rule shall be accomplished in the light of larger social goals, specifically in terms of the principles of access and governance. *Participation,* the political analogue to allocation, refers to the breadth and degree of significance of such access, which is what is normally meant by the term *structure of authority.*

The political system is obviously linked to the social system in several ways. Its "driving force" derives from normative and structural imbalances at the general societal level. Its information, we have said, derives from these. But the political system is a special subsystem, in the sense that it has a capacity to change the social system of which it is a part. How a society responds to the problems of development and order is in part a matter of how the political system determines the response. With this formulation what begins as an apparently simple statement becomes very complex. Not only does it involve an elaborate set of political and social relationships analytically defined, but it implies that the concrete units follow a specific order of generality and significance.

By examining any development sequence as a departure from any point of order (equilibrium), we can determine the pattern of discrepancy between equity norms about allocation and role stratification in society as a whole. By observing the particular relationship of political norms and the distribution of political roles (political elite roles) in terms of how well they restore the normative and structural balance for society as a whole we can determine the efficiency of different types of political systems. Persistent failure to restore the balance will lead to a new relationship between political norms and participation, and a different political system.

How these normative beliefs about participation are distributed represents discrepancies and generates conflicts. No matter how integrated, however, they will always be different from the actual mechanisms of participation both for society as a whole, i.e., in role stratification, and in the degree of access to decision-making possible for competing elites. To analyze the latter we need to cut through specific institutional mechanisms to include possible participation outside of more familiar organs such as political parties in relationship to legislative bodies. That combination is so persistent that we tend to universalize its practice, but we need to remain sensitive to other alternatives. One basis for the charge of ethnocentricity leveled at contemporary pluralists is that they take Western institutional mechanisms as substantial evidence of universality.

We do not deal with questions of legitimacy in this analysis, preferring to draw attention to what constitutes the source of political norms. Such an emphasis turns attention away from mechanisms and toward the relationships between our two sets, the one social and the other political, with political information as the link. A crucial assumption is that relevant information about the discrepancies between equity of allocation and allocation differs from other kinds of knowledge. The discrepancy itself creates a political obligation, i.e., a political norm.[4] The content of political information in society corresponds to a demand for recognition at the political level and defines rights. Populist information means citizen "rights." Interest information means the right of specific groups to make their demands explicit and heard. Technical information means the right of those who have special knowledge to have it applied. Restating the structural theory, then in its simplest terms, *equity of allocation is to allocation as political norms are to political participation.* The linking variable is information. This gives us a minimal equilibrium statement of the structural theory which we can diagram. (See Figure 1.1)

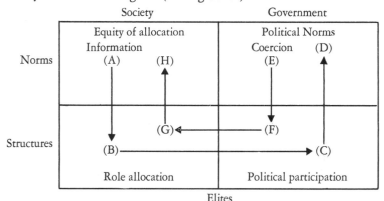

Figure 1.1. The structural theory of politics

The arrow A-B indicates how information arises. The line B-C indicates how this is divided into types, populist, interest, and professional. The line C-D indicates how it is translated into messages involving obligations, i.e., informational warrants for government. Thus, the line A-B in Figure 1.1 indicates the *source* of political information, which we have described as the discrepancy between public beliefs about the equity of allocation and allocation itself. This we have classified into three types,

4. Of course, not all information received by government is treated as an obligation. Governments do not simply act on information. Information recognized but not accepted as an obligation implies postponed or alternative actions or coercion.

populist, interest, and professional. However, such information cannot properly speaking be information until it is converted into messages. The line B-C represents the *conversion* process, and we see this being accomplished by members of the elite of any society. Finally, at the point at which these messages are accepted by government they become obligations, or, more properly, they define the norms to which government grants greatest credence. The line C-D is a transformation of messages into normative warrants. In this manner the legitimacy of political norms is reinforced by virtue of its responsiveness to information, a communication sequence itself requiring a source, a conversion, and a transformation.

Furthermore, an opposite process that follows a reverse procedure is at work. This is *coercion,* by which we mean punitive actions by government against groups or members of the society. It is supposed to reduce the consequences of uncertainty, although it may actually generate more uncertainty in the process. Coercion is applied as follows. The source, E-F, is the activation of some previously defined norms of legitimacy— such as preserving the society from destruction or from some principle of potentiality or belief, such as the universality of an ideology or a goal. The conversion to punitive action is undertaken by an elite responding primarily to government rather than to the society, F-G in our diagram. The end process is G-H or the restriction of permissible norms in society.

The effect of coercion on information is to eliminate its source. The information transformation process is stopped. Conversion into messages does not occur. The discrepancy between widely held beliefs about the equity of allocation and its discrepancy with respect to allocation is not registered. Populism becomes a ritual expression of loyalty. Interests are defined by government. Professionality becomes a form of espionage.

The restriction of norms of equity is the object of coercion because it means the obligation of society is fixed by government action. This is one way to establish order. It is otherwise in high information systems, where the obligation of government is defined by society. As we shall try to show later on, some political systems emphasize coercion and others information.[5] Much will be said about consequences in political systems that emphasize coercion in preference to information. Perfect coercion in theory might equal perfect information or its perfect absence, which is the same thing. No system could in practice eliminate political uncertainty. The real question is how to deal with it when attempting to maximize development and order.

5. This critical distinction has been advanced in a rather less systematic way in my previous writings.

We turn now to the concrete units represented in the structural theory. The first, the largest unit under examination, is society. The second, the smallest subunit of society with a defined responsibility for the maintenance and adaptation to the unit as a whole, is government. The third—the elite—is a linkage group that is more general than government and less general than society. We use the term *elite* with reference to access to decision-making not with any reference to prestige.

To summarize once again, the model consists of six variables, all of them interrelated: equity of allocation, role allocation, political norms, political participation, information, and coercion. The first two variables define the source of information and identify obligation in political terms. The third and fourth variables define the political system and its effect on the principles of equity in the degree to which it applies coercion. The three requisite concrete units are society, government, and elites. Other concrete units will be referred to as they affect the flow of information and coercion.

THE BOUNDARIES OF THE MODEL

Although many questions are raised by this formulation (the structural consequences of inadequate information and coercion for both society and the political system, for example), for the moment it is important to put the model in a context by locating the parameters within which it is seen to operate. These are, of course, analytical rather than concrete.

The reason development and order are dependent variables in our theory is that they are the two problems attendant upon choice that have the greatest significance for political behavior in real societies. It becomes the task of government, or a group that creates the appropriate governing instrument by changing the political system, to maximize development and order. The response of government to limitations imposed by development and order depends on the manner and amount of information and coercion employed. In theory the solution to maximizing development and order would be for a change in allocation according to any change in belief about equity of allocation to occur at every increment of development. This would imply a political system that in principle would function on the basis of high information and therefore high participation. As an ideal type or formal system it would be perfectly responsive to societal problems resulting from development and it or the government would respond to an information "market" so as to create order.

But in reality there is a set of boundaries that, related to but independent of development, must be made explicit. Returning to our reference to norms, structures, and behavior: it is a key assumption here that norms change dialectically and structures functionally. Although it is true to say that both will change in response to development and in the demands for differing principles of role allocation that arise in a developmental context, this is not the whole story. That is why norms and structures show so many incongruities. Norms are not mere reciprocals of structures. Indeed it is a common weakness of both capitalist and socialist ideologies to assume that a process like industrialization, when pursued in a suitable structural manner, will eventually achieve order. But we now have opened a Pandora's Box that would require us to pay attention to the behavioral aspects of norms and structures, the terms under which socialization and desocialization occur, and the conditions under which political perceptions change. This is part of the behavioral task to be "located" by the structural theory. What we see is not some evolution toward a specific normative order emergent from the appropriate structural one, as with the Marxian vision of the penultimate stage of communism, but the idea that normative change is continuous and dialectical. It is unceasing because behaviorally the dialectics of meaning change the content of symbols, ritualizing some that were once rich in meaning, downgrading others so that they fall into disuse, and generating new ones. Such a normative dialectic presupposes a complex of behavioral factors that can be correlated with generational changes and thresholds of symbolic relevance. Work here will increasingly come to depend on psycholinguistic theories in what constitutes a new and fascinating behavioral ground.[6]

On the structural level and most clearly manifested in postindustrial society, we see a new multifunctionality of institutions as well as their proliferation and differentiation. A host of historical sociologists from Durkheim to Parsons assumed that one of the chief characteristics of industrial as distinct from rural society was the growth of functional specificity. But what is happening in addition is that contemporary institutions—educational, workplace, community—are gradually coming to be more functionally diffuse in their consequences, but not in the same way as in more traditional societies, where the same act or institution performed so many functions. The term *institutional diffuseness* is more appropriate because the same instrumentality may satisfy a number of functions. To avoid confusion, however, it will be better to distinguish the older use of the term from the more contemporary experience by speaking of *institutional multifunctionality*. Bodies that appear to embody specific functional purposes like redevelopment boards, planning commissions, and boards of

6. See particularly Claude Lévi-Strauss, *The Savage Mind* (Chicago: University of Chicago Press, 1969) and *Structural Anthropology* (New York: Basic Books, 1963).

education all have multifunctional consequences and not merely of the latent variety. This involves many more demands on individuals. The new multifunctionality may result in behavioral dysfunctionalities. We mention these points not only to show how the structural and the behavioral relate, but also to suggest why dialectical and functional changes overlap with but are not purely dependent on development and order. Both the behavioral "causes" of dialectical change and the multifunctionality of institutions need to be the basis for separate and special inquiries, the one through work on symbol formation and its relation to norms and the other in research on organizational behavior.[7] Both these aspects of change are described in Figure 1.2.

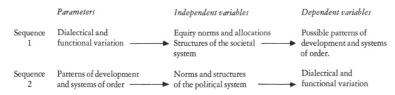

	Parameters	Independent variables	Dependent variables
Sequence 1	Dialectical and functional variation ⟶	Equity norms and allocations Structures of the societal system ⟶	Possible patterns of development and systems of order.
Sequence 2	Patterns of development and systems of order ⟶	Norms and structures of the political system ⟶	Dialectical and functional variation

Figure 1.2. The behavioral context of the structural theory

We have placed the theory in a structural context in order to conceptualize what we regard to be the total problem of political change.[8] We leave the behavioral for another time and to others working more experimentally; discoveries are now being made that are appropriate to a larger theory. Hence our reference to functional and dialectical factors will be in terms of consequences not causes. Our main analysis, which concentrates on the terms of the structural theory itself, is based on a comparison between the problems of postindustrial societies such as the United States and Britain, or increasingly the USSR and Japan, and the problems of modernizing societies. Thus, behavioral problems will be defined and not analyzed. They will become relevant, for example, when we speak of a "loss of meaning" or a decline in political commitment or belief and the search for new ideas. Indeed, if a purely structural approach would incline us toward a "secular-libertarian" model of the political system, the behavioral variables will help us to understand the forces that work in an

7. See, for example, the essays contained in J. R. Lawrence, ed., *Operational Research and the Social Sciences* (London: Tavistock Publications, 1966), and James G. March, ed., *Handbook of Organizations* (Chicago: Rand McNally and Co., 1965).

8. See my article, "Political Studies and the Search for a Framework," in Christopher Allen and R. W. Johnson, eds., *African Perspectives* (Cambridge: Cambridge University Press, 1970).

opposite direction, toward the "sacred-collectivity" model, in which the measure of man is the community and the standard of value contained in an ideal.[9] Hence, although we cannot treat behavioral variables systematically here, we will refer to them particularly as they are relevant to normative change.

DEVELOPMENT AND ORDER

How does development, or expanding choice, occur? Choices expand as a result of men's capacities to increase their control over nature, to be less the victims of it and more the masters. Such a capacity is a function of the kind of information people have at their disposal. The more highly organized or theoretical, the more powerful it is. The more innovative and imaginative, the more quickly it has an effect. If development is a process of growth that reduces scarcity and enlarges choice, implied is the growth of differentiation and specialization. Industrialization is a condition of high innovation on the basis of rapid generation of new information and its application through a technological infrastructure. Modernization can be described as the extension of roles and information generated in an industrial context and applied to a nonindustrial one. We thus divide development into two growth stages: industrialization, where such innovation is high, and modernization, which is derivative.

The "moving edge" of development is where information is generated at the fastest rate and applied with greatest consequence, a situation that occurs in industrial societies.[10] If we define industrial societies as those with the capacity to generate new knowledge at an exceptionally rapid rate and to apply it by means of a technological infrastructure to the expansion of choice, then industrial societies represent the special case that determines the whole process of development. Industrial societies are innovative with respect not only to the amount of information created but to the quality of it as well.

The universal consequence of industrialization is the spread of knowledge and with it the roles most functional to its application. It is this "halo" effect that describes modernization. If modernization is the dissemination of knowledge and the roles appropriate to it, such roles would include those of teacher, planner, engineer, civil servant, economist, and so on. The spread of the roles is intrinsic to the spread of knowledge. Ideas, conveyed in large measure by the printed word, cannot be received by an

9. See my study, *The Politics of Modernization* (Chicago: University of Chicago Press, 1965), pp. 31–33.

10. See the discussion of the role of information creation in Clark Kerr's *The Uses of the University* (New York: Harper & Row, 1966), pp. 87–88.

illiterate population. The special ideas of economists, agronomists, and statisticians cannot be received without an understanding of special theories. Hence, the appropriate spread of roles results in schools, universities, technical institutes, etc. This development of infrastructure, which originates in the need to receive knowledge and information, is that part of development we call modernization. When modernization reaches a point at which the various institutional receptors of information are no longer passive but take an active role in information creation, then we can say that the society is highly modernized. When the society's technological structure is sufficient to translate the information it generates into concrete production, we can say that the society is industrialized.

Our notion of order[11] is more Marxian than Hobbesian. The "war of all against all" is usually considered to be one outer limit to the concept; anomie is the other. But this combination is too broad for what we have in mind. We want to trace specific political relationships between norms and structures to evaluate alternative solutions to the same analytical problems, with disorder seen as the punctuation mark between solutions. This leads us to identify periods of order between revolution on the one hand and more ordinary outbreaks on the other. An example of the latter, strikes (the organization of political movements that may resort to extra-legal or punitive activities), can be seen as arising from a discrepancy between norms and structures, or a disagreement over how norms and structures will be interpreted and adjusted within a period of order. Order, in our use, is a condition of congruity between norms and structures that

11. The term *order* is a confusing one. From one standpoint it has an ominous ring implying a kind of gray dullness, an existence with no life to it. Order implies control, totalitarianism. It can also imply a peaceful, happy community of free souls whose compatibility constitutes noncoercive order. The confusion stems from the common pairing of two terms as antithetical as *freedom* and *order*. In some circumstances freedom is a form of order; in others it is not. Implied in our theory is that where beliefs in equity of allocation and allocation are in balance, order results from freedom. Where such equity notions and allocations are incongruent, then order may be organized coercion. Freedom is not the opposite of order.

Development intensifies inequities; there is no automatic allocation response to an increase in available choices. This is why the relationship between freedom and order is variable. Society may require a period of "unfreedom" in order to prevent disorder while it expands development and thereby provides a more equitable allocation of choices at a later stage. The key here is the coercion variable. How much coercion can be applied before development is reduced? How can freedom be employed so that coercion is not necessary? The paradox is haunting, and answers are not readily forthcoming. To make freedom an absolute value in the early stages of development may simply serve to slow down the expansion of choice. The penalties then are fewer opportunities. To make order an absolute goal is to retard development.

reflects itself in the absence of overt violence. It is an analytical construct rather than an empirical state of affairs, although the former derives from the latter. In a certain sense we are restating an old problem that Marx saw as a relationship between superstructure and infrastructure. Our view is in keeping with his in the sense that the relationship between norms and structures is seen as having diverse characteristics. The normative is considered in terms of the point of view of the members of a system and refers to the gathering and distribution of ideological predispositions by means of which meaning is "attached" to structures. But such meaning does not correspond automatically to the structures themselves, which are also subject to autonomous dialectical variation. Though meaning no doubt can never be too far removed from some structural base, it may over time endow the structures with quite different qualities in the eyes of the members of the society.

If we accept the view that a number of different adjustments are possible, congruity of norms and structures to each other can be seen as continuously changing, phasing in and out. When they are "in" we can speak of a highly integrated system. When they are "out" we can speak of a society that, lacking integration, manifests this lack in "disorder," i.e., in conflicts and violence. Thus disorder is an empirical correlate of the lack of order defined analytically.

One of a number of consequences of disorder is that making policies aimed at restoring the balance becomes a specific political problem for government. If too great a discrepancy exists between widely held beliefs about equity and actual role allocation, then the remedial alternatives are to change the concept of equity or to change the pattern of allocation, the former ordinarily much more difficult to do than the latter. If neither can be done, then one can expect not only disorder but also a change in the political system through which either fresh and different concepts of equity or allocational modifications occur, depending on the character of the political system.

We said earlier that our theory refers to relationships at the societal level and at the level of elites and governments. At the societal level are general norms embodied in ideologies, and structural allocation according to roles; at the other level is the political system. Incongruity at the more general level becomes a political problem at the second. Failure of the political system will mean disorder in society and the possible change of the political system to another type. However, the process can be seen in reverse. Where the relationship between political norms and structures becomes incongruent, conflict and confusion between decision-makers will weaken the ability of government to make decisions, which in turn will undermine the normative-structural basis of society. Marxians will be particularly sensitive to this formulation because it implies the notion that government is of much greater consequence than either Marx or Lenin implied and that it is not only a "permanent" feature of the political landscape, but one of the two "concrete structural requisites" of civil society (the other being the family).

By deliberately considering development and order in the same phrase, we want to emphasize that development produces many possible alternative choices with respect to resolving incongruities between norms and structures, but by doing so also introduces many potential incongruities. Development provides not only the stimulus for incongruities but also new solutions. But it does not do so automatically. Hence the focus is to learn how such opportunities can be realized and how different types of political systems select appropriate strategies. With the present formulation we will view imbalances in society and the political system, the dynamic relationship between them, and the opportunities and penalties embodied in development itself.

EQUITY OF ALLOCATION AND NORMATIVE CHANGE

The term *equity* concretely includes the ideologies that define norms of appropriate distribution. For Marx, this meant superstructure. For Weber, it was an independent variable of his theory. The most general aspect of equity is that it involves nonempirical ends. It refers to absolute principles of right and wrong, good and bad, which can be said to contain a state of political grace, whether ecclesiastical or mundane. Not easily pinned down in terms of some concrete form of achievement, what is involved is the realization of higher purposes and motives. But equity is also empirical. It is a statement of evaluation about allocation that represents a distribution of preferences between consummatory and instrumental values. Referring to particular distributional ends, it measures benefits, pay-offs, and achievements, such as higher wages and shorter hours, higher output, productivity, and increased opportunity. This second aspect of equity measures the developmental efficiency of a political system. The part of equity that relates to ultimate ends or "meaning" we call *consummatory*. The part that relates to concrete ends we call *instrumental*. The relationship between consummatory and instrumental values is intrinsically unstable. Congruity between them is difficult to sustain, even if it is achieved momentarily, because beliefs themselves are unstable.

Political meaning embodied in equity is a result of a dialectical relationship of terms. Sometimes this takes the form of a "debate."[12] Some of the anarchist groups of the last century will serve to illustrate what we mean. Although unsuccessful in accomplishing their purposes, they tried to combine a "religious faith with a rational philosophy" by which through a "violent transformation of society" they hoped to produce a reasonable community of men.[13] The troubled social reaction was due less to their likelihood of success than to the fact that their ideologies, specifically moral, called attention to the dubious inequities embodied both in prevailing beliefs and in allocational practices. Eric Hobsbawm has described some of the more picturesque of these political movements. These include the robber band led by a "Robin Hood" (social banditry), the Mafia, millenarian movements, and labor sects. What these have in common is that they feed on social unrest or disorder. Unable to redefine their norms in terms of the prevailing structure, they indicate profound dismay at the way choice is allocated.[14] Sects, religious reform movements, and millennial movements all are carriers of normative change. Organizationally they may be religious or political. No matter how spiritual and other-worldly the moral belief they uphold, however, their consequences are ultimately political. Political prophets may be stylistically different from religious ones, but their messages are designed for more or less the same audiences. The simplest way to identify norms is to locate heresies and conflicts over orthodoxies, such as those that preoccupied the Church Fathers or characterized the bitter debates over theoretical questions in the Second Internationale. In these the dialectic is embodied in its consummatory aspects. History is strewn with such conflicts of principle: royalists against republicans, absolutists versus conciliarists, Guelfs versus Ghibellines, Protestants against Catholics, Trotskyites against Stalinists.

12. I use the word *debate* advisedly. Normative matters are rarely debated. They are more usually the result of a dialectic of conflict that results in a dialectic of meaning. What a person chooses defines his normative priorities and gives specific meaning to his life. But such choosing is not a solitary affair. It is conditioned and formed in concert with others. This is why a changing normative condition takes on a dramatic quality. The arena for a normative change is usually a big public one. It is a revolution, a war, or some other profound event that identifies the issue, punctuating history with epic moments.

13. See James Joll, *The Anarchists* (London: Eyre and Spottiswoode, 1964), p. 13.

14. See E. J. Hobsbawm, *Primitive Rebels* (Manchester: Manchester University Press, 1959). How sect development works at the normative level is interesting; for example, in France in 1834, when legal revolutionary activity had ceased, a League of Outlaws was formed. This organization in turn gave birth to the League of the Just, which became the League of the Communists, for which the *Communist Manifesto* was written. The transition described was from a brotherhood to a modern organization with a normative ideology, from 1834 to 1846.

It has been customary to divide such norms into two main types, such as sacred and profane, idealistic and practical, to distinguish ends that are nonempirical from those that are concrete and practical. But these distinctions do not cover all that we have in mind. In this customary view, traditional societies that employ magic extensively or use shamans or witch-doctors may be carrying on highly instrumental activities, the instrumentalism depending on an interpretative experience, symbolically and ritually stated, that seems to go well beyond "scientific" tests of instrumentalism. (The same would apply to an industrial society.) That is, there may be no clear and rational means-and-ends relationship between certain ceremonials and their intended consequences, especially since the ceremonial act rather than the specific content of the actions (dancing, incantations, the use of beads and chalk, etc.) may be the crucial factor. In our terms *instrumental* would refer to activities that imply mastery rather than mystery, control over specific experiences and events. *Consummatory* embodies meanings that endow those events with some larger implication. The importance of such larger meanings is a behavioral question, but one of our assumptions here is that it is precisely this "need" to define a universe of meaning which makes possible a universe of control. The one without the other is not conceivable.

More specifically, equity of allocation refers to specific ideological statements that identify, elaborate, and particularize views about how choices should be made and distributed. That is, they contain priorities of meaning with rewards seen as contingent upon some considered view of harmony in the social universe. Some may be embodied in religious ideologies. Some priorities may be properly "political." Such a view draws attention to how ideologies splinter and break off one from another. An ideology will contain a synthesized relationship of general values germane to the community, whether stated in utopian, scientific, or revelatory terms, and it will have some application of the principles to modes of distribution. In this way the normative element will utilize either a traditional statement or a hortatory interpretation of structure, or some mixture of both.[15]

15. Our analysis of ideology is both functional and symbolistic. In the first instance, the concern would be with the relationship between ideology and structure, with ideologies seen in terms of their usefulness and appropriateness, according to various structural patterns and tendencies. However, the matter of meaning can be seen as partly independent of structure. Meaning in this sense is diverse, for any ideology will contain several levels, aesthetic, emotional and connotative, as well as rational, practical, and denotative. This is one reason why ideology is so confusing. It becomes important because it seems to convert reasonable demands into sets of evocative and emotional symbols. Political ideology has the effect of putting complex, individually held sensitivities on the same plane. But precisely because it

Moving to the political system, with respect to political norms, we are concerned to view the ideologies more specifically with reference to the principles of access and governance. Some of these principles—such as parliamentary control over the executive, judicial review, and parliamentary government—have been studied. Embodied in mechanisms, such principles are endowed with special qualities that are often simply inaccurate or not necessarily true. Certain common fallacies develop, in which the idea of a thing, like the two-party system in relationship to democracy, becomes the thing in itself, i.e., the two-party system *is* democracy; in this way the concept of democracy comes to depend on the mechanism. But whether fallacious or not, the principle is an expression of how political participation *should* occur, which is why forms like judicial review take on a certain authority. Then it is found shocking when such mechanisms are rejected in the name of the principle they commonly stand for (as when Tanzania opts for an ideology of one-party democracy and familistically based economic organization).

Whatever the particular combinations of such principles, we shall attempt to distinguish between the wider political ends that constitute pictures of an appropriate form of participation and the beliefs about their advisability, basing our attempt on the functional consequences of the mechanisms. It is precisely here that the distinction between consummatory and instrumental values becomes important for the analysis of political norms.

One would expect to find some consistency between societal norms about allocation and political norms about representation. (Hence our statement of the relationship in the model.) But particularly under conditions of rapid change, this expectation may not be met. Then there may be severe cleavage between norms and structures in society and norms and structures relating elites to government. Even more likely is horizontal cleavage between societal and governmental groups, cleavage that divides them both. To the degree that it is vertical, i.e., between society on the one hand and government on the other, as in cases of societies where changes in the political system have occurred in a manner not directly related to the ideology of the society, then either the government must trans-

---

simplifies what is complex, it is subject to continuous reinterpretation. The dialectic is thus both a source of definition and a cause of misunderstanding and controversy. In this sense there can be no end of ideology, no ultimate appeal to reason, for every ideological appeal is rational according to some criterion, mystical or matter-of-fact. Ideology, then, is always an aspect of roles. It does not refer to "attitudes" as such. In this context a question like "what is the effect of ideology on behavior?" is irrelevant.

form the society or it must itself be changed into another form. Nkrumah's
Ghana, Soekarno's Indonesia, and the USSR in 1917 are examples.

Dialectical changes of a normative sort occur not only in society but
in the more restricted political arena. This complicates the model considerably, for the problem is how to study all these combinations. Our
suggested answer involves the analysis of both levels simultaneously
through the dialectical examination of ideologies in which the meaning of any one in any concrete case is based on the observer's involvement
in a normative dialectic of his own. The specific analytical problem is to
use a singular normative experience in one's own cultural environment to
examine others in one's own or in an exotic culture. A dialectical method
allows us to locate key allocational constructs (property relations, authority
relations) and enables us to see the levels of contradiction, conflict, and
intersection, including the identification of mythic elements and how they
are expressed, their sequence in the ideology (the beginning or the end as
in the golden past, the debased present, and the golden future), and the
logical structure implied in the statement (as with Plato's *Republic).*

How to use a dialectical approach in a nonmystical manner is a question
that remains to be solved. The comments made by Lévi-Strauss in his
analysis of the myth of Asdiwal are suggestive but not specifically helpful.
This myth describes the vicissitudes of Asdiwal, a superhuman being,
born of a union between a human mother and a god father. Provided with
human vulnerabilities and some special supernatural weapons, he travels
about the region of the Skeena Valley in Alaska defining by his various
predicaments the life, strategies, and alternatives open to people, as well
as the ambiguities and limits imposed by both the human condition and
the natural environment. In a fascinating and intuitive exercise Levi-
Strauss suggests certain polar opposites, both specific and general, that can
be abstracted by the analysis of the myth. Specific ones include heaven and
earth and degrees or stations in between, such as peak and valley. Other
specific comparisons are high and low, water and land, sea hunting and
mountain hunting. Lévi-Strauss continues with this analysis and develops
global alternatives, female-male, east-west, high-low, famine-repletion,
movement-immobility, which he says provide the shared criteria of what
is significant when the people of the society examine both their condition
and its latent possibilities.[16] Of course such reciprocities are not stacked

16. Whatever one thinks about what Lévi-Strauss has done in the case of this
particular myth, the same method can be applied to founding myths, revolutionary
ideologies, and other powerful political belief systems. For example, in some founding myths, like that of the founding of Ile Ife in Yorubaland, the sex of the founder
is ambiguous. This is particularly important when the mythical founder fosters a

up like so many packages in a supermarket, to be picked over at the appropriate hour by the analytical customers. They are difficult to identify in a concrete sense. Even when one particular set is seen in contrast to another, there is a danger that they will be seen as simple reciprocals, capable of sustaining only one reciprocal relationship. It is bound to be more complex than that because norms must be considered to have a fluctuating historical content. For example, consummatory ends embodied in socialist ideologies during a period of harmony between various socialist groups in the days of the Popular Front might be downgraded in favor of the instrumental advantages of coalition against a common enemy. At another point in time, the differing consummatory values formerly suppressed may break out and prevent solidarity and cooperation over instrumental objectives. The best we can say is that a dialectical method that can make use of normative reciprocals to identify operating political beliefs will locate permissible and impermissible norms.

The terms *consummatory* and *instrumental* are designed to initiate analysis into normative conflicts occurring in any concrete case, since a dialectic is at work between the consummatory values and the instrumental values. As consummatory values lose their meaning, become perfunctory, and are ritualized or fragmented by increasingly subjective perception, instrumental values develop. Partly there is conflict between beliefs and partly a decline in belief.[17] Such a projected analysis would require identification of "real" ideological groupings. For example, it might be possible to consider in our analysis four strategic groups that have participated in normative conflicts in China: the "old guard" of pro-Soviet revolutionaries whose consummatory values were forged in the civil war; the bureaucratic or technocratic managers whose instrumental values were based on getting the job done; the revivalist youth mobilized in the "red guards"; and military zealots who cherished order. Assuming that consummatory values are represented by the "old guard" and the "red guard" and that instrumental values are represented by the army and the bureaucracy, we can put the

---

descent system. In this the comparison to the myth of the Virgin birth becomes obvious, particularly when that particular myth is seen in the context of its political impact as a counter-ideology to the idolatry of the Romans and the legitimacy of Hebrew religious beliefs. We can examine such aspects of ideologies specifically when we come to the case studies themselves. Our purpose now is simply to indicate what the normative dimension implies and how the consummatory-instrumental distinction is capable of further articulation.

17. The point is similar to the one raised by R. H. Tawney when he wrote about the separation of economic from ethical interests. See R. H. Tawney, *Religion and the Rise of Capitalism* (London: John Murray, 1926), p. 238.

"dialectic" in the following terms: "red guard" versus "old guard" (consummatory values); army versus bureaucracy (instrumental values); "red
guard" versus army (consummatory versus instrumental); "old guard"
versus bureaucracy (consummatory versus instrumental); "red guard"
versus bureaucracy (consummatory versus instrumental); "old guard"
versus army (consummatory versus instrumental).

Dialectical process is based on the formation of normative principles
which negate others in the form they have hitherto taken, i.e. the identification of permissible norms by means of the identification of impermissible
norms. For example, in the antebellum South, slavery represented a permissible norm embodying racial principles of inferiority and superiority,
while abolitionism referred to such principles as impermissible. Slavery
became an impermissible norm. The transforming process resulting from
this dialectic resulted in a new and more directly political one, namely,
states' rights versus national unity.

In the USSR, the conflict over capitalism versus Bolshevism or Leninism has reappeared in the form of conflicts over principles of decentralization versus principles of centralization. In many African societies, ethnic
norms compete with national norms, transformed into regionalism or
sectionalism versus nationalism and nationalism versus pan-Africanism.

A more explicit dialectical chain might divide Marxism and liberalism
as dialectically opposite normative systems, the one holding that the collectivity is primary with the individual deriving from it, the other holding
that the individual is primary with the collectivity a summation of individuals. In turn, Marxism divides into its Leninist and Revisionist forms in
which the terms of the collectivity become the focus of normative conflict.
Leninism divides into what loosely can be called the Trotskyist and Stalinist
positions and the normative implications of bureaucratic statism. In turn,
Stalinism divides in the form of Titoism and Maoism and the degree of
"economism" and type of participation as well as the "meaning" of revolution. As well, Stalinism gives way to competing instrumental ideologies,
i.e. the "Goulash communism" of Khrushchev and the managerial communism of Brezhnev. Where "liberalism" re-emerges, as in Czechoslovakia, it is smashed.

Such dialectical chains can be traced out not only in terms of directly
conflicting norms, but also in the defining quality of those norms, i.e.,
their embodiment of principles which are consummatory, and thus contain fundamental normative "end-states," or instrumental, specifying
ends, rather than end-states, in the sense of objectives or goals. The importance of such an analysis is that norms are inextricably linked with
behavior and structure insofar as roles are functionally defined and institu-

tionalized positions in a social system. That is, structure is made up of roles embodying norms. Behavior is shaped by roles insofar as action is socially structured.

However, this is not to be construed as implying that norms are regarded as the sole independent variables in the present system. It should be clear that, in our analysis of the relations between function and dialectic, we come closest to the Marxist epistemological tradition. A functional analysis defines a field of truth based on human needs with structures created by the attempt to satisfy those needs. In short, it deals with man's work in relation to himself and the generalized consequences of that in the choices available in the roles that organize and regulate activity. A dialectical analysis deals with the binary manner of gauging meaning, i.e. the moral measure of an experience in terms of its opposite. This is man as a cognitive being. The truths involved are different but related. In the last analysis, politics consists of the dialogue between them. Perhaps the best statement of this point of view is found in Kolakowski's essay, "Karl Marx and the Classical Definition of Truth," where he says, "It is probable in any event that a certain method of analyzing human cognition, in everyday perception as well as in art and science, could be worked out upon precisely this basic idea of Marx: that man as a cognitive being is only part of man as a whole; that that part is constantly involved in a process of progressive autonomization, nevertheless it cannot be understood otherwise than as a function of a continuing dialogue between human needs and their objects. This dialogue, called work, is created by both the human species and the external world, which thus becomes accessible to man only in its humanized form. In this sense, we can say that in all the universe man cannot find a well so deep that, leaning over it, he does not discover at the bottom his own face."[18]

ROLE ALLOCATION AND FUNCTIONAL CHANGE

Role allocation deals with the way roles provide access to resources and benefits. Rather than examine directly a flow of goods, services, and power, we translate them in terms of their accessibility to roles. Roles represent a system of claims, with each role being a kind of promissory note. The holder of it expects to receive his due. If he wants more he must change his role. Role changing is what is meant here by *social mobility*.

18. See Leszek Kolakowski, *Toward a Marxist Humanism: Essays on the Left Today* (New York: Grove Press, 1969), p. 66. See also the discussion of the dialectic by William L. McBride, especially Jean-Paul Sartre's view of the participant observer or the "interiority" of dialectical knowledge in *Fundamental Change in Law and Society* (The Hague: Mouton, 1970), pp. 152–63.

One implication of our approach to role allocation is that the special roles most functionally relevant to development per se are particularly linked to the achievement of instrumental ends. Therefore, during a period of development the most important roles are those most useful in producing instrumental output. Such roles normally take on significance at the expense of less useful ones. Several types of allocation systems may develop alongside "emergent" ones based on functionality. Others not based on functionality become residual.

Role allocation in this model needs to be examined at two levels, societal and governmental. On the societal level an increase in development does not necessarily mean that choices will be redistributed. More likely, the rich will get richer and the poor poorer. Social mobility may increase, but not necessarily for all. Role allocation can be evaluated in terms of two criteria: the germaneness or nongermaneness of sets of roles in a stratification system; and the degree of permeability of the boundaries around various sets. Germaneness refers to functionality for development. Permeability refers to social mobility. The least germane with the most limited type of functional consequences with the firmest boundaries are caste role sets and ethnic role sets. Such groupings are exclusive, segmentary, and closed. A caste system is a vertical stratification of ranked castes with no social mobility. Groups differentiated by ethnicity form a horizontal system in which movement from one group to the other is almost impossible. Recruitment is almost always by birth. We can call this kind of role allocation *segmentary stratification.*

Next in order of germaneness and permeability is the type of class based on occupation, in which occupation is the key to all other aspects of life and where boundaries between classes are difficult to pass through. This is a condition common to societies in an advanced stage of modernization or early industrialization. This concept of class is closest to the Marxian idea and is solidaristic. Relationships within each type are said to be fused, whereas between classes they are hostile. We can call this kind of role allocation *fused stratification.*[19]

A more open class system is based less on occupation than on education, which allows diverse occupational choices. Permeability is great, depending on qualifications. Functionality is the basis of ranking. Such groupings tend to form not in large-scale fused classes but in small competitive mini-classes. We call this kind of role allocation *differentiated stratification.*

19. The present use of the term *fused* is different from the one employed by Fred Riggs. He characterizes whole societies as fused (in contrast to diffracted). We apply the concept to a particular type of class. See Fred W. Riggs, *Administration in Developing Countries* (Boston: Houghton Mifflin Co., 1964), pp. 23–25.

Finally, there is the most open of all on the basis of qualification and germaneness, the functional status groups, which maximize functionality and include various kinds of technocrats. Though they represent a small sector of any stratification system, for a variety of reasons their significance is out of proportion to their numbers. Since they represent a group that continues to grow in size, we will call them an "emergent" stratification group.

Thus, there is a tendency toward functionality that increases with development.[20]

TYPES OF POLITICAL SYSTEMS

We have stated earlier that the political information and coercion relationships between society and government are transmitted by elites. We also suggested that where the maximization of political information was the emphasis in decision-making, it embodied norms or principles of wide access. These in turn define relevant communicators. The norms thus identify the character of political obligation and locate those to whom obligation is a recognized responsibility. The application of coercion reverses the process. Then obligations are defined by government and held to be binding upon the members of the society.

Because these distinctions play an important role in the following analysis, we should distinguish further the characteristics of political norms from more general norms of equity before we discuss types of political system. The norms differ in the order of generality and in the referents. Norms of equity, which define equity of allocation, center about how much equality shall prevail in society as embodied in the ensemble of roles. Such roles can be ranked in terms of the equality of their distribution, i.e., stratification. This view is similar to the emphasis on class in socialist thought of the late nineteenth century, particularly in relation to

20. Functionality may have different consequences in various settings. The role of a lawyer may be entirely relevant in an industrial society, where the settlement claims over scarce goods and services must be handled with relative dispatch. But a lawyer's role in a traditional setting may be quite the opposite; it may help to hedge with restrictions and litigation for its own sake what otherwise might help development. The lawyer in Latin America or Africa tends to personify a status rather than a set of tasks, which is functionally a very different matter. The same may be true for an economist or a planner. The planner who is trained at MIT and goes to Peru may find that his role is changed from that of a task-based expert to a status that prevents him from working. This may be one reason why many technocrats turn into politicians. They cannot get results by means of their expertise but they can do something if they can gain political power. Technocratic status may provide them with the resources to manipulate the political situation and so accomplish some of their original purposes.

the role of property, ownership, and occupation. Both capitalism and socialism as ideologies embody broad distinctions about the appropriate role stratification.

The four political norms that for us are the most general are (1) realization of social potentiality; (2) maintenance of control; (3) maintenance of beliefs; and (4) prevalence of principles of negotiation or bargaining. These will always include large ideological distinctions but will be focused more narrowly on principles of access to decision-making. Indeed, these four are the substance of political norms. Here we are less interested in distinctions between broad ideological positions like socialism or capitalism and more in the terms of appropriate access to decision-making, the forms this should take, and the permanence of the arrangements. This kind of concern is embodied in issues of how much and what kind of representation there will be between society, elites, and government, and more specifically, how elite participation will function vis-à-vis information and coercion. Under these circumstances, the dialectic of political conflict tends to occur in a manner somewhat different from the more general conflict over norms of equity, precisely because these larger ones tend to be embodied in the smaller ones. Such issues are raised in the context of mechanisms of rule and what they imply. Judicial review, the multiparty system, proportional representation, referendums, legislative control over the executive, the party as a leading instrument of change, the organization of mass and line, etc.—each of these specific mechanisms of rule have a consummatory and an instrumental side. On the one hand they are methods of making and defining appropriate policy; on the other they define the limits of executive power.

Whatever form they take they can be summarized in our analysis as principles of access to decision-making. The content of those principles, as described above, have a dialectic of their own. They embody larger principles of equity translated into information. How and the degree to which such information serves to define the obligations of decision-makers to the society as a whole will vary considerably. Such variation stems from the type of elite participation and the degree of coercion applied. This aspect of the political system is structural. On the basis of how much elite participation there is, the ideal of representation and its actualities can be compared and the ways participation occurs can be studied.

The types of political system are described in terms of whether or not political norms consist of predominantly consummatory or instrumental values and whether political participation is predominantly hierarchical or pyramidal. Political norms are beliefs about political access and participation. They are embodied in such terms as *democracy, aristocracy, monarchy, communaucracy.* They define an ideal of how authority should be distributed.[21] The combination of consummatory values and hierarchical authority in elite-government relationships is a mobilization system; instrumental values and the same pattern of authority is called a bureaucratic system (including in that term military regimes). Where there is a combination of pyramidal authority and consummatory values in the elite-government relationship, we call the system theocratic; such authority with instrumental values results in a reconciliation system. Each type of system has a special characteristic. The mobilization system is mainly concerned with achieving some defined pattern of *potentiality* that is regarded by political leaders as their mission. The bureaucratic system is largely a *control* mechanism; it has few wider purposes. The theocratic system is preoccupied with sustaining a pattern of *belief,* and the reconciliation system is concerned with *bargaining.* A shift from one emphasis to another implies a different use of coercion and information. For example, in order to achieve potentiality, mobilization systems tend to be highly coercive. In order to bargain appropriately, a reconciliation system needs to maximize information to indicate interests. A bureaucratic system would apply coercion to sustain control.

These statements can be phrased as hypotheses. If a political system is of the mobilization type, it will employ a high degree of coercion to realize its potentialities. If a system is of the reconciliation type, it will maximize information in order to have more effective bargaining. If a system is of the bureaucratic type, it will employ coercion to maintain control. If a system is of the theocratic type, it will use information in order to remain sensitive to any falling off of belief. These hypotheses, and the notion that there is an inverse relationship between coercion and information allow us to go further in specifying how political systems change from one type to another. If there is a mobilization system, coercion will be high and information low. A low information system will not be capable of adequate decision-making. Similarly with a bureaucratic system, if information is low the political system will not realize its potentiality in the first instance or maintain control in the second. At that point whatever the originating system, it will need to change to another. In the case of theocratic and reconciliation systems, if there is an excess of information, or if information cannot be utilized, what is needed to maintain the system is the application of coercion. Information without the capacity to coerce is likely to produce uncertainty because of the randomization of ends. If either of these conditions—an information glut or a miscellany of ends—should

---

21. These types are described in detail in my *Politics of Modernization.*

occur, information becomes a source of confusion, bargaining breaks down, and belief fails. Once again the prevailing political system type will change to another.

We do not consider the types of political system as "real" in the sense that they are concrete. They represent "predominant" relationships or tendencies found in any actual relationship between government and elites. Such relationships are most visible where the "systems-problems" in each type are found in the actual case. The more "reconciliation" a system is, the more it is based on system bargaining and the more likely it is to suffer from an information glut and an incapacity to act. The more "mobilization" a system is, the more it will show a tendency toward the use of coercion as a policy directed toward achieving potentiality. In illustrating the theory it will be useful to begin with extreme cases of each type in order to demonstrate the properties ascribed to the hypothetical case. Cases that fail, like Peron's Argentina, are especially interesting. Examples should be selected because they serve as promontories for the analysis of others. Less clear but more valid illustrations are precisely those where the political system changes quickly from one type to another, and where change in the political system is a dynamic factor, in countries at a developmental point between late-stage modernization and industrialization, for example. The political system aspect of the theory draws particular attention to the terms and conditions of transformation of late modernizing systems to industrialization. Which is the best political system for this? The search for an answer provides us with one point of inquiry. Having suggested some types of political systems, the particular goal crucial to each, and the propensity of each to employ coercion and information, we can conclude this chapter with some hypotheses about their suitability for handling normative and structural imbalances, and threats to development and order.

Mobilization systems stand out historically as political engines of drastic change. They bear down on the problem of development with the total resources of a community, if development is an explicit goal. Their purpose is to bring together the kingdom of the damned and the republic of the saved. The kingdom of the damned has been the special burden of the proletarians in the nineteenth and early twentieth centuries, the blacks in contemporary United States, marginals in Latin America, and more generally, third world peoples against imperialist powers. The consummatory values appropriate in each case include Marxism as a faith, blackness as an ideology, Castroism as a strategy, and nationalism as a crusade. The primary emphasis of the mobilization system is on the realization of potentiality—not any potentiality, to be sure—but particularly that of the most offended group or class. Through its realization all other groups will be saved. The method used is reallocation.

But difficulties stand in the way of realizing the mobilization system concretely. We said that in acting coercively the system begins to lose information. In particular this information loss is of the populist type; lack of support will be disguised, which in turn affects the reliability of other types of information. As well, the transition from a kingdom of the damned to a republic of the saved implies a rather fundamental change in the moral position of the oppressed group. From the oppressed it becomes the oppressor. It then loses its moral initiative or momentum and from then on consummatory values decline. More than likely a competitive in-strumentalism will set in that pushes the system in a bureaucratic or even reconciliation direction. Efforts to sustain the values without coercion, i.e., a theocratic system, are very rare indeed. The mobilization system then handles the consequences of development; by identifying oppressed groups it makes them into a mechanism for total reallocation. Information loss and instrumentalization are this system's vulnerabilities.

Bureaucratic systems, which also respond with coercion, characteristically take the form of military or paramilitary regimes. (Paramilitary regimes would include highly instrumentalized single-party systems in which the party bureaucracy is the agency of rule.) The bureaucratic system em-phasizes control rather than potentiality. Its object is to contain threats to order while allowing development to occur more or less by itself or, in some more recent military governments, with some direction or plan-ning. Like the mobilization system the bureaucratic will eventually lose information. If it reduces coercion to have more information, it tends to make compromises with various groups, bringing it toward a reconciliation system. This explains why so many military regimes end by turning power over to civilians in a reconciliation framework. They do not know what to do with power, and sheer coercion is insufficient. If they increase coercion, they are likely to generate bands of outcasts capable of acts of daring, feats of valor, i.e., counter-groups with consummatory values. This is pre-cisely the condition under which guerilla warfare flourishes. Such situations are not likely to be controlled easily. The bureaucratic system that cannot control loses its raison d'être and becomes vulnerable to a system change— ordinarily in the direction of a reconciliation system.

The reconciliation system has as its key characteristics a bargaining rela-tionship between various pluralistic groups, the number of which pro-liferate, coalesce, split, and recombine in pursuit of highly instrumental ends. The one ultimate consummatory value necessary to such a system is commitment to the rules of bargaining. If the rules are broken by all, anarchy results. Reconciliation systems are high information types that have at their disposal knowledge about support, interests, and professional and technical matters. The knowledge may help them alleviate the stresses and strains of development. It may also show political leaders that there is not much they can do, that the terms of the situation are hopeless. The reconciliation system is likely to be vulnerable to all three alternative types. In a republic that emphasizes rules over men, theocratic visions of new human relationships are likely to emerge. Reconciliation systems, then, by creating a consummatory vacuum, open the way for both theocratic and mobilization counter-groups. Millennial movements, religious salvation communities, love communities, encounter groups, political militants, terrorists—all these may appear in reconciliation systems. The need to fill the consummatory vacuum is one basis for them. The other is that information becomes glutted by sheer volume (the case in highly industrial countries) of available information, and a political ceiling is quickly reached when alternative actions are exhausted.[22]

The theocratic *impulse* is perhaps more alive today than at any time since the sixteenth and seventeenth centuries, but as a type it has never been less possible. Essentially, theocratic systems are noncoercive, because of unanimity on consummatory values. To take issue with them is to be cast into exile or out of the community entirely. Ecclesiastical societies in seventeenth-century New England represent one type of theocratic system. Others include Arabic tribes after the death of Mohammed. And we could also include various utopian experiments in group living.[23]

Like the mobilization system, the theocratic system is faced with the problem of the ritualization of values. As belief declines, ends are instrumentalized; coercion must increase or the community will fall apart. The assumption in the theocratic system is that by virtue of living in the community redemption will occur, so the need for coercion would never arise. The fact that redemption is rarely ever accomplished on a long-term basis is one reason for the failure of the theocratic system. But its failures should not cause us to dismiss it. One major task of social analysis is to discover, for example, why such theocratic communities (the religious can be political as well as ecclesiastical) as the Israeli *kibbutzim* work. Such small-scale theocratic systems may eventually turn out to be protypical of future arrangements.

22. Our assumptions about norms in a reconciliation system are very similar to those of Michael Mann in his article "The Social Cohesion of Liberal Democracy," *American Sociological Review* 35, no. 3 (June 1970): 423–29.

23. See Charles R. Crowe, "Phalansteries and Transcendentalists," *Journal of the History of Ideas* 20, no. 4 (Oct.-Dec. 1959): 495–502.

Radicalization and Embourgeoisement

Modernizing societies are characteristically poor and what they have is badly distributed. In a reconciliation system the knowledge of this condition will spread as development occurs. Transistor radios, the expansion of literacy, the shift of significant parts of the population from the villages to the towns, the growth of a class system—all help to spread a sense of the imbalance between equity of allocation and allocation. This is exacerbated by knowledge of how people live in richer industrial countries. As modernization occurs, then, a sense of relative deprivation and role conflict increases. How do the visible consequences of growing wealth in the form of some pattern of skewed allocation arouse antagonism? In an African setting, for example, it was characteristic in more traditional times for a chief or an elder to live like his subjects. He might have had more retainers and slaves and his compound might have been larger and able to hold more people; a measure of splendor might have surrounded the court. But for the most part he would live in a fashion similar to that of his kinsmen and fellows. At festive occasions he would likely be required to distribute largesse. With modernization all this changes. Regalism, seniority, and status come to mean social separatism and altered life styles. Where once a rich man simply had a bigger compound with walls spreading out a bit farther to take in more members of the family, a rich modern man builds upward. Vertical cement structures, part fortress, present imposing and formidable façades that rise above the walls of neighboring compounds of houses, the vertical line implying a different pattern of stratification. This suggests a behavioral phenomenon. Let us define two universal behavioral patterns as follows,

Embourgeoisement is a behavioral position in which motivation is directed toward the acceptance of an existing ensemble of roles and increasing individual social mobility within it. The normative position is highly instrumentalistic, with preference based on short-term interests and interests primarily economically based. *Radicalization* is a behavioral position in which motivation is directed toward the rejection of an existing ensemble of roles and the creation of new ones embodying new normative prescriptions. It is oriented away from instrumentalistic interests and short-run objectives and in favor of long-run consummatory values and their distribution throughout a collectivity. Emphasis is on collective rather than individual mobility. *Radicalization for embourgeoisement* is is a form of embourgeoisement aimed at removing barriers to social mobility and the realization of interests which accepts the prevailing ensemble of roles but attempts to redistribute or reallocate them.

If a society is in a period of modernization, the preoccupying equity principles or values of the society as a whole will be centered about material benefits and their distribution, even if the regime is a revolutionary one. Competition for roles defining access to rewards of power and prestige is the characteristic of embourgeoisement behavior. The hypothesis is not intended to apply only to modernizing countries. Insofar as there is a modernizing sector of an industrial society, the predominant values and principles of equity would be those involving material benefits and their distribution. Hence, despite the rhetoric of revolutionary worker's movements in Europe and the United States in the 1930s and the language of militancy in the black movements in the United States today, there is militancy in favor of embourgeoisement. This helps to explain the phenomenon of working-class conservatism, a phenomenon that, if our hypothesis is correct, will increasingly apply to blacks, or other modernizing marginals.

In highly industrial societies, however, an alternative and opposite pattern of change in the general variable of equity of allocation is visible. This might be called a change in meaning, a filling of a consummatory vacuum that occurs with a certain material surfeit. It is revolutionary in consequence in the sense that individuals either try to drastically overhaul existing values in order to change the structural terms of life or search for new values. Both of these would involve great changes in the structural system on the basis of which roles are allocated. Relations between men and women are changing in industrial society; there are changes in child-rearing, occupational, and educational patterns. As such changes occur there is as well a redefinition of the nature of obligation.

Similarly with the idea of participation: the assumption in organized life is that participation in any large-scale society must be limited. (The vote is an example of a momentary or short-term activity representing participation.) With radicalization the desire spreads for more participation in decision-making. Such a desire for involvement in decision-making comes less from below, from the worker sectors of society, then from above, from the industrial elites and managerial groups. Management replaces bosses. A bureaucracy replaces the manager. The lack of demand for worker participation in industry and for a share in political decision-making rather than bargaining for benefits is precisely one of the characteristics of embourgeoisement and is as true in socialist as in capitalist countries.

In industrial systems it is the bourgeois radicals of the literary-intellectual tradition who are looking for different principles of social and political equity. They seek a new basis by which a community can reallocate its benefits and allow fuller political participation. Such bourgeois radicalism can incorporate such widely differing concerns as the nurturing of the physical environment, an interest in art and its distribution in society at large, and a concern with taste. It increasingly comes to see the industrial society not simply as philistine, but destructive, with violence, war, and death its ultimate consequences. Such a pattern of radicalism is primarily limited to industrial countries. Extended to the more developed modernizing societies such as those of Latin America among the educated elites, it takes on an especially significant normative character. There the bourgeois radicals are the sons of the rich, particularly the rich industrialists and financiers. Among them can be found most varieties of Marxists, Catholic militants, and residual fascists.

What we are suggesting is that as development occurs the normative and structural imbalance that it creates can be described in terms of equity of allocation. Since most concrete systems have both an industrial and a modernizing sector, embourgeoisement and radicalization can be seen as two competing and continuing behavioral consequences of the search for equity. Such conflicts over equity form one source of political problems. The business of creating a new system of order requires generalized political norms that can reflect this embourgeoisement-radicalization dialectic, encompass it, and render it compatible with people's wants, needs, and interests. That means that not any set of political norms will do. Which norms can be congruent within this dialectical boundary is one of the questions with which our structural theory must deal.

THE RATIONALE OF THE THEORY

The original empirical purposes of the model were to provide a framework for comparative research on West African and Latin American development cases.[24] Using case studies we hope to show how the classic moral problem of how man confronts freedom can be defined in terms of the expansion of choice. Expanding choice quickly and effectively is the modernizing problem; what to do with the potentialities of choice is the long-term moral issue. Thus, the theoretical variables were selected to be consistent with the issues themselves.[25]

A more specific issue associated with the problem of choice and freedom concerns the relations between rich and poor countries. Increases in

24. See my very preliminary effort in "Radicalization and Embourgeoisement," *Journal of Interdisciplinary History* 2 (1971).

25. Those interested in this problem will find a discussion in my essay "A Paradigm for Political Analysis," in *Some Conceptual Approaches to the Study of Modernization* (Englewood Cliffs, N.J.: Prentice-Hall, 1968).

development make modernizing societies more dependent on industrial ones. This observation requires us to include industrial societies in our concerns and allows us to suggest a general characteristic of modern imperialism. A country with a very limited developmental infrastructure may be utterly dependent on a metropolitan or industrial country for protection, capital, and technical assistance; but, in the last analysis, it can restrict its demands and survive with very little. It is functionally self-sufficient. In other words because it needs all, it can use little and can survive in modest circumstances. But the more highly modernized a country becomes, the more it needs aid and the more at the mercy of the external industrial world it becomes. It cannot control prices of basic marketable commodities, particularly cash crops, on which it typically depends for income. It needs the technical assistance, capital, and other resources that only industrial countries have in any abundance. Because a modernizing country has already achieved some industrial infrastructure, it is ordinarily linked to an external corporate structure whether of private capitalism or state socialism. Such corporate structures may have semi-autonomous status. In short, the dependence of a modernizing society accelerates with the complexity of its development. Development in effect generates a new form of imperialism as the fundamental nature of the relationship between modernizing and industrial societies, an imperialism in which there is complicity on both sides, each trying to gain advantages and not reckoning with handicaps. This is why anti-imperialism is such an important political weapon of modernizing societies. It is the only defense open to them, a normative defense in the face of structural vulnerability. Indeed structural options in modernizing societies are drastically altered once development becomes a goal of policy. This problem of freedom and imperialism is thus another of our concerns.

A third concern combines the other two. Roles most functional for development tend to be "locked" into role systems that are integral parts of the corporate and social structures of industrial societies. The training, orientation, and associations of occupants of these roles is thus "outward" rather than "inward," lacking responsiveness to domestic needs. Development generates internal role conflict by virtue of its unevenness. Functionally relevant roles oriented "outward" are locked into antagonistic relations with functionally irrelevant roles that represent public needs; or they may hive off to form enclave communities, separate from and virtually independent of the society of which they are a part. Such problems are not made explicit in economic theories of development, in which statistics of development using aggregate functions ignore the social dysfunctionalities of this form of conflict. Moreover, most social and political theories fail to relate the shifting fortunes of various individuals and groups in terms of the changing significance of roles that use up scarce resources and lead to "functional strains." How to solve both external dependency and internal dislocation are in our view the most pressing concrete political problems of modernizing societies.[26]

If the matter were simply economic, then the solution would be to ascertain the correct combination of the factors of production and eliminate dysfunctionalities in the system. Under such circumstances, all that would be necessary would be to fit the "juridical" to the "economic." With a good fit between the former and the latter, the relationship of development to order would be solved.[27] But the problem is more complicated than that. There is no one-to-one correspondence between a political system and an economic one. The growing diversity within various socialist countries is a testimonial to that, as are the various recent types of planning, decision-making, and strategies appropriate to various investment priorities. There are plenty of approaches, socialist, mixed, and capitalist, in countries both highly industrial and modernizing. But strangely enough, the analysis of politics remains utterly conventional. The analysis of political life has lagged behind the study of political consequences. This is why it is useful to try another approach, and consider a political system in terms of the balance between development and order. The political goal is to harmonize the two and maximize them both; in this way the two can serve as guides for the evaluation of the performance of real systems.

So far we have concentrated on the problems of modernizing societies and saved the most important concern for the last: how to live in a universe of great choice, the problem of highly industrial societies. Here we define our concern in primarily normative terms by suggesting that the

26. The histories of developing countries can thus be seen as a series of attempts to deal with such matters—in the context of a precarious legitimacy—as they try to maintain orderly development, or optimize both development and order. Political solutions take several different forms. Military regime, bureaucratic state, one-party democracy, parliamentary government, "communaucracy"—these are some of the names by which such attempts have been known. (Others are Kemalism and Bismarckism, with Japan different from all the rest.) Tanzania experiments with a specific form of village democracy, *Ujamaa*. Ghana returns to parliamentary government after years of Nkrumah. Latin American fashion currently dictates a return to the military regime. In effect each country, faced with the general problems of structural dislocation and external dependence, tries to find its own solution. If it reaches a political "ceiling" beyond which it can not do much more, having used up its political capital and incurred new obligations, the regime will either falter and be overthrown, or hang on accomplishing little.

27. See Charles Bettelheim, *Planification et Croissance Accélérée* (Paris: Maspero, 1967), pp. 17–24.

dialectic of meaning in highly industrial societies will lead to a continuous redefinition of precisely the values that endow society with its solidarity and individuals with a sense of their own identity. We also assume that the dialectic on these matters quickens in pace and ideological solutions replace each other more and more rapidly. This will lead us to the notion that radicalization is at work in highly industrialized systems, a process permanent in form and ever changing in substance.

To summarize, we want to be able to evaluate the diverse consequences of development, the effects it has on people in different kinds of societies. If one query is how best to foster development, another is how to live with the consequences. When development causes grave injustices and discomforts, people react. Sometimes their reaction is violent—assassinations, coups, coercion—sometimes despairing. The task of our theory is to make choice more comprehensible and amenable to improvement, for we want development to lead to increased efficiency and social pride.

2. Equity and Allocation in Modernizing Societies

The three central hypotheses that so far have been mentioned can be summarized as follows. (1) As modernization proceeds the potentiality for embourgeoisement increases, and as industrialization increases so does the potentiality for radicalization. (2) The greater the degree of industrialization the greater the need for information by decision-makers, and the greater the degree of modernization the greater the need for coercion. (3) The greater the degree of coercion the smaller the amount of information available to decision-makers. These three hypotheses are linked to the dynamics of development and constitute universal paradoxes that can usefully be considered in terms of two stages, modernization and industrialization.

Taking these hypotheses one further step we will argue that as development proceeds the pressure for embourgeoisement comes from "below," whereas the pressure for radicalization comes from "above." Moreover, our proposition that there is an inverse relationship between coercion and information is based on the assumption that risk varies inversely with knowledge; that high risk implies low knowledge (or high stakes with some knowledge); and that coercion is a political consequence of high risk. Finally, embourgeoisement and radicalization will result from changes taking place at the normative and structural levels of societies as they develop. Coercion and information will result from the more specific responses emphasized by particular types of political system as they seek to establish order.

MODERNIZING SOCIETIES AS DERIVATIVE

Opportunities for choice are a function of development, and development takes two forms, industrialization, which is dynamic and innovative as a consequence of the allocation of new information to technology, and modernization, which is derivative. In general, development offers choices between higher and lower rates of savings (with consequences visible in types of economic growth) and long-term or short-term priorities (insofar as the system becomes rationalized and predictable rather than magical and demonic). Preferences need to be clarified and priorities established for investment in heavy or light industry, durable or consumer goods, and so on. In addition, development means social choices. Individuals have more opportunities to choose their styles of life with respect to geographical location, housing, education, occupation, financial autonomy, membership in voluntary associations, and so on. Growth in opportunities means continuous changes in allocation. Certain powerful coalitions, for example, may skew the allocative process so that development is itself inhibited, a common condition of many Latin American countries in a late stage of modernization. As a source of variation, then, industrialization is dynamic, universalizing, and continuously disruptive. Industrial societies are innovative in the sense that their central activity is the production and utilization of new forms of information; modernizing societies, because of their derivative character, are in a continuous state of dependence. They may improvise with great skill, but they will not change until they are able to become innovative. By this criterion only two countries in the past generation have passed completely from the modernizing stage of development to industrialization—Japan and the Soviet Union.

Accepting the view of development as a linear progression allows us to divide the choice variable into three stages. The stage corresponding to the highest choice can be described as industrial. (Postindustrial societies, a fourth stage, exist only as some special characteristics of a few very highly industrialized countries in which they form a particular "value-problématique." In them there is a decline in choice and a feeling of powerlessness.) The lowest choice stage, which is characterized by the absence of development, we call traditional. The various choice stages in between we call modernizing.

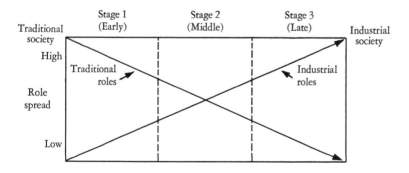

Figure 2.1. Stages of modernization

Figure 2.1 suggests a sequence in which the increasing spread of roles and changes in sets of roles lead a society from a traditional system to an industrial one, a process that can take many forms. In the nineteenth century the form was mainly commerce, and it led to various types of colonial center-periphery relationships. Such linkage roles as those of educator, civil servant, and professional helped to mediate both between the industrial center and the modernizing periphery and between the traditional and modern sectors of society. This was true everywhere in Asia, Africa, and Latin America, although, of course, the relations with the center differed in each case.

A universal pattern with complicated consequences is to be found in middle-stage modernization. The expatriate quality of modernizing roles disappears with the appearance of a large and growing reservoir of mobile and aspiring local candidates. Mixed role sets produce a wider choice of alternatives and result in role ambiguity, particularly in the cases of modern roles such as civil servant and technician, which may lack functional relevance in a nonindustrial environment. As roles split, subdivide, and lose their boundaries it becomes difficult to maintain standards of performance, and values not necessarily related to role performance are emphasized. Functional criteria may be less important in the middle stage of modernization than in earlier or later stages.

In the later stages of modernization, however, functional criteria reappear and are crucially important. Increasingly, the boundaries of roles are set as the roles become relevant preconditions for industrialization. Certain roles become strategic. As functional significance becomes important as a result of the growth of opportunities for the employment of skills, there is likely to be a normative shift toward instrumental values of functionality and consummatory values of development change. The proportions of these values will vary from case to case, but in all societies some tendencies or pressures for appropriate remedial alterations in the relationship between government and society will be created. Hence, as modernization proceeds both potential structural antagonism and the number of normative claims increase.

If these stages of modernization have such characteristic differences, it should not be difficult to identify the stage of a particular society. The chief indices would be modernizing roles and their proportion and distribution in a system. Roles with the most durable boundaries, such as those in business, bureaucracy, and education would be the most suitable indicators. In later stages, another important index would be the proportion and distribution of technocratic roles, particularly those associated with planning and development. Both sets of roles provide a modernization profile, although for a comparative analysis a weighting system would have to be devised.[1] With such role criteria in mind, most countries of sub-Saharan Africa may be placed in the first stage, and most Latin American countries in the second, with a few—Brazil, Argentina, Mexico, Uruguay, Chile, and Cuba—about to enter the third stage, the point of transition from late modernization to early industrialization. Countries that have made the transition are Poland, Yugoslavia, and possibly Taiwan—all of which have become technologically innovative and have begun to export industrial surpluses. Countries like Argentina, Brazil, and Mexico remain stuck at the border between derivative and innovative societies.

Such late-stage modernizing societies, remain in a disadvantageous position.

With very few exceptions, these countries must depend, initially at least, on outside investment for capital. Some internal savings from a more efficient agriculture are theoretically possible but are seldom realized in practice. Most modernizing societies first generate savings by exploiting some useful primary product, where their comparative advantage is greatest. Producing an export commodity appears to be a first step in the right direction, especially if demand is inelastic. With the development of an exportable commodity comes a rise in internal demand. The expansion of the domestic market increases demand for educational and training facilities, the elaboration of a transport and distributive network, better communication, and so on. All of these activities increase investment opportunity. In most former colonial countries, expatriate farmers, trading companies, or other entrepreneurs have been quick to identify profitable fields for investment, in spite of their vulnerability to the money markets of primary industrial centers, with their leads and lags and the drastically fluctuating prices of the international commodities market. This dependency on foreign capital should not matter if industrialization is the goal; in fact it may be both politically and economically useful. In this sense, the pejorative use of such terms as "colonialism," "neocolonialism," "imperialism," and "neoimperialism" is not appropriate. Industrial centers create the inter-

---

1. This need for weighting raises a practical question about the appropriateness of treating roles that are functional in an industrial system as if they must have some necessarily similar functions in a nonindustrial setting. The point is a good one because our theory does contain implications of functional teleology that in fact can scarcely be avoided. On the one hand, we do not intend to make roles into substitutes for some set of functional imperatives. On the other hand, if we treat roles as having some institutional persistence, then it seems fair to expect them, like Pirandello's six characters, to search for ways to perform functions for which they were originally intended, even though the scene may be different.

national capital market that allows modernization to proceed by generalizing economic growth.

But in other senses the pejorative use of these terms is appropriate. They do have a sociological and political relevance that is more significant than mere ideological or informal use would imply. The survival of such organic links of economic dependency can prevent political equity. Production and consumption, for example, have somewhat different meanings in modernizing and industrial societies. In industrial societies, production and consumption are viewed as two aspects of the same process, the manufacture and distribution of goods and services. It is possible to analyze the inter-dependence and complexity of, say, the factory system, the pattern of distribution deriving from it, the level of technological innovation, and the reinvestment of resources to achieve the next stage of development. But if we apply the same economic analysis to modernizing societies, because of certain political and sociological factors the comparison with industrial societies breaks down. One factor is the vulnerability of modernizing countries. Another is the growth of social inequality within them.[2]

In the derivative modernizing society consumption largely consists of overseas purchases of finished products or of finished components to be assembled locally. On the whole, import substitution does not reduce dependency. In rare cases where the volume of exports is great, the dependence of modernizing societies on any one foreign country may be reduced by selective purchases from many sources. But the typical modernizing society remains simply one customer among many and subject for its economic health to the health of the industrial society from which it buys. Industrial societies are occasionally dependent on modernizing ones for some products (e.g., Middle East oil), but such days of dependency are numbered, with the number of irreplaceable items steadily being reduced. Industrial countries, then, rely less and less on modernizing ones for raw materials, but their own overseas markets continuously expand. Modernizing countries, in contrast, remain in constant danger of a balance of payments crisis against which there are few internal reserves or alternative resources. Increasing indebtedness results. For these and other reasons, such as growing unemployment, modernizing societies exist in a world environment that in spite of outside aid and multilateral alliances is essentially hostile. Furthermore, they have few mechanisms of defense to maintain equilibrium.

The derivative character of modernizing societies has many consequences. In political terms, it allows an industrial society to play a "monitor

2. Marx had a remarkable insight into this problem very early. See Karl Marx, *The Grundrisse,* ed. David McLellan (New York: Harper & Row, 1971), pp. 43–46.

role" at the expense of modernizing countries. It also assures that many of the problems of industrial societies will increasingly arise in modernizing ones, the more so as the latter approach the point of transition to industrialization. The adaptive strains produced by combinations of internal and external inputs create political problems that can never be adequately resolved by centralized planning, because the modernizing society has little control over the externally induced pressures of industrialization. Development may occur, but the relationship between allocation and equity may be upset and may produce a threat to order.

The predicament is difficult to resolve. Given the great costs of economic growth, few countries can be autarchic. Indeed, the alternatives open to a society that wants to develop are few. If a country exports primary products in order to generate capital, its short-run rationality is likely to produce long-run irrationalities as the process of development continues. Since demand for its primary products is relatively elastic, expansion of production is likely to cause prices to drop. Increased investment in such products will therefore increase vulnerability rather than reduce it; hence the need for "political" rather than economic solutions.

The pursuit of what appears to be an economically rational course of action may also result in "social" dysfunction. Development policies that maximize income in order to sustain a good balance of payments position and stimulate the flow of investment capital are usually designed to stimulate internal growth. They are likely to increase consumption as well and enlarge the market. Larger incomes are often directed toward consumption of imported goods or investment in industrial countries rather than toward investment in domestic industry. The fortunate individuals whose personal incomes are rising characteristically are more concerned about minimizing the consequences of underdevelopment to their style of life than about using their increased capital for socially useful purposes. The economic consequence of this concern for status consumption is a slower rate of industrialization. The sociological consequence is embourgeoisement. The political consequence is greater and greater inequality, accompanied by skewed allocation of the expanding opportunities for choice. These, then, are some of the internal responses to externally induced modernization.[3]

3. If we illustrate the consequences of the derivative character of modernizing societies in the context of entrepreneurship (whether individual or corporate), we find that the rationality of the entrepreneur or the rationality of the firm may be quite perfect. One does not need to look for an absence of Calvinist ethics or for some nonrational traditional preference to account for this. The pursuit of rationality under conditions of a derivative society may result in nonrationality from the point

The vulnerability of modernizing societies thus tends to be self-perpetuating. Investors distrust a vulnerable economy. Public and private domestic investors, eager to improve their living standards, favor high and quick returns, a preference that tends to produce inflationary pressures that in turn stimulate the demand for consumer goods and further diminish funds available for domestic industrial growth.

Under these circumstances of disorderly development political instability is the characteristic outcome. Often, governments respond with grandiose plans that attempt to solve all problems at once. In the face of increasing socioeconomic inequality, they must allocate an ever higher proportion of income for social welfare in order to placate a public increasingly aware of "relative deprivation." These costs, once incurred, are politically difficult to limit. Efforts to shift the balance of expenditures in the economy toward production would realistically require political restrictions on welfare, government expenditures, and public consumption, along with strict controls to prevent inflation; but few governments take these measures. Long-term developmental planning is also costly, since as modernization increases, so do the opportunities for gross errors in planning. Hence, the pursuit of a short-term rational development is likely to create long-term political difficulties, while long-term planning may be impossible under such frangible circumstances.

If this description is applied to two of our types of political systems, it is clear that a reconciliation system's approach to equity-allocation imbalances will lead to stagnation, exploitation, and corruption, slow growth in the industrial sector, and gradually increasing external vulnerability. A mobilization system's approach will lead to misallocation, waste, and error. In both, roles functional to industrialization will continue to emphasize consumption over production except when high modernization already exists. The one will show political inequality through the skewed allocation of power, whereas the other will show economic inequality through the skewed distribution of income.

In both cases the high proportion of modernized occupational roles in bureaucracies and the proliferation of government services will have the effect of shipping off funds from production into social welfare and other services. This kind of allocation, a form of normative appeasement, creates its own difficulties. A large and parasitical "pseudobourgeoisie" grows. Yet

---

of view of the system as a whole. Hence, a corollary of our notion of modernization is that increased vulnerability is the result of attempts to balance international payments, allocation of expenditures into quick and safe sources of capital return, and high emphasis on consumption expenditures. Some of these consequences are discussed in René Dumont's *False Start in Africa* (London: Andre Deutsch, 1966), passim.

how can this be avoided? Few leaders are able to afford the political consequences of restricting consumption in favor of major investment, particularly when the immediate industrial climate is not favorable. Long-term plans, when there are shortages of trained manpower, minuscule domestic markets because of inadequate purchasing power, and gaps in the basic infrastructure, are likely to lead to waste, inefficiency, and demoralization.

These and other real limitations, such as the lack of skilled middle managers and entrepreneurs, confront most modernizing societies at a time when they are most vulnerable to industrial ones (although they may be less dependent on them because of a lower degree of embourgeoisement). A highly modernized society is dependent because of large government expenditures, heavy overhead costs, huge recurrent expenditures for social services, inflationary pressures, and costs of import substitution. All of this makes it difficult to jump into industrialization. Whatever the stage of development, a derivative society can never be independent as an innovative society can.

These, then, are some of the political problems induced by modernization: increasing dependence resulting from the superior technology and knowledge of industrial countries; embourgeoisement resulting from randomization of intermediate roles and proliferation of role sets; overemphasis on consumption and short-term bargains rather than on long-term solutions, interspersed with periods of drastic remedial planning. This manner of describing the complex process of modernization embodies a point of view. It emphasizes the continuous subordinating pressure by industrial systems on nonindustrial ones.

The basic problems posed by modernization can be identified here without invoking certain theoretical shibboleths that have become part of the literature of modernization. For example, some "radical" theories of modernization suggest that the spread of functional industrial roles at the expense of traditional ones is accompanied by a growing contradiction between rich countries and poor ones. This contradiction sharpens the poor population's awareness of relative deprivation. Modernization then increases alienation, resulting in the progressive radicalization of the mass and particularly of certain strategic marginals whose number and strength increase as modernization proceeds.[4]

Modern conservative theories suggest that there is a "trickle-down"

4. This is the approach contained in the idea of a peasant or *campesino* revolt as a means of radical modernization, and also in the "strangle the cities" theory and organizational Leninism, occurring (conveniently enough) under the hegemony of the radical intellectuals (à la Gramsci). We doubt that the peasantry (replacing the working class) will be headed by a dictatorship of the intellectuals.

effect produced in hitherto traditional societies by outside investment, leading to domestic commercialization and the growth of a middle class, which combined with democratic political mechanisms ensures stability, the prime condition for further growth.

Something is obviously wrong with both approaches. For a variety of reasons those who should be radical because of deprivation are quite often among the most conservative in a population. Or, perhaps more frequently, they are able to hold conflicting ideological positions simultaneously. Nor is the response of a modernizing society to inputs of foreign investment generally equable. Indeed, increasing modernization is most often associated with rising unrest.

Taking a different view, we suggest that modernization produces an embourgeoisement of the population resulting in its deradicalization. Embourgeoisement produces structural complexity and stagnation requiring a radical political method of change. Both are based on the relationship between development and allocation and can be presented

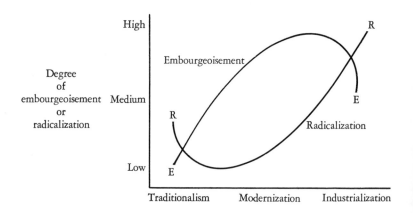

Figure 2.2. Some behavioral consequences of development

graphically. (See Figure 2.2.) These hypotheses can now be combined in terms of allocation or access to resources. By this means, it should be possible to explain our hypotheses about role randomization and conflict during modernization and to make projections about the consequences for stratification.

MULTIFUNCTIONALITY AND STRATIFICATION

The descriptive surrogate we use for allocation is stratification. Simple functional theories of stratification tend to be based on reciprocity, a principle that may be useful for analyzing small-scale traditional societies but does not serve for studying modernizing ones. Reciprocity notions fail to describe class relationships during modernization, because at that time functional specificity combines with multifunctionality and no single set of functional attributes can be applied to a particular class. This is especially true during late-stage modernization, which is characterized by a high degree of "intermediate functional substitutability" (below the level of highly generalized functional requisites), as well as by a variety of mechanisms able to fulfill the same functions. For example, there are many appropriate and visible alternative ways of providing transportation and communications. Such a wide range of social strategies is available in highly developed choice situations that any strictly functional definition of reciprocity or class conflict is simply not applicable.

Highly modernized systems embody a multibonded system of class that includes competitive clusters of groups that may be mutually hostile and at the same time related in diverse functional ways. Multifunctionality not reciprocity is the key to this concept.[5] Thus, our four main stratification categories are seen in terms of two variables, *mobility* and functional significance, or *germaneness*.

Segmentary stratification. This preclass situation is characterized by a permanent boundary around each group, or a lack of mobility, and criteria other than germaneness for membership. It may be "horizontal," as with African tribal groups occupying adjacent geographical areas, in which case we call it "ethnic." Or it may be "vertical," or layered, as with the hierarchy of Indian castes, in which case we call it "caste." Both have highly ritualized boundaries, with ritual expressing primordial attachments deriving from race, language, and religion. Ritualized norms reinforce the structural character of caste by reinforcing solidarity within and hostility toward those outside.[6]

5. It is not that the older notion of class should disappear but that it ought to be applied as originally intended and not tinkered with too much. That is, it should refer precisely to the common membership in a group that derives from a relationship to the means and modes of production, the consequence of which is a consciousness of life chances and normative proprieties, reciprocally defined. Such a notion of class, Weberian as well as Marxian, is at base a liberal one in which class, class interest, and motivation are considered to be different functions of the same phenomenon.

6. In a caste hierarchy within a single system it is possible that shared norms will define some castes as "chosen people" and others as ritually unclean, or what Weber called "pariah people." Normative religious situations may involve negative and positive reciprocities. Something of this sort may extend to other stratification situations, such as those involving patron-client relationships (for example, *haciendados* and *campesinos* in Indian areas of Peru). We could then speak of the relationship between patrons and clients as similar to that between castes. See T. Shibutani and K. M. Kwan, *Ethnic Stratification* (New York: Macmillan Co., 1965), pp. 82–115.

Fused stratification. In this condition a boundary exists between groups through which some mobility is possible, but difficult, and considerable functional germaneness is accepted as a criterion for group membership. As a result of common work and life chances, occupationally determined membership in a group or class produces a subculture with shared outlook that is clearly identifiable and in sharp contrast and conflict with other groups or classes. Not only is it difficult to move from one class to another, but once achieved, the move exposes the actor to ridicule and hostility from both his new and old classes. Class consciousness, then, is a characteristic of this type of stratification.

In a "class system" (in the Marxian and Weberian usages of the term), each class is engaged in sometimes hostile but also reciprocal relations with other classes based on the integration of their roles in the productive systems. Today the fused system is typically found where there is early-stage modernization with large rural classes, a small industrial proletariat (a somewhat larger subproletariat in urban areas), a large urban bourgeoisie, and a small aristocracy. Often the aristocracy and the rural peasantry form one set of reciprocal relations (patron-client), the subproletariat and the urban bourgeoisie a second set, and the industrial proletariat employed in expatriate industries along with the reciprocals (owners) of these industries, a third set.[7]

Differentiated stratification. This type of stratification implies great diversity in a society that rests on a more functionally complex and more "distributive" set of group relations than did the systems discussed so far. Membership criteria do not necessarily stress germaneness to a greater extent than in a fused system, except in the sense of giving greater significance and power to professionality and skill. Mobility is based on competition. Occupation is still crucial, but recruitment is by education for positions functionally relevant for the society as a whole rather than narrowly related to the process of production. As the society becomes more industrial, membership in a class is not dependent upon any one factor, such as occupation (place in the productive process), but many: education, place of residence, cultural attainments, religion, income, travel, and so on. Once the transition to industrialization is made, education becomes the most important qualification. Although some nongermane residual caste-ethnic characteristics (such as religion or race) may continue to be important, in general the trend is away from such "anachronistic" aspects of social stratification and toward an emphasis on instrumental values.

7. See Barringon Moore, *The Social Origins of Dictatorship and Democracy* (Boston: Beacon Press, 1966).

Structurally, differentiated classes lack stability. They are continually being broken up so that their boundaries are blurred. Small groups are arranged and rearranged in order of increasing professional power, and prestige is more narrowly differential as more and more positions proliferate. The groups on which this system is based are mainly interest groups. Hence, instead of solidaristic classes, there develop functional interest groups that favor instrumental values. This is why we say that the differentiated system is competitive, mobile, antisolidaristic, and pluralistic. In such a system, class is multibonded and Marshallian.[8]

Functional stratification. This type of system is a postclass phenomenon. It is found at the apotheosis of modernization—industrial or postindustrial society—when roles of critical functional significance have come into being. Many of these roles are found in specialized status clusters involving those creating information, such as scientists, research workers, and mathematicians, and those applying it, particularly in government, such as highly trained technocrats acting in supervisory, mediating roles.[9] In modernizing societies they are also to be found in groups whose status is based mainly on germaneness (expertise). Such roles are in practice the most closed and in theory the most open; that is, they are ordinarily open to all capable of going through the elaborate education and training required. These special status groups are characterized by their own technical languages (jargon), a sense of the boundaries of knowledge in their fields, and some sense of their wider significance in the social structure, particularly as the transition from late-stage modernization to industrialization begins. Normatively, they are completely instrumental except when obstacles to their role performance arise. They tend to see the universality of their expertise, with the result that professional solidarity is combined in them with instrumentalism. Structurally, they form professional groups and sustain supporting links and associations with their

8. See T. H. Marshall, *Citizenship and Social Development* (New York: Doubleday and Co., 1964).

9. See my discussion of career roles in *The Politics of Modernization.* It should be pointed out, if it is not already obvious, that the present set of stratification categories utilizes the more recent work of many writers on the subject. Perhaps the most important for our purposes is that of Ralf Dahrendorf. See his discussion of quasi-groups and the relation of these to imperatively coordinated associations. Dahrendorf makes the point that social classes and class conflict are present wherever authority is distributed unequally over social positions, a position with which we agree. See his *Class and Class Conflict in Industrial Society* (Stanford, Calif.: Stanford University Press, 1959), p. 247. See also Suzanne Keller, *Beyond the Ruling Class* (New York: Random House, 1963).

counterparts in other industrial societies through various international bodies. (See Figure 2.3.)

Stratification type	Characteristics	
	Structural	Normative
Segmentary	Set boundaries Fixed membership No mobility	Primordial attachments (e.g. race, tribe, religion)
Fused	Well-defined boundaries Limited mobility Solidarity	Ideologies
Differentiated	Weakly articulated boundaries Lack of solidarity	Interests
Functional	Well-defined boundaries Ease of mobility for those with germane attributes Solidarity within the social unit	Professional expertise

Figure 2.3. Normative and structural characteristics of stratification

By juxtaposing the characteristics of the types of political system and the stratification categories, we should be able to evaluate the effects of modernization on political systems, and vice versa. Only structural characteristics will be discussed here. We deal later with claims to representation by elites.

An important distinction between stratification categories can be made in terms of their bases of solidarity. The solidarity of the fused stratification system is based on similarities of predicament that lead to shared sentiments and bonds, the phenomenon described as "class consciousness." It can only occur when class boundaries are so hard that an individual who passes from one class to another is conscious of it and is proud or ashamed of his change.

In a differentiated system there is little fraternal loyalty to class as such, but instead there are practical attachments to friends, associates, and acquaintances. Such attachments may be quite superficial, but they help to determine status within a class. However, more important than class to the members of differentiated groups is the immediate social unit that limits and defines their conduct. General standards are important, in-

cluding civic postures. Manner and style, then, are substitutes for the
class consciousness and the feeling of general responsibility to a particular
class found in fused systems.

In fused systems even when class boundaries are a bit vague, there is an
identifiable awareness of class position, which is mainly indicated by
occupation. Groups may bear descriptive names like "proletariat" and
"bourgeoisie." Whatever the division, an awareness of class may accompany a sense of disjunction between equity and allocation. This sense of
inequity need not lead to class conflict; indeed, it may help to break up
fused relationships. Coalitions not polarizations are the result of development advancing far enough for education to be the key to "reallocation."
Occupation is also a distinctive characteristic of differentiated systems, of
course, but in them social mobility depends to a much greater extent on
education. As a society moves toward differentiated stratification, we assume that the role of education becomes increasingly important. However,
only a highly modernized system can absorb its educated elite.

The progression of segmentary, fused, differentiated, and functional
stratification categories is linear in the sense that each type is the result
of the society's degree of development. But the particular mixture of types
in any given case gives rise to different and nonlinear political inputs.
Ethnicity, for example, seems to count in functional status hierarchies in
Latin America and Africa and to be present but less important in the
United States. Tribe, race, caste, and religion may be present in societies
in all stages of development, in many possible combinations. In a situation of fused stratification, where occupation and income constitute the
main criteria of membership, there are many other possible secondary
distinctions between rural and urban persons, large landowners and
peasants, owners and workers, combines and small businesses, and so on.
In the differentiated type, the situation is even more complex. Although
differentiation is based on certain standardized criteria, education being
the most important, this system is also the most open and, because of its
multibonded character, contains some residual aspects of segmentary or
fused situations. In Nigeria, for example, an Ibo Catholic surgeon is generally of somewhat lower status on a differentiated scale than a Yoruba
Anglican surgeon. And as we have seen in the other categories, such distinctions are not restricted to modernizing countries. In Britain a man
recognized as a gentleman on the basis of residual fused criteria who occupied a differentiated schoolteacher's post would probably be higher on
a differentiated scale than a doctor in a fused system Welsh mining community.

Hence, although criteria germane to class become most important with differentiated stratification (and later with functional stratification), the criteria for this type are not necessarily simplified by this fact or even limited by it.[10] Since distinctions in this category are extremely subtle, their measurement becomes complex. Such complexity is increased by the frequent reevaluation of status rankings that occurs in a differentiated system. Particularly in industrial societies, distinctions of rank are revised vis-à-vis the frontier of knowledge, with theoretical scientists ranking higher than applied scientists.

Our discussion of modernization suggests that development produces a kind of allocational or stratification lag. Ranking that originated with caste or ethnic associations may retain not only a sentimental attachment based on primordial loyalties but also power based on the role of these associations as organizational boundaries for interest groups. Hence a stratification system may endure in spite of drastic changes in collective mobility and a host of related phenomena that inevitably accompany development.

Comparison of fused and differentiated types of stratification should not imply a conflict between them. For example, the fused type is not necessarily "working class" and the differentiated, "middle class." Nevertheless, conflict between types is possible. Fused-system groups of all levels, "upper" and "lower," may see the growth of differentiated groups as a threat. A particularly obvious example is the alliance of fused-system businessmen and workers against differentiated and functional status groups that form an educational elite. Education and style are then objects of envy, anger, and abuse, and are seen as threats to a class system based on occupation. In various early-stage developing societies, it is possible to find a fused-system upper-middle class composed of teachers, journalists, businessmen, civil servants, and lawyers, conscious of their vulnerability, cultural as well as economic, existing alongside rural ethnic groups such as tribes and urban marginal groups loosely organized along caste or ethnic lines. Alternatively, the marginal groups may show many differentiated characteristics, including subgroup competitiveness and an acceptance of gradations between occupational alternatives based mainly on degrees of education. For this group, clerkships, storekeeper posts, junior civil servant positions, and other lower-level jobs have class corollaries in residence, education of children, changes in church affiliation, and so on.

There is no inevitable stratification pattern of allocation for each degree or stage of modernization. Nor is there a hierarchy appropriate to each developmental type. As a general tendency, however, the greater the de-

10. We might also suggest that fused-system prestige is collective, that is, class determined, whereas in differentiated systems prestige is individualized.

gree of development, the more the differentiation phenomenon becomes a function of the upper levels of society rather than the lower. Even here there are problems of formulation. For example, a differentiated structure may change into a fused one, particularly under conditions of late-stage modernization. The range of mobility of lower-level differentiated groupings, such as those found in the *barriadas* outside Lima, may become restricted by the limitations of geography, which formerly provided new opportunities for population shifts from rural to urban centers, mountain to valley areas, and so on. As the boundaries grow rigid, real or pseudo-subproletarian fused groups are likely to grow out of the former differentiated groupings.

Whatever the changes in rank or position of various classes, distinctions based on the relevance of occupation and education continue to hold because of the strategic role of information and knowledge, new or derivative, in modernization. Even in early-stage modernizing societies, education is widely accepted as the main route to mobility. In highly industrialized societies with differentiated stratification systems, its role is even more decisive. In early-stage modernization, education may actually lead to unemployment, particularly in countries with high levels of illiteracy and few occupational alternatives. An individual may be prohibited from entering the labor market by virtue of his superior education, in part because he will not do the work of the uneducated but also because an insufficient number of posts are available for the educationally qualified. "Educational unemployment" is a common occurrence in early-stage developing countries with lower-level differentiated stratification. Such a predicament confronts many African countries today, not least because of the derivative character of their economies.[11] In industrial societies, as the competition for upper-level positions in the differentiated hierarchy increasingly is decided on the basis of education, advantages derived from an earlier fused system playing a smaller and smaller part, the opportunity to be part of the "meritocracy" will be based on equal entry and unequal dropout.

As a society becomes more industrialized, then, it moves away from caste toward functional status groups, and away from the Marxian fused system toward the Marshallian differentiated groupings. Extensive over-

11. Behavior in differentiated systems is very similar at lower and higher levels, although the style and manners in each case may be different. There is preoccupation with education on the one hand and with consumption on the other. The scale of consumption is lower in developing societies, but its manifestation in conspicuous waste is similar to the phenomenon of discarded automobiles and elaborate mansions of highly industrialized societies.

lapping will always occur between segmentary, fused, differentiated, and functional status groups, because one type does not necessarily disappear as another appears. Multiple membership is possible. Newly differentiated groups, showing great mobility as a result of functional germaneness, can coexist with segmentary and fused groups. This coexistence produces the complexity without coherence that we described earlier; it may or may not be characterized by conflict between classes within each type of stratification or between the types themselves.

This brief discussion of the multiple and overlapping aspects of stratification should help to clarify the pattern of pluralism that is produced by development and that may be explained in terms of allocation. In any of the stratification systems, there is the possibility of challenge from the traditional and agricultural caste groupings, whose leaders are skilled at the manipulation of primordial or class normative attachments. There is also the possibility of conflict from industrial workers whose experience of struggle has resulted in an anticommercial outlook. Alternatively, those occupied in commerce may also hamstring the new status elite, which is interested in more efficient means of development, by their antiplanning, short-term entrepreneurial propensities. Thus, in order for development to proceed, pluralistic coalitions must exist between diverse groups.

Multiple access to functionally significant roles is another potential source of conflict. Similar groups, instead of working together, are likely to become competitive with each other, as well as with older, less functionally significant groups that have nevertheless retained popular support. Thus there is a continuous need during modernization to search for convenient affiliations and mutual support. For example, roles associated with types of agricultural or industrial labor that have become visibly residual during the later stages of modernization do not disappear. Rather, those who occupy these roles look for new leaders to mobilize other forms of "relevance." If labor-saving devices minimize the need for an unskilled labor force, this search for relevance may, for a time, cause featherbedding and other protective activities. Of course, as industrialization proceeds and substantially fewer industrial workers are required, there will be role attrition, not only because roles have become residual but also because the functional significance of some industrial positions, particularly managers and technical personnel, will grow even if their proportionate numbers do not, thus creating a new rank of roles. These roles are likely to be separated from residuals of a fused system or others involved in the basic production process.

Agricultural roles tend to become more functionally significant in one sense and less in another. Their significance grows if agricultural productivity is a major source of investment funds for development. However, no matter what form the organization of agriculture may take, it is ordinarily more efficient than it appears on the surface, whereas the social system associated with it is less efficient especially insofar as it remains traditionalistic. Improving agricultural efficiency by introducing modern machinery and techniques may therefore also change the social structure. The enormous capital expense of modernization will rock the economic structure; unskilled farm laborers displaced by machinery will be forced to undergo rapid urbanization in a situation in which inadequate numbers of jobs await them. Agricultural roles are extremely varied. They may be seen in terms of patron-client relationships or involved in various types of corporate, community, or communal holdings. Membership in these groups may be based on caste or ethnic characteristics, on the nuclear or extended family, or on shareholding.

In contrast, commercial roles are much less varied. In early-stage modernization, they form preponderantly fused middle or upper classes that seek to generalize their significance by pressing the claims of their interests. Hence, the ideology of nationalism in early-stage modernizing societies is associated with expanding opportunities for a local bourgeoisie. This fused middle class enlarges as development occurs. Related ideologies of nationalism view middle-class commercial roles as the stabilizing centers of gravity in new nations. At this stage education counts for less than occupation, since command over resources, human and national, is embodied in an occupational role.[12] In this view, the middle sectors expand at the expense of the aristocratic and rural patron sectors.

This is the classic liberal definition of development: not that a fused system becomes differentiated, but that all fused groups eventually blend into an "extended middle." Indeed, much American overseas aid policy is based on this notion. Our contention, however, is that modernization, instead of throwing all classes into one, is more likely to produce another pattern[13] in which civil service roles proliferate and come to embody more and more of the specialized attributes of functional status groupings plus highly instrumental values. Since the major structural problem during modernization is a lack of organizational skills, especially at the middle

12. This was particularly characteristic of very early-stage development, such as that undertaken by West African nationalists in the 1920s and 1930s.

13. See Morris Zelditch and Bo Anderson, "On the Balance of a Set of Ranks," in Joseph Berger, Morris Zelditch, and Bo Anderson, eds., *Sociological Theories in Progress* (Boston: Houghton Mifflin Co., 1966), pp. 248–49. See also Alain Touraine, "Management and the Working Class in Western Europe," *Daedalus,* Winter 1964, p. 332, in which he speaks of "conflictual participation" as the characteristic of a "new" working class.

and lower levels, the expanding network of bureaucratic roles is actually a way of organizing resources. What does *not* occur is a class struggle between fused groupings, for group alignments are more complex than that. Nevertheless, this proliferation of the civil service creates a perpetual pull in favor of a bureaucratic type of political system. Pluralism plus bureaucracy rather than class conflict is the result.

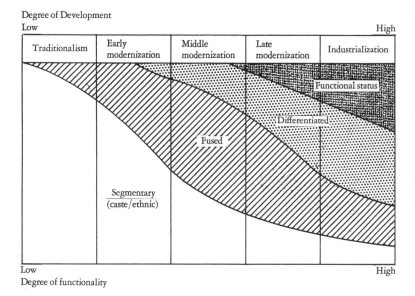

Figure 2.4. Stratification and pluralism

Figure 2.4 emphasizes the overlapping pattern of relationships that are continually becoming more complex, the changes in the functional germaneness to industrialization of each type, and the decreasing likelihood of conflict. Turning now to the normative dimension of choice, we find that the picture is also interesting. Modernization is accompanied by a shift away from primordial attachments of race, religion, and language, all nongermane to development and associated with more or less ritualized boundaries. At the fused level of groupings, there is growing solidarity and class awareness involving the articulation of moral issues within a political subculture. These fused groups do not form a "working class," however, but a commercial middle class or, in the classic sense of the word, a bourgeoisie. As modernization continues, the normative emphasis on solidarity and class awareness changes to an emphasis on instrumental values, reflecting the growth of interest groups and an increase in the types of activities leading to accommodation rather than conflict, and reconciliation instead of persistent hostility. Lower-level fused groups remain small even after industrialization has begun because new technologies are not labor-intensive. Competition arises for various germane attributes. A permeable differentiated system recruits from residual fused and segmentary types on the basis of educational attainment. As the society moves closer to industrialization, certain highly instrumentalized functional status roles become strategic. The normative consequence of structural pluralism accompanied by instrumentalization is the conversion of values into interest and the creation of groups that support or challenge this conversion: the condition of embourgeoisement. This is why we suggest that modernization produces embourgeoisement in a bureaucratic form.

EMBOURGEOISEMENT AND BUREAUCRACY

The preoccupation with occupation, mobility, short-term coalitions, and consumption creates a frame for the response we call embourgeoisement. It should be clear from the start that this is by no means a condition limited to capitalistic forms of modernization; it applies equally to socialist forms. It leads to bureaucratism, opportunism, and corruption, to efforts to provide for family, friends, and associates and to reduce risks in what is seen as a hostile and demanding environment. But embourgeoisement does not necessarily imply irresponsibility. It is possible to find the most responsible elements in a society involved in coalitions that will favor their work. For example, engineers, plant managers, and other technicians in socialist societies, in a desire to regulate and make more predictable the immediate world of their expertise, may attempt to reduce the ambiguities of role conflict, thereby minimizing the effects of political actions that are a response to ambiguity. This may have politically, dysfunctional consequences, although it may be highly successful economically, as when the most productive managers of an industrial plant in China are judged, from a political point of view, to be irresponsible bourgeois elements, opportunists, or worse.

Embourgeoisement occurs when there is an intersection of instrumental values with functionally accommodated roles. A certain degree of role stability is necessary, and the perpetuation of such stability soon becomes a goal. The result is an emphasis on rewards, including respect, dignity, and a style of life that underscores traditional virtues. Expenditure on items to symbolize these virtues, such as houses, furnishings, and clothes, is a familiar characteristic of embourgeoisement. This is why the "consumption function" is important for our analysis.[14] If there is corruption in the bureaucracy, it leads not to satisfaction but to a self-righteous, even angry, defense by bureaucrats who blame the confusion in society for their behavior.

Obviously, there are different styles of embourgeoisement, each determined by the society in which it occurs. In countries in the early stages of modernization, embourgeoisement tends to emerge in political and business roles. In middle-stage modernization, embourgeoisement is frequently found in professional roles, such as those of doctor, lawyer, teacher, professor, and senior civil servant. In later stages of modernization, it touches the new technocrats. This progressive quality of embourgeoisement should not be understood to imply that those affected first become less bourgeois as more and more roles are involved. Rather, we suggest that the process is progressive and cumulative.

Embourgeoisement is an important aspect of modernization for more than stylistic reasons, however. It has the effect of exaggerating the consumption function without correspondingly affecting the production function.[15] It occurs as classes become multibonded (based on a variety of criteria), as group boundaries become increasingly fluid, and as fixed identifications or loyalties are replaced by competitive group affiliations— that is, when society is divided not by powerful antagonistic classes but by competitive interests. In a fused system, conflicts of interest are likely to be converted into conflicts of values (primordial or ideological, as the case may be). In a competitive, pluralistic, and multibonded class system, however, the process is reversed: conflicts of value are likely to be converted into conflicts of interest.

The embourgeoisement hypothesis can be restated as follows: the greater the degree of modernization, the larger the number of pluralistic and competitive instrumentalistic groupings in the system and the less likely a successful revolution. What results is not polarization but pluralism. However, a contrary hypothesis is equally plausible: the greater the degree of modernization, the more extensive the proliferation of roles originally derived from an industrial setting, the less effective the government's

14. See, for example, Pi-chao Chen, "Individual Farming after the Great Leap: As Revealed by the Lieu Kiang Documents," *Asian Survey* 8. (Sept. 1968): 724–91.

15. The reason for this effect of embourgeoisement is by no means simple. It has both functional and dialectical aspects to it that have not been properly explored except in some very superficial ways (as in Milovan Djilas' argument about the rise of the "new class" and in writings as diverse as those of Trotsky and Burnham). As a practical matter, however, the way modernization proceeds determines in some measure the results.

ability to coordinate social life and cope with the growing chaos. In this hypothetical situation, pressure for a revolutionary solution must come from above.

SOME POLITICAL CONSEQUENCES

We have said that, in general, the growing significance during modernization of differentiated groupings and embourgeoisement does not eliminate other groupings. Where castes remain, they constantly seek to extend their relevance. If this fails at the structural level, it may still succeed at the normative—where primordial loyalties to race, religion, culture, and language are represented. If the normative relevance is supported by some strategic role advantages, these advantages are likely to take the form of either roles appropriate to primordial attachments (e.g., in the church or in the army) or residual claims to property (e.g., like those of fused-system landowners). Which of the two forms emerges will depend on whether the residual segmentary stratification system is horizontal or vertical.

If the segmentary system is vertical, it is likely to be transformed from a caste to an estates system, in the sense that its component parts have legally defined boundaries, rights, and obligations. If our theory of embourgeoisement is correct, as modernization proceeds caste norms shift from consummatory to instrumental values—in other words, from primordial rights to interests. As instrumentalization increases the vulnerability of traditional groupings to modernization, the vertical system tends to rely on its special institutional supports to resist. Surviving reciprocal class and caste relations prove useful for this purpose. When the highest castes are linked solidly with the lowest classes in patron-client relationships, as in southern Italy and many Latin countries, a united front is created to combat the threat of modernization.[16]

Caste relationships of the vertical type are based to a great extent on kinship. By means of a virtual monopoly on cosmopolitan education, higher castes have often retained access to government more successfully than their numbers or functional significance would suggest. When these higher castes form an aristocracy, it is possible for them to manipulate political life so as to deflect modernization insofar as it threatens them. Obstacles to modernization may thus be inherent in the vertical caste system.

The horizontal segmentary system for the most part is composed of

16. See Michael Parenti, "Ethnic Politics and the Persistence of Ethnic Identification," *American Political Science Review* 61 (Sept. 1967). See also Sidney Tarrow, *Peasant Communism in Italy* (New Haven, Conn. Yale University Press, 1967), and Edward Banfield, *The Moral Basis of a Backward Society* (Glencoe, Ill.: The Free Press, 1957).

ethnic or tribal groupings occupying the same political space. Examples are Nigeria and the Congo, where such horizontal groupings pose the problem commonly known as tribalism—competition between tribes at the expense of the larger society to which they all belong. The result of tribalism in times of modernization may be civil war or secession. And tribalism can have other effects on modernization through its tendency to allocate political offices, fellowships and university places, and other positions to fellow tribesmen, for example. On the normative level, this type of system puts tribe above nation and thereby casts doubt on the legitimacy of the nation. On the structural level, it causes basic cleavages in social allegiances, so that each new strain divides society along the same lines.[17] Hence, conflicts over development, local government, education, and so on, which inevitably accompany modernization, reinforce separatism and pose the political problems of unity and legitimacy. In sum, the threat posed by modernization to the primordial loyalties and functional significance of ethnic groupings results in the attachment of their members to groups or individuals whose normative status is given precedence over that of society as a whole and whose structural status is separatist and exclusive.

In our fused stratification category, the contemporary modernizing situation is very different from the Marxian notion of reciprocal functional relations between increasingly polarized occupational groups. It has already been suggested that in the early and middle stages of modernization it is likely that the fused system will lean more toward the middle class (defined as a modernizing group with roles drawn directly from an industrial setting and with caste as its reciprocal) than toward other classes of the fused type. In short, modernization does not provide a dramatic confrontation between a powerful group of industrial captains on the one side and a large group of industrial proletarians on the other. Instead, the class that comes to pre-eminence is urban, commercial, familial, and solidaristic to the extent that it feels vulnerable to downward mobility (that is, to falling into the ever-present reservoir of lower castes and classes) and is in an ambiguous position vis-à-vis higher castes and classes. The dominant middle group in the fused stratification pattern is likely to desire upward mobility into a "modern" style of life and will ask that other groups identify its success with the general development of the country. (Liberal and religious normative values support this group's view.) At a later stage of modernization, this is the class most likely to

17. Perhaps the best illustrations are to be found in Africa, with the Biafran war being the most dramatic and tragic.

turn into a differentiated group, with a small fused group of the proletarian sort standing in opposition.

When a large nonsolidaristic bourgeoisie is confronted with a small solidaristic working class, the working class is more likely to search for a place on the general differentiated mobility ladder by the threat of revolutionary disorder than to undertake a revolution that would actually create sufficient opportunities for upward mobility. Moreover, opportunities are slow to expand when a particular combination of segmentary, fused, and differentiated groups exists, resulting in a stratification stalemate imposed by pluralistic group activity and competition; in such a situation, lower groups must settle for short-term gains on the basis of temporary coalitions. To put the matter differently, as the number and type of groups multiply, marginal gains become more difficult to achieve and the society reaches an allocation stalemate.

Finally, we come to the new status elites, those occupying what we have called "career roles." Among the most important of these are the technocrats, whose functional significance becomes greater as modernization proceeds, and certain bureaucrats. Technocrats are underemployed in most modernizing societies because of the lack of supporting facilities, material and human, that would enable them to contribute to development. As a result, they lose heart and tend to abuse their roles or to become politicians. Bureaucrats are also likely to follow this course, but for opposite reasons; they most often have too much to do and become resentful. There are exceptions, of course. For example, the old Indian civil service could draw from a middle class of the fused type and thereby sustain its high quality even after the original conditions favoring its historical evolution had diminished.

We can also mention another role that has political consequences of great significance—that of the intellectuals, who represent universalized ideological norms with differentiated class references, or, in some cases, residual caste references that they reject. Most intellectuals in modernizing societies come from bourgeois groups of the fused or differentiated type, but they reject the competitive instrumentalism of the differentiated system. Hence, it is the intellectuals who become the carriers of consummatory values and represent revolutionary innovation. Their ideologies, all-embracing to be sure, are particularly designed to link them to lower caste or residual fused groups, as when young radicals in Buenos Aires adopt Peronism or the cause of "the workers." Quite often, though, their ideologies and activities mobilize residual caste groups against them, resulting in the appearance of polarization without its substance, in the sense that upper "residuals" are posed against lower "marginals" while the bulk of the population continues to move toward a differentiated type of competitive mobility situation. The problem for government is how to avoid becoming imprisoned in the various maneuvers of such groups. If it fails, it becomes exposed and vulnerable to a takeover by any organized group with the capacity to move quickly and immobilize its opposition. Not mass revolution but coup d'état is the consequence of modernization, and not by a mass public but by an elite. This is what we mean by revolution from above. Late-stage modernization thus contains the possibility (it is no more than that) of both stagnation and coup. It is an interesting predicament for both populist revolutionaries (especially those among the radical bourgeoisie) and all governments of the nonmobilization type.

Our comments may be summarized. In the most general terms, the structural processes just described involve the adoption of function as the principle of role allocation at the expense of reciprocal obligation; the normative processes involve secularization at the expense of the sacred. All of our stratification types tend to follow this sequence, but the transition is never clear-cut. The particular modes of differentiation and values will vary from place to place. In addition, the secularization of traditional values opens up a normative space into which new norms can be introduced, although (from a behavioral point of view) not very easily. The resulting political problem of society is a lack of solidarity, a high degree of competitive bargaining among members with few internalized restraints, and an emphasis on short-term gains. This is the classic situation of the reconciliation system.

The political problem of the modernizing society is thus posed on two levels. First, how will modernization be achieved? Second, what political system is it likely to support? According to our discussion, political instability may be the most favorable condition for further development.

We are now in a position to state what is perhaps the most important paradox of the modernizing society, particularly in its late stages. The allocation pattern has created pressures for embourgeoisement. These in turn have exercised a pull toward a reconciliation system. But a reconciliation system would limit development because it does not allow the concentration of resources for rapid growth. The most appropriate type of political system for development would be the mobilization system. *Thus developmental pressures tend to produce a dysfunctional political system, and the system that would be most functionally useful is very difficult to put into practice.* The most common resolution of this problem in modernizing societies is through some variant of a bureaucratic system.

If our assumptions about embourgeoisement are correct, we should be able to specify certain propositions about the process at various stages.

In the case of industrialized societies, the spread of embourgeoisement coincides with the resolution of the allocation crisis: increases in the social product are accompanied by greater opportunities to exercise choice over roles, together producing a collective mobility for the entire system, including an increase in access to various status roles. In late-stage modernizing societies, however, this mobility occurs primarily between differentiated roles; there is little increase in the opportunity for movement from fused to differentiated groupings. The result is a shifting of the allocation crisis downward, with the following effects. Differentiated groups confront fused groups more sharply. Fused groups develop a particular set of counternorms. Differentiated groups become instrumentalized and try to form alliances that cut across residual segmentary and fused stratification lines. Revolution from below becomes increasingly less likely, but revolution from above, which seeks to bridge fused and differentiated group differences and conflicts and which makes particular use of status elites functionally related to industrialization, becomes more acceptable. Thus, the likely effects of embourgeoisement during late-stage modernization are revolution from above, with tendencies toward a mobilization governmental form; or the emergence of a bureaucratic system. If a bureaucratic system materializes, it will be vulnerable to many of the same pressures that gave rise to it in the first place, and it is likely to be replaced by a system closer to a reconciliation type under which the allocation crisis will continue more or less as before.

A mobilization system is most likely to succeed at the point of maximum embourgeoisement in late-stage modernization, but not by mass revolutionary action. Its leaders are likely to be bourgeois radicals, whose links are with status elites (technocrats) and whose ideologies are populist, socialist, nationalist, or national-socialist. Modernizing societies, then, become revolutionary through bourgeois radicalism, a phenomenon frequently commented upon but insufficiently analyzed. A mobilization system, however, is least likely to be able to cope with embourgeoisement. Hence, the political paradox of modernization: embourgeoisement creates the conditions both for a mobilization system and for its demise. This we regard as the crucial political predicament encountered by governments in all modernizing countries.

What these comments suggest is that revolutions from below in the form of people's revolts that begin in armed rebellion and end in general social disruption are less likely than we might assume. Popular rebellions or mass movements are more a nineteenth-century phenomenon than a contemporary one. In our view, normative and structural conditions during modernization are much more likely to result in an aggressive, highly instrumentalized and increasingly mobile population that may not necessarily be productive or entrepreneurial in the real sense of the term but may be dominated by narrow self-interest, commercialism, and the desire for mobility. Looking for security rather than for innovation, the population will tend to live off commercial activities of the type common to derivative economies. Such results of modernization are fostered by large urban areas with small industries at the periphery and a rural hinterland, conditions that are found on a relatively modest scale in Dakar, Accra, Lagos, and Nairobi, and on a larger scale in Buenos Aires, Santiago, Mexico City, and Lima.

A second proposition about revolution and radicalization becomes relevant when purposeful developmental goals are frustrated by functional randomness and normative polarization. Functional randomness or even role incompatibility as a consequence of modernization paves the way for revolution from above, particularly if a normative vacuum accompanies randomization. Then coups d'état and forays from any organized source are more likely to succeed. Long-run success, however, is possible only if the new régime can generate enough popular support to create an effective restructuring of roles along more immediately functional lines and a normative system that affects motivation. Ideologies of revolution from above may be of any political shade. There might be a revival of "corporate" normative theories, not dissimilar to fascist ideologies, based on a dialectical tension between nationalist and socialist ideological pulls; the structural units of such a system would be functional corporate groups possessing external institutional support. Indeed, fascism (stripped of some of its more atavistic characteristics, perhaps) might reappear as an ideology with considerable relevance, to be preferred to some of the more anarchic theories of socialism.

RADICALIZATION FROM ABOVE

The analysis so far makes certain assumptions about the normative and structural consequences of development during modernization. Choice is enlarged. The range and number of roles potentially open to members of society increase. Competition for these roles intensifies. Institutional groupings mediate the growing competition either by trying to monopolize and control entry or by eliminating it. Such change wears away at established notions of equity. Older and more traditional ideologies are broken or die and are revived in new forms. Those appropriate to a more fixed and stable order give way. There is a general downgrading of consummatory values in favor of instrumental values more relevant to development and to competition between interest groups. Under such circumstances, if the equity-allocation relationship is at all responsive to expanding choice, embourgeoisement should combine successfully with a reconciliation system to minimize the difficulties of transition to industrialization, liberating many sources of participation and involvement, stimulating growth and activity. That, of course, is the liberal ideal. It lies behind such programs as the Alliance for Progress, not to speak of other types of aid designed to expand choice, make allocation more flexible, and allow greater public participation on the basis of instrumental values related to development. According to this ideal, development is its own reward.

But if other assumptions are also correct, the success of this pattern is exceedingly rare. For one thing, the equity-allocation relationship is characteristically different from the responsive ideal, with previous advantage leading to a more or less successful monopolization of increased allocation opportunities rather than to an expansion of choice. Institutionalized mediating groups restrict the downward flow of role allocation, not in simple class terms but by means of coalitions that limit immediate benefits to the cooperating parties. The smaller the coalitions, the greater the benefits for their participants. No fixed membership is necessary, however, and the pattern of coalition can include representatives of all groups able at one point or another to generate populist, interest, or professional sources of power. As modernization increases, so do the possible coalitions, and although it can be argued that in the long run this is in itself a form of reallocation, it may be the very long run indeed.

Moreover, such bargaining between groups creates conditions of corruption. Groups become gamblers, with equity determined entirely by highly instrumentalized and short-term bargains. In terms of general social norms associated with choice, there is lack of trust in others and a minimum of reliance on law, courts, and other civil procedures. A consummatory space is likely to appear alongside such extreme instrumentalism, representing a longing for some sort of moral rejuvenation, a new beginning. Hence, when development follows this pattern, one behavioral consequence is the need for innocence—the desperate desire to be fresh, to have direct relationships btween individuals, and to do away with the hypocrisy and the atmosphere of fraud that permeate political life. This is particularly the case among those whose fundamental roles, as civil servant, technocrat, or university lecturer, have about them some generalized commitment to the future and to the development of the society as a whole (that is, to the industrial part of the modernizing society). These persons are likely to be the most corrupted by such a situation because they are inevitably co-opted in one way or another by various interest

groups or coalitions. But not always: it is interesting that a significant proportion of the radicalized leadership in modernizing countries consists of
teachers, doctors, lawyers, and civil servants. When they in effect "jump"
their roles to form counter-elites in which highly consummatory values
require selfless devotion to the state and to the objectives of development,
a radicalization process has begun. These elites embody different ideas of
equity to be realized by a reclassification of roles according to criteria of
germaneness to industrialization or some other objective standard. These
are the sources for the mobilization system. The ideological pulls come
from groups that are unwilling to strike the bargains offered to them and
that resist being co-opted.

In general, two factors militate against the mobilization system. One, as
we have suggested, is the flexibility of the coalitions that can offer immediate benefits and advantages to all with some education and a bit of a
following. The other, a characteristic weakness of the mobilization system, lies in the relationship between development and allocation, namely,
the limited accountability of those controlling choice to the elites created
by development. Except as bands, guerrillas, or other small underground
groups, where camaraderie and hierarchy can be successfully combined, a
lack of political participation prevents involvement in the society. Even
the most successful mobilization system is plagued by the problem of
pseudoparticipation, which in turn creates an imbalance in the relationship
between norms and structures. The consummatory values associated with
revolutionary purity soon give way to instrumental values, and the pressures to return to some form of reconciliation system grow.

At this point, it is interesting to consider cases in which the response to
development has in one way or another been kept within bounds, so that
the development-order relationship has not been upset. Two notable cases
are the Philippines and India. In India the British legacy of a powerful
civil service plus the extension of instrumental values to include the
proprieties of government provide the most interesting illustration of two
types of political systems (reconciliation and bureaucratic) operating
effectively, one inside the other.

The great difficulty with the purely bureaucratic system is its combination of hierarchical authority and instrumental values, which increasingly
requires reliance on coercion (unless it is possible to revitalize primordial
racial or religious or nationalist values to reinforce the instrumental ones).
Under some circumstances this is possible; Egypt, for example, relies
periodically on intensifying the conflict with Israel for this purpose. Without such dramatic confrontations, however, the normative tendency is in
the other direction. It becomes impossible to obtain the necessary public

response to government-defined development policies. Bureaucratic systems are not capable of generating any "big push" into industrialization unless they receive unusual amounts of outside assistance, as, for example, did Taiwan.

In general, then, we can suggest the political tendencies that are most pronounced in the transition from early to late modernization. (See Figure

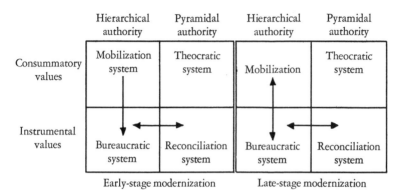

Figure 2.5. Responses of political systems to modernization

2.5.) Systems originating in the mobilization form (such as Ghana, Guinea, and Indonesia) or reconciliation form (such as Nigeria, the Congo-Kinshasha, and Sierra Leone) show periodic tendencies in the early stages of modernization toward bureaucratic systems, in a military or some other form. Bureaucratic systems show a continual tendency toward the reconciliation type, producing a pattern of instability characteristic of late-stage modernizing societies. However, some bureaucratic systems (Peru) also generate tendencies toward the mobilization type (Cuba, China), which in turn shows bureaucratic tendencies.

These varying tendencies during modernization when combined with the embourgeoisement hypothesis lead us to a tentative conclusion about political response to development. Continuous variation in the type of political system is itself an important characteristic of modernization. It has the effect of altering the relationships between society and government and by this means opening up, for a short time, at any rate, a new set of options. Hence, with respect to modernizing societies, political instability, seem as the continuous rearrangement of political relationships, may itself be both a result of modernization and a cause of further development.

3. Equity and Allocation in Industrial Societies

The analysis of modernization so far has led us to define certain stratification systems through which we might operationalize the allocation variable. By stressing the more derivative characteristics of such systems, we were able to suggest certain structural tendencies. The relationship of norms and structures is continually changing, with each part in some measure varying independently of the other, and it provides an important focus for empirical research on concrete societies, particularly for comparative research dealing with the responses of different types of political systems to highly generalized problems.

How far norms and structures can diverge is an open question. In all concrete systems the mechanisms of adjustment are ordinarily flexible enough to respond to changing needs. In addition, the dialectic over norms most often occurs when there is a threat to legitimacy. If such threats can be met by reviving old consummatory values or instrumentalizing basic value conflicts, the political system may be preserved even when there is dissatisfaction with its structures. Precisely because of the wide range of possible strategies and combinations, we need to penetrate below the surface of events, instrumentalities, and techniques of rule to identify analytically some limits to the alternatives.

INDUSTRIALIZATION AS A DYNAMIC PROCESS

Industrialization is dynamic in the sense that industrial societies generate new knowledge at an exceptionally rapid rate, apply it to all aspects of social life, and at the same time produce exportable industrial surpluses. Although a country such as Israel may have very high research potential, if that potential cannot be utilized at home, the country is still not industrialized. If a country produces an exportable industrial surplus only because of the presence of the branch of a foreign industrial firm as in Latin American countries, it is not industrialized, although it may be industrializing.

An industrial society is already bourgeois (whether in socialist or capitalist terms is irrelevant). Insofar as modernization and industrialization proceed together, the conditions of embourgeoisement are present. However, since the occupational structure of an industrial society reflects a hierarchy of roles based on their relation to knowledge and information functions, the result is not only bourgeois but meritocratic. A bourgeois meritocracy embodies a functional definition of merit that combines open recruitment with unequal role distribution. Consequently, any rejection of roles functionally related to information triggers a search for new meaning and contributes to a continuous redefinition of equity. This is because roles related to information creation are, in industrial societies, self-legitimating. Rejection of them by those eligible for such roles creates the bourgeois radicals. The greater the degree of industrialization, the more meritocratic the stratification system and the more widespread the search for meaning.

The continuous redefinition of a society's consummatory values is evidence of what we mean by radicalization; the legitimacy of the system is being questioned. Like embourgeoisement, radicalization is caused by a normative-structural imbalance. The hypothesis we suggest is that the more industrialized a society becomes, the greater its crisis in meaning. Since an industrial society is based on high information, the type of political system best able to facilitate information formation would appear to be a reconciliation system. But this type is the very one that because of excessive instrumentalism is always in danger of losing its legitimacy; as a result it is vulnerable to pulls from other types (particularly bureaucratic and mobilization systems). This political vulnerability highlights the fundamental predicament of highly industrial societies, namely, that high degrees of embourgeoisement produce radicalization. Moreover, this predicament can confront governments in all highly industrialized societies whether they are capitalist, socialist, or guided by a combination of ideologies.

The continuous crisis in industrial society is puzzling primarily because it is difficult to conceive of industrialization as a predicament rather than as an achievement. It is as if those who live in industrial societies see their past not as a landscape studded with monuments to their accomplishments, but rather as a combat zone littered with casualties. The political effects of this disillusionment are just beginning to be visible both in countries like the United States and in slightly less industrialized ones like Japan and the USSR. The phrase "postindustrial society" expresses a sensitivity to the need for new and different political solutions to the problems of industrialization.

Consciousness of a predicament is one of the distinguishing characteristics of an industrial society. Within modernizing societies a widely accepted view—particularly by leaders—is that industrialization is the final solution to the problems that plague them. The advantage of such a view is a certain programmatic innocence in which general agreement is easily reached about policy objectives and developmental goals. Few such illusions persist in highly industrial societies. The competitive pace of new knowledge contributes to the functional vulnerability of roles; they are no longer linked together in groups based on solidarity but are locked into networks in which the parts are as replaceable as those of machines. The vulnerability of the individual is increased; new marginals are created as old ones disappear; political inequities multiply.

The multibonded character of differentiated classes in an industrial society contributes to status incongruities but also makes them less important. Although there may be many routes to a particular rank or status, one route may have been crucial for obtaining other characteristics. Occupation was in this category for roles in the old fused system. Education is similarly salient for differentiated roles in industrial societies. Hence we can pick out salient (and therefore desirable) roles and use them not only to determine a wide range of other class characteristics but also to define mobility within the stratification system. Of the changes that may occur in the shift from modernization to industrial society, therefore, two will stand out; the increase and spread of status incongruities and the expansion of salient roles.

The stratification picture is complicated by the fact that no industrial nation is without its modernizing sector which, in the context of stratification in an industrial society, is composed of marginals. The issues of political life are confused because the needs of both sectors are so different. The modernizing sector wants embourgeoisement—in particular, greater social mobility. It does not, however, challenge prevailing concepts of equity unless mobility is denied it. At the far end of the spectrum, at the top of the industrialized sector, the new technocratic elite shows signs of becoming antibourgeois. That is, its radicalization has begun, accelerated by increasing concern over the dehumanizing consequences of a functional universe, created, of course, by its own activities.[1] Between these two sectors, modernizing and industrial, is a wide range of groups, each of which defines equity in a different way. The result is a curious dialectic on the normative level between opposite structural groups: prosystem marginals versus antisystem bourgeois radicals. Hence, the same forces that generate embourgeoisement in modernizing systems produce the opposite result in industrial ones, where the difficulties are compounded by the way industrial countries coexist with modernizing ones,

1. This "technocratic alienation" is widespread among biologists, physicists, engineers, and others engaged in military research or in activities producing such consequences as air pollution, water pollution, and urban decay.

by the way industrial countries coexist with each other, and by the fact that both systems do not follow in a simple manner the tendencies just described.

CHARACTERISTICS OF INDUSTRIAL ROLES

A truly instrumentalist society is impossible without complete internalization of shared norms by members of the system (if only because of the randomization of ends). Complete internalization of norms requires an effective socialization process built on a stable structural base.

Until recently it was widely believed that knowledge was open-ended and that information, applied through an expanding educational system, was capable of extending the area of rational control over empirical problems. Thus, industrial society appeared to possess the secret of self-validating moral purposes and a view of knowledge so dynamic that it created its own demands and its own categorical imperatives.

But new knowledge does not necessarily replace old knowledge. Nor does knowledge follow narrow grooves of expertise. As it expands, it creates new paradigms, signal systems, word sets, and overlapping theories. Input-output models, stimulus-response models, the concept of feedback, and other types of systems theory spread from research to applied fields as diverse as engineering, psychology, and business planning and marketing. With the application of knowledge, a mutually comprehensible language makes its appearance. Although it is useful, it creates insiders and outsiders. Generalized models become core theories that can be borrowed and applied from subject to subject. Eventually, this process gives rise to metalanguages. Metatheories also form, establishing boundaries of participation for special elites that have gained access to power by monopolistic control of technical knowledge. Such functional elites are the ultimate result of concentrating on instrumental ends. Knowledge, therefore, extends the process of instrumentalization but at the expense of consummatory values.

Traditional democratic theories are becoming obsolete because they are based on the assumption that any normative problem can be solved by enlarging political participation, leaving questions of meaning to chance. Unfortunately, the solution is not that simple. The industrial process, by generating new knowledge, continuously superimposes multibonded and functional elite classes and groups on an existing network of groupings based on ideologies and interests. Antagonisms and coalitions with complex political consequences result.

Because of its strategic role in industrial society, then, knowledge creates a functional hierarchy and multibonded classes composed of small nonsolidaristic groupings defined by multiple criteria. It also creates unique sets of marginals.[2] These marginal groups are likely to be found in residual areas of society such as castes or among newly debased fused or differentiated groupings. For them, opportunities to participate are severely limited. Some never attempt to participate. Those who try and fail are likely to fall back on primordial norms to fill the normative vacuum and to respond to populist appeals. It is the marginals' attachment to primordial norms that enables politicians to manipulate them in order to attack technocrats or other intellectuals who represent rationalistic instrumentalism and, derived from it, liberal economic presuppositions. This conflict over instrumentalism increasingly identifies the main areas of political controversy. Its dialectical forms are knowledge versus anti-intellectualism and elitism versus populism, which are incorporated in a specific ideological package appropriate to the political culture of the society. The growing instrumentalization of values is accompanied by a search for simplistic, consummatory formulas. Not the end of ideologies but their proliferation is the chief normative problem of this stage, heightening the instability already engendered by science and technology and the substitution of new knowledge for old. If our assumptions are correct, the industrial society is characterized by increasing instrumental clarity and power based on new information and by greater consummatory confusion and power based on populism. Occupants of nonfunctional roles, or roles losing functional significance, are susceptible to reactionary or conservative norms, whereas individuals that reject instrumental criteria are attracted to radical or revolutionary norms. That is the main point of the present discussion of radicalization as a crisis of meaning for highly industrial societies. The *industrial society becomes a universe of calculation for its elite and a universe of chance for its mass.*

If the liberal tradition underlying the democratic ideology of representa-

2. Problems of mass society are not characteristic of highly industrialized societies. It is in modernizing ones or in the modernizing sectors of industrial societies that there is undisguised nonparticipation. Industrial systems, on the contrary, are individualizing; they articulate alternatives for different skills, provide more opportunities for choice, and as a result intensify the burden on individuals. It is not mass man who is the problem of industrial society but increasingly personalized man who makes his claim to be treated in all his variability and complexity. This claim has the effect of enlarging the scope and number of roles of the technical status elites. Screening, evaluating, and testing in order to study how human beings achieve satisfaction in their work, their leisure, and their family relations all become relevant. The computer, symbol of wickedness, one of the culprits of the mass society hypothesis, is in that capacity a myth. Such machines, on the contrary, make it possible to take into account individual variations of increasing numbers of people.

tive government (capitalist or socialist) accepts that instrumentalization is capable of creating its own self-validating and universalized ends manifested in a stable set of rationalistic consummatory norms, our discussion suggests several reasons to doubt this view. The instrumentalization of norms produced by an increasingly rationalistic universe of information leaves too great a meaning gap. Purpose and action are divorced. Preoccupation with short-term objectives, the breakdown of moral constraints, and the personalization of failure are some of the consequences of this divorce.

Pluralism, a structural imperative of highly complex systems, becomes the instrument of false values and slipshod solutions. Many ardent advocates of purer forms of democracy attack pluralism because it increases the structural coherence of a system at the expense of its normative coherence. For example, growing instrumentalization may result in the proliferation of interest groups that cater to a range of more or less functional demands; if the elites of these groups have access to decision-making and their sources of power are hardened into fixed stratification categories, this in itself becomes a source of inflexibility in the system that seriously weakens its ability to develop. Hence, the response to development in industrial society is twofold: it results in the establishment of functional claims as the basis of allocation; it fosters instrumentalization at the expense of consummatory values. The modernizing sector of an industrial society holds to such values if increased social mobility is possible for its members. The industrial sector responds by dividing into two main groups —one that favors instrumentalization and intensifies it by performing certain roles and the other that rejects instrumentalization and seeks either to revive fading consummatory values or to create new ones. These two groups arise to fill the normative space created both by immobilities in allocation and by equity conflicts resulting from excessive instrumentalization. Although industrial society should be a situation of wide choice for any individual, this normative confusion turns opportunities for choice into an illusion.[3] Disorderly development is thus endemic in an increasingly rationalized universe.

EMERGING ALLOCATION PATTERNS IN INDUSTRIAL SOCIETY

This interpretation of the industrial crisis can be linked to our form of structural analysis more specifically. We have defined information as a key variable in determining hierarchy, a meritocratic hierarchy that di-

3. If an industrial society reaches the stage when the production of goods and services continues to increase as real choices decrease, we refer to it as "overdeveloped," or "postindustrial."

vides society into three main clusters—functional status groups, multibonded class groups, and functionally superfluous groups. As we go from the most functionally relevant to the least, the role of information changes. Each group has a different information function. The first group provides professional information. The second provides interest information, and the third provides populist information. The three groups overlap and are linked in various ways to form the concrete basis of alterations in a society's notions of equity, allocation, and order. Each group is capable of internal subdivision. At the highest level, the functional status elites include those who produce information through research, such as physicists, medical research workers, computer research scientists, and increasingly, social scientists, particularly economists and psychologists. These roles create new concepts and new techniques of research, and they are also concerned with application of research. They are institutionalized in universities, independent research complexes, and academies of science.

Closely associated with the highest functional status roles are the applied scientists and administrators of scientific knowledge. These include experimental scientists—space engineers, for example—and a variety of specialists closer to the production side of industrial life than to research but dependent on new knowledge and techniques, such as technocrats, high-level administrators, and highly specialized entrepreneurs. Such roles are often interchangeable between universities, commercial enterprises, and governments. Indeed, one can identify them by their relative closeness to university centers, since the academy is the most institutionalized corporate group concerned with both research and recruitment of candidates for all roles pertaining to knowledge.

The multibonded class groups can be similarly subdivided, although they comprise a much wider range of positions and roles. The roles are differentiated either in terms of the functional significance of a role vis-à-vis the industrial process, particularly whether it is declining or becoming more significant, or in terms of the degree to which education allows nonfunctional aspects of life to become important. The first criterion is a means of judging whether a role has industrial importance, and the second, whether a role is part of a fused or differentiated class.

Division among the functionally superfluous groups, tends to take caste-ethnic forms. These groups are marginal. One of the consequences of industrialization is the continuous creation of marginal groupings. The marginalization process does not mean simple downward mobility. It is possible for individuals to move downward in a ranking of roles without becoming marginal. The concept of marginalism is related to the problem of functional superfluousness in which, in terms of societal needs, an individual can make no recognized contribution by means of his roles. In modernizing societies this often occurs as the functions of chiefs, religious figures, elders, and others are displaced (i.e., when formerly useful roles lose their original purposes). In industrial society this is more a result of such occupations as those of unskilled laborers. However, there are more complicated ways in which marginalization occurs. Engineers or physicists may become functionally superfluous when their skills become outmoded or when they fall behind the theoretical advances of their fields. In other words marginalization may be a function of obsolescence in terms of specialized knowledge. This is "high level" marginalization. The person involved may or may not find it possible to be reabsorbed in a different functional role.

Marginalization needs to be distinguished from collective downward mobility, which occurs when a set of roles becomes less functionally significant. Such collective downward mobility has occurred among such professional roles as those of doctors, and commercial roles such as salesmen, small businessmen, brokers, and the like.

The most salient groups in industrial society are those most closely related to the creation of knowledge and its application. These groups consist of scientists (pure and applied) and technocrats (including entrepreneurs and senior organizational leaders). The next level of groups is involved in the translation of knowledge into industrial and commercial life; in highly industrial societies, the roles in these groups are mainly of the differentiated type and are ranked according to social distance and functionality. At the opposite end of the scale, the functionally superfluous groups represent marginals in the system.

In postindustrial societies a new group has arisen between the functional status groups and the differentiated groups—the bourgeois radicals, who reject the functional standard of ranking. If they are reactionaries, they attempt to revive fading or historical consummatory values, as have Stalinists in the USSR, nationalists in Poland, and right-wing conservatives in the United States. If they are revolutionaries, they create new consummatory values or provide old ones with new meaning, as have poets, students, and writers in the USSR and the bourgeois radicals in the United States, Britain, and France.

Coalitions are increasingly viable between bourgeois radicals and technocrats. In Czechoslovakia, for example, the economic reforms suggested by Ota Šik and others were designed to improve industrial performance. Support from high-ranking technocrats for the reforms also opened the way for a reinterpretation of consummatory values. Thus instrumentalization is not a one-way process. It can result in a decline in consummatory values, but it can also call forth a new consummatory-instrumental synthesis.

What does the meritocracy look like in terms of our structural theory? Let us compare it briefly with earlier descriptions, such as those of Marx or Weber, that used objective categories denoting a class type together with an expected form of action, or that of W. Lloyd Warner, which used statistically significant characteristics to establish class rankings, including social prestige and style. Marx and Weber suggest categories such as subproletariat, peasantry, proletariat, bourgeois, haute bourgeois, and aristocracy, each constituting a distinct subculture, a source of consciousness, and a particular relationship to the mode of production. The pattern of reciprocal exploitation between classes, as they become polarized, is set during a system change. But in this specific prediction, Marx was wrong. And he was wrong insofar as he based his revolutionary theory on a simple theory of polarization.

Marshall and Warner were concerned with the multiple characteristics of class in a highly industrial society. Particularly in the case of Warner these characteristics were subjectively defined by the members of the unit under analysis. Statistically significant points of reference included various social structures, family, clique, voluntary association, and kinship, which were then combined in a descriptive ranking—lower, upper lower, lower middle, middle middle, upper middle, lower upper, and so on. Using this approach Warner paved the way for a new evaluation of the concept of class that allowed Lipset and others to focus on the reverse of the Marxian hypothesis of class polarization, namely, an all-embracing middle.[4]

If the early Warner approach (and much of the later literature on stratification, which represents variations on his model) has many weaknesses, it does not ignore the qualitative changes that take place in the character of stratification as industrialization proceeds. Although the specific Marxian thesis was wrong, the dynamic use of class categories was valid. Combining both approaches should create a new pattern that does

4. See the useful critique of Warner's approach by Ruth R. Kornhauser, "The Warner Approach to Social Stratification," in R. Bendix and S. M. Lipset, eds., *Class, Status, and Power* (Glencoe, Ill.: The Free Press, 1953). See also W. L. Warner and P. S. Lunt, *The Social Life of a Modern Community* (New Haven, Conn.: Yale University Press, 1941); Gerhard E. Lenski, "Status Crystallization: A Non-Vertical Dimension of Social Status," *American Sociological Review* 19 (1954): 405–15; and S. M. Lipset, *The First New Nation* (New York: Basic Books, 1963), p. 125. Lipset points out that the original and gloomy emphasis by Warner on the rise of inequality in the 1930s is replaced in his later work when social mobility had increased. See W. L. Warner and J. C. Abegglen, *Occupational Mobility in American Business and Industry* (Minneapolis: University of Minnesota Press, 1953).

greater justice both to the actions of classes involved in modernization and to qualitative changes in social life. Our criteria of functionality and mobility (or weakly articulated boundaries) establishes a general progression from segmentary to fused to differentiated to functional status stratification types occurring as a result of modernization. Since modernization works from the industrial center to the traditional periphery, the progression today does not follow the same pattern it followed in Western Europe, for example. Most modernizing societies have a small proletariat and a large commercial class of the fused type. They may have small numbers of functional status elites that are nevertheless extremely important because of their functional control of the sources of power.

What is the emergent pattern for industrial society? It is the meritocracy. If our categories are valid, ranking within the meritocracy is as follows. Marginals, continuously replenished and redefined, are at the bottom, barely participating in the system. Their share in the allocation of resources is minimal and their functional utility zero. Next are the fused groups, whose collective mobility is downward because the groups are derived from occupation rather than education and whose hierarchy is based on functional significance (e.g., doctors and entrepreneurs at the top, salesmen in the middle, workers at the bottom). Differentiated groups come next, consisting of multibonded classes. Within the category, there are "miniclasses." Whereas fused groups are solidaristic and engaged in reciprocal relations (whether in the form of polarized conflict between workers and management or of mutual dependency between patrons and clients), differentiated groups are competitive. Beyond the multibonded differentiated groups are three divisions within the functional status category. The first is composed of bourgeois radicals who repudiate the entire system but who by virtue of high education have potentially high functional significance. They redefine functionality. Next is the administrative elite whose function is transformation, that is, the transformation of new knowledge into corporate or institutional form. These two groups are competitive. At the top is that part of the functional status elite which creates new information. It can be divided into two, the pure and the applied. This gives us a pattern presented in Figure 3.1 that includes the older patterns within it, utilizes the implications of the Marxian theory, and takes into account the limitations of the Warner approach.

This formulation suggests that with increasing embourgeoisement in the middle sectors of the fused and differentiated stratification systems, two types of bourgeoisie appear (one solidaristic, the other competitive). Fused groups can either move up into fused ranks or differentiated ones or be pushed into marginal status. The tendencies of this marginal group

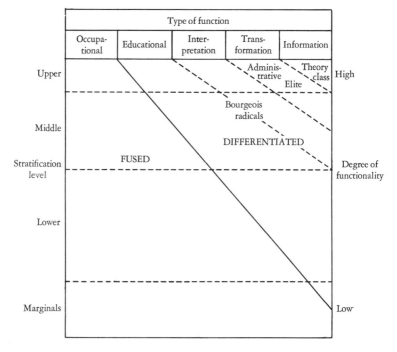

Figure 3.1. Allocation in the emergent meritocracy

are toward embourgeoisement if the movement is upward and radicalization if it is downward, the latter taking the form of primordial loyalties and a reemergence of caste-ethnic affiliations (nativism, Christianity, primitive Stalinism, and so on). The process at work in the fused sector is the redefinition of functionality; occupation is being divorced from a relationship to property or ownership, and education (the acquisition of technical skills) is being given priority over occupation.

The functional status elites are open to radicalization, whether toward the left or the right. They do not need to search for functional significance but for a wider context of meaning for their skills. The radicalization of this elite is likely to occur as instrumentalization reaches excessive levels and leaves a consummatory vacuum. It begins with the bourgeois radicals but is likely to spread. Moreover, insofar as the bourgeois radicals are poets, writers, artists, and other highly creative persons, the search for style among the upper differentiated groups and the functional status elites provides a meeting ground for the search for meaning of the latter and the radical attacks of the former. Indeed, style takes on a new character in a highly industrial society. At earlier stages of industrialization, style was traditional; that is, it amounted largely to conspicuous consumption. But now among functional status elites it is equivalent to a search for new meaning. Innovation in the arts, and the criticism of society which that often implies, becomes important in the process of radicalization. Some governments attempt to defend themselves against these radicals by making them marginal, while others co-opt them through commercialization.[5]

Allocation in industrial societies is based on competition between functional claims. The marginals have the least functional relevance and the theory class, with its information function, the most. The administrative elite has a transformation function that is necessary to society in order to generate an output or a project. The bourgeois radicals have an interpretative function, ranging from criticism to revolutionary rejection. The competition between classes in a fused system is perhaps less and less significant in an industrial society, where it is replaced by competition between fused and differentiated groups (or in other words, between occupation and education).

STRUCTURAL SOURCES OF RADICALIZATION

Industrial society offers many opportunities for choice but in doing so distorts allocation in ways that violate universalized egalitarian norms. In socialist countries, allocation is skewed by political power (particularly by that embodied in party and bureaucracy). In capitalist countries, it is skewed by unequal access to wealth. Both conditions are self-perpetuating. The question of public or private ownership, although important, is not crucial. Conservatism and radicalism manifest themselves (and for similar reasons) in both the capitalist and the socialist systems.[6]

Given the emphasis on new knowledge as a key characteristic of industrial society and the basis of its continual innovation, it is not surprising that education and educational institutions become strategic for the balancing of norms and structures. Precisely because competitive inequality is built into educational achievement the more egalitarian the access and the less egalitarian the results, the greater the "violation" of ideas about equity and the more "perverted" the actual pattern of allocation. We say "violation" because in all industrial societies there is a normative pull

---

5. In the USSR, for example, the Soviet government has put writers and other critics in mental hospitals or forced them to do physical labor.

6. See the description of student disturbances, for example, in George Z. F. Bereday, "Student Unrest on Four Continents: Montreal, Ibadan, Warsaw, and Rangoon," in S. M. Lipset, ed., *Student Politics* (New York: Basic Books, 1967), pp. 108–13.

toward social leveling in comprehensive or integrative schools that competes with the structural tendency to rank on the basis of achievement. Ability determines rewards in direct proportion to its functional value for industrial society. The value changes: for example, the overpowering functional need today is for creative skill and imagination, so these talents are at a premium and are the new sources of inequality.

The ways inequity and skewed allocation are manifested are many. In political terms, arbitrary powers may be applied in the name of egalitarianism. The present tentative trend toward liberalism in some socialist countries, such as the abortive tendency toward reconciliation systems in countries like Czechoslovakia, is apparently in response to the sorry record of arbitrary actions. In the United States economic not political misallocation is the core problem among the urban poor and the black population.

That both kinds of inequality are anachronistic in any highly industrial society should go without saying. The liberal solution favored in the West relies on the notion that wider political participation by underprivileged groups will improve the situation (through changes in taxation and increases in services, welfare, and educational opportunities). But this solution has little hope of success unless it is combined with a different consummatory emphasis. Structural changes, too, have not been sufficiently rapid to repay patience with greater collective mobility. Even in Britain, for example, after successive Labor governments, some nationalization, and enlarged social services, the distribution of private wealth helps to sustain a skewed system of allocation in which roughly 7 percent of the population owns 84 percent of the wealth.[7]

Normative interpretation of these startling figures is more complex than it appears. Taking a rather traditional socialist position, Robin Blackburn cites the Vauxhall case—in which workers, hitherto regarded as generally positive, "calculating," and reciprocal (instrumental) in their relations with the firm, "exploded" in a militant (consummatory) conflict with management—as evidence that coercion and exploitation were in reality the bases of worker relations with their employers. From our standpoint, Blackburn's interpretation is incorrect; the events do not support an either-or proposition that the workers were either cooperative or coerced. Both are possible. Indeed, it may be that a calculating and highly instrumentalized relationship based on reasonable and reciprocal gains had actually stimulated feelings of coercion and exploitation by emphasizing, in normative terms, the crisis of equity. The radicalization

7. The *Economist* study from which this example is derived is analyzed by Robin Blackburn in "Inequality and Exploitation," *New Left Review,* no. 42 (March-April 1967): 4.

process occurs in industrial societies because events generate intensities of passion that are translated into powerful ideological expression. These political ideologies may wax strongly only temporarily. In other words, in industrial societies, crises can arise not only because of narrow conflicts of interest but also because of the erosion of consummatory values by instrumental ones and the structural proliferation of interest groups that combine to generate a search for new and drastic solutions.

Action—strikes, mass confrontations, violence—may itself be sufficient to assert or redefine meaning in a satisfying way, and the revolutionary moment may pass. (This is the likely result of much student activism.) We should not be tempted, therefore, to build our notions of political equity on the superficialities of mass action. Nor should we be lulled into assuming political stability. Industrial societies confront a permanent crisis of a sort largely absent in modernizing ones. Dialectically, the crisis is brought about by the instrumentalization of values, which encourages competition to fill the consummatory vacuum. Functionally, it is a result of the proliferation of competitive and pluralistic groupings, which becomes counterproductive.

With reference to whether there is any justification for considering instrumentalization a problem in socialist systems, the Czechoslovakian experience would be relevant, but little empirical data is available. As the most highly industrialized socialist country, one that was embarking on a liberalization program (interrupted so dramatically by the Soviet invasion), it would have been a perfect case study. However, considerable data is available from Yugoslavia, which in our view moved from a modernizing stage to early industrialization in the last decade.[8] One of the most important norms of specifically Yugoslav socialism was worker participation in management. A self-validating consummatory value, it was based on the idea that fulfillment came from working in a situation free of exploitation, whether from capitalists or managers. But from 1960 to 1964 the relative importance of work as motivation declined sharply in favor of wages, and self-management remained the least valued single objective.[9] In addition, management, whose significance had originally been based on its revolutionary role and an involvement with consummatory values, was seen simply as a barrier to greater efficiency.[10] Growing instrumentalization

8. See Misha D. Jezernik, "Changes in the Hierarchy of Motivational Factors and Social Values in Slovenian Industry," *Journal of Social Issues* 25, no. 2 (1968).

9. Ibid., p. 109.

10. Jezernik says that "after the revolution was won and industrialization started, the country was short of professionals; people without proper professional education had to be promoted. And secondly, when industry became nationalized, revolutionary

produced circumstances in which a system of beliefs failed to validate empirical actions.[11] The Yugoslav case also shows that ideologies that presume an identity between the larger rationality of nature and the particular requirements of social life create so many problems at the consummatory level that they cast doubt on the original synthesis.

Whatever the form taken in Yugoslavia, instrumentalization prepares the way for such normative dialectical confrontations as those between Catholicism and Calvinism, capitalism and socialism, socialism and revisionism. Although they are perplexing, they invariably follow a particular sequence. First, a comprehensive normative synthesis represents legitimacy. It links instrumental actions with consummatory values, associating nonempirical and empirical ends in the context of proprietary limitations on conduct and behavior. The result is a validated set of ends defining equity. Second, when over time this comprehensive system begins to break down into its consummatory and instrumental parts, the instrumental becomes more important and the consummatory more perfunctory. The gap between them can be covered over for a time, but eventually opportunities arise for the creation of a new set of consummatory values. If these new consummatory values are to be successful, they have to correspond more adequately to changes in structure and functional needs than the set they are to displace. This final stage in the sequence defines radicalism.

In the context of our emergent meritocracy such a sequence illuminates a predicament of all industrial societies: that except for moments of equilibrium the functional needs of society based on industrial life re-

---

cadres distinguished by their revolutionary zeal and political reliability were brought into managerial positions. As long as modernization did not take place and workers did not become 'spoiled' by material incentives, these ineffective managers did not disturb anybody seriously. Now they are becoming the main obstacle, nearly the unsolvable problem; they do not want to quit their jobs voluntarily and they sabotage the hiring of young competent professionals who could menace their positions." Ibid., p. 110.

11. Another example of this failure is provided by the decline of Calvinism as a moral basis for business action. This is not a matter of belief versus science. The consummatory values associated with Calvinism could hardly be regarded as antiscientific, for all its fatalistic theology. Indeed, Calvinists saw in the scientific investigation of nature a "duty of love." In time, however, these very investigatory impulses became quite divorced from practice. Calvinism initially served as a specific warrant for science against religious orthodoxy. Today it is a bar to science where it is not totally remote from it. See R. Hooykaas, "Science and Reformation," in S. N. Eisenstadt, ed., *The Protestant Ethic and Modernization* (New York: Basic Books, 1968), p. 215.

main in conflict with the normative needs of society based on consummatory principles of equity. Thus, permanent contradiction is the characteristic condition of industrial society. Ideologies introduced to resolve contradictions often end in solidifying them. Ideological conflicts, then, seem to be perpetual, though their venue and their intensity but never their vitality may change.

STRATIFICATION GROUPS IN INDUSTRIAL SOCIETY

Having identified a characteristic predicament of industrial society, we turn now to an examination of the groups that vie for roles in this society.

The functionally superfluous caste and ethnic groups, or marginals, comprise tribal, ethnic, language, and nationality clusters that have a pronounced identity or classification and are encircled by ritualized constraints on their mobility. These constraints may be partly due to subcultural solidarities based either on primordial consummatory values, as in the German communities in Russia, Canada, and the United States; or on cultural prejudice, as against Negroes or Indians in the United States; or more likely, on a combination of both, as with Jews in Western Europe.

In the process of industrialization, upper caste and ethnic stratification rankings lose even residual functional relevance, theoretically making way for open entry. A differentiated type of system emerges, with the top rank based on functional relevance and continually expanding as choice expands. Thus, individual mobility and collective mobility are simultaneously possible. However, few members of segmentary groups can make the transition to a differentiated group. Functional irrelevance is their more likely destination. Ethnic boundaries persist, especially when a fused pattern of upward mobility is the only sort available. Negroes can move into top-level positions in the United States, for example, only if they have had access to education and housing in areas that permitted their enculturation in white society. Those who are functionally superfluous are cut off from active competition by the negative qualities of a ghetto existence and the related behavioral consequences of discrimination. The closer equal access appears to be, the more devastating their condition. As industrialization increases, these caste and ethnic residuals become increasingly hostile to one another, unless they can find some common enemy. Since a single class enemy is impossible to find in industrial societies, which are formed along multibonded class lines, anger is unstructured, highly generalized, and random. In a meritocracy, no matter how democratic, there is no comfort in being at the bottom. Indeed, even solidarity disappears entirely at that level. Functional significance is nega-

tive—violence, crime, sexual challenge—and contrasts so strongly with
the norms of the rest of society that this lowest common denominator is
viewed by some as the moral center of society, with a monopoly on a certain kind of truth.[12] When this occurs *the functionally superfluous marginals become a key group for normative, not structural, reasons.* They
are able to define negative or positive values for the rest of society.

In industrial society, class identity is undermined as roles emerge for
the upwardly mobile. *Residual fused groups,* which are collectively im-
mobile, lose their position by standing still. When this happens, fused
groups become politicized, the stimulus being the threat of their own
irrelevance in the face of increasing specialization. The most important
example is the old fused bourgeoisie in the United States, the group that
for generations had its functional base in occupations essential to industrial society—businessmen or bureaucrats whose success was based not on
special training but on hard work, skill, thrift, and all the notions of how
wealth and well-being should be won. For this group, occupation determined place in the social structure. Organized in various corporate
bodies, devoted to shared concerns, such fused groups seemed to be permanently balanced against other fused groups—for example, employers
and trade unionists. The key to the fused form of industrial society was
enterprise not education. Opportunities created by enterprise furnished
the meaning of society itself.

It is precisely this group that suffers most in the late-industrial period.
Missing are such clear demarcations as blue or white collar, by which class
reward and position were distributed. Less important is the assembly line,
that bogy of earlier forms of industrial enterprise, with its presumed
alienating characteristics. Instead, specialization occurs in a "situation
chain" in which infinite hierarchical gradations involving minute increments of status and power provide motivation. Puzzled and pressed by
the complexity of the paths of status in the industrial hierarchy, the fused
middle class responds by working less hard and thereby losing its purpose.
But it is still better off than the differentiated middle class. For this group,
there is little psychic leisure; the cares of the office cannot be left behind,

12. Indeed, in the United States, where this process has gone further than elsewhere, the functionally superfluous must resort to caste or ethnic boundaries if they
are to have any sense of community. Many are black. Superfluous whites derive status
through racial violence. Kinship associations in rural areas and localized populist
vigilante groups direct violence against blacks and convert color into a caste mark.
Superfluous blacks, on the other hand, have had until recently the local church, which,
in the absence of other institutions, formed a corporate focus in the ghetto. However,
church participation is declining today, and a substitute is being found in political
groupings whose demands are for "black power."

for relevance involves continual competition. Although the behavioral consequences are negative, there are important structural ones in the emergence of continuous interest-group conflict. The old fused middle class is increasingly split because of specialization, which emphasizes training. Part of it moves into differentiated groupings by virtue of educational and other advantages. Part of it moves downward into lower fused or differentiated sectors. Such downward mobility is likely to produce temporary radicalization expressed in terms of primordial norms. Even primitive managerial roles come to require technical skills. Any operating post develops "input voraciousness," and an enormous organizational structure is required.[13] Whereas the fused bourgeois may be a displaced person in the society he has helped to create, the differentiated individual is likely to be victimized by the situation chain. Let us examine these aspects of post-industrial society in terms of our third stratification category.

The *differentiated groups* constitute the core of the developmental bourgeoisie within the industrial sector of society. The main criteria for mobility within this sector are functional performance and education. Among the most functionally relevant groups, there is a growing consciousness of style, manners, taste, and mode of living. The members of these groups have multiple group affiliations based on various interests—residence, school, service club, alumni association—all of which cut across narrow occupational lines. Characteristically, such subgroup affiliations, or "miniclasses," have loose and flexible boundaries and relatively open membership. Miniclasses rank achievement on a graduated and increasingly complex continuum, whose ultimate criterion, no matter what other characteristics are taken into consideration, is functional relevance.

Each subspecialty, organizational unit, and type of work has behind it some group or corporate organization that is part of the corporate structure on which industrial output depends. The combination of miniclass and corporate structure results in very small degrees of differentiation within this stratification type. But this does not create anomic or alienated men in the Marxist sense of alienation, where work may include negative rewards, such as lack of self-esteem. In a multibonded miniclass system, since occupation is only one of the factors determining a total status position, occupational rewards are not the sole stimulus for work. They alone

---

13. One sees this in a modern army, where the actual combatants are a relatively small group compared with the organizational staff and personnel necessary to equip and place the soldier on the line. The same is true of virtually any other field operation or industry.

do not account for the intense intellectual, social, physical, and psychic efforts frequently made by members of differentiated groups.

At each point in the multibonded hierarchy, the corporate agency works as an interest group, defining what might be called a corporate structure of group life. The corporate group, by intersecting the main points of the stratification hierarchy, helps define many of the bonds of the miniclass. If education is a key to miniclass position, corporate affiliation is a point of intersection with other bonds, including not only narrow professional associations but also clubs, neighborhood associations, old-boy associations, and so on. Hence, technical specialty, religious affiliation, social club— all depend in various ways on corporate affiliation to fix an individual's position in the multibonded hierarchy. The hierarchy defines his main interests and acts as a mechanism for further social mobility. As the corporate group becomes more of a social group, it is no longer just a work place but a social universe.

The *functional status elite* is a small group with miniclass roles that has achieved high status by its generation and application of new knowledge. This group, which we call a "theory class," is not a class at all but, rather, a small self-sustaining and slowly expanding group that has been differentiated from the rest not only by the nature of its activities, but also by its various informational languages and theories. It has its own hierarchy based on scientific and technical criteria: pure versus applied science, qualitative versus quantitative science, natural and physical versus social science. It is outside any single corporate grouping but uses many of them, particularly government agencies and universities. This group's control of information differs from administrative management's: it represents a new form of political power, already highly developed in the USSR and the United States. The membership of functional status elites is divided on the basis of the distinction between pure and applied science. The main emphasis of the theory class is on research and creativity, the underlying assumption being that new information is better than old and innovation superior to application. Utilitarianism is not highly regarded, since that is the function of the technician rather than the scientist. Pure scientists, clustered in research institutes and universities and, increasingly, in large industrial corporations and certain governmental agencies are separated from others by the abstract nature of their work. Their findings become the energy for industrial development.[14]

14. The social sciences show a reversal of this order of priorities. Applied natural or physical sciences, such as engineering, are quite likely to serve as the basis for theoretical models in the social sciences (as with cybernetics theories). The false starts and inadequacy of pure theories in the social sciences have limited their claims

In spite of its high degree of differentiation, the functional status elite has certain unifying features. Entry is open and is based on competition and less and less on advantages of birth. Indeed, in status elites in both the United States and the USSR the proportion of members from immigrant stock (in the former) and the fused working class (in the latter) is quite large. As a group, the functional elite theorists are no longer nervous philistine technocrats. If anything they are divorced from the technocrats and the rest of the population by a heightened capacity for appreciation of creativity. They show fluency in language and a sense of style. The cultural model for this elite is a mythical aristocracy (sometimes cultivated deliberately in universities). Where such roles are concentrated, they provide a pattern of social life—a desire for more grace in academia, an interest and perhaps a participation in the arts, a devotion to a certain life style. This stylistic pattern is seen as a necessary part of professional life, especially as a contrast to professional communications, conferences, and meetings. But more than just style the functional status elite requires the ability, as well as the propensity, to think and communicate abstractly. The models used by specialists, although they originate in a particular field, overlap epistemologically to create technical languages that not only are highly abstract but also represent a hurdle for others, part of a curriculum to be studied and examined by those who wish to enter the theory class.

The functional status elite should not be regarded merely as the top of a standardized differentiated stratification hierarchy. It may not have more social prestige than other groupings; it does not have the trappings of an administrative elite or the scale of life of an old fused aristocracy. But because of its capacity to create new theory, it is a monitor as well as a creator of new information. Increasingly, too, those of the theory class (particularly in socialist societies) are trying to find ways to make realistic opportunities available to the functionally superfluous at the bottom. The normative sanction of this group and its activities is a unique and impersonal patron-client relationship similar in some respects to the medieval lord-serf relationship. It is an open feudalism in which under the ideologies of democracy and socialism, the concept of service becomes a vali-

---

to functional significance. Social scientists have tended to elevate technique to the level of theory in order to achieve the purity that distinguishes research in the material and physical sciences. The pure social scientist is rare indeed and, where he exists, is regarded as more of a luxury than a necessity because his theories are too speculative. It is therefore the high-level practitioner—the social science technocrat—who is able to mobilize large resources, whether through institutes of applied studies, private foundations, or government-sponsored research. Increasingly he is invited by industry to take consulting or even managerial roles.

dating norm. In theory at least, the patron is at the bottom and the client at the top: those who occupy roles in the theory class increasingly describe their functions as service to the public and, most particularly, that part of the public in greatest need. In the name of public service, the client, the occupant of the functional status role, claims a certain exemption from ordinary rules from his patron, the public as a whole, which pays for the client's privileges. He needs academic freedom, for example, a concept that now extends beyond universities and encompasses highly specialized agencies of government engaged in secret work (such as the RAND Corporation in the United States and, no doubt, equivalents in the USSR).

Our emphasis on the growth of professional elites should not obscure the fact that segmental or fused groupings are still an important part of the social system in an industrial setting. Indeed, the very existence of such groups helps bring about some of the conditions that create functional status roles. The urban poor and the caste and ethnic ghettos generate experts in urban development, integration, and education. Structural changes result. Groups that in principle may be polarized are instead broken up into overlapping interest groups, each looking to experts for support. Trade unions protecting the interests of a residual fused group employ economists and other specialists, thus creating both differentiated positions and a few functional status roles that will give the unions access to the power and style of the theory class. Many members of the new functional status elite seem to be showing their concern for society by designing military hardware, weapons system, and space vehicles. But there are others, particularly in the social sciences, who are concentrating more and more on the need of marginals.[15] Such responsibility to society is necessary for the theory class if it is to justify its existence and, above all, if it is to sustain its inspiration of creativity. Whereas technical matters may separate these groups from society, the appreciation of creativity in all forms is a force that unites them. But they are more than the new patrons of the arts; they are clients with power, serving the patrons who may lack grace and knowledge but have their claim to power in numbers.

15. It may be worth pointing out that the notion of putting an educational elite to work on behalf of the strategic marginals of society, that is, the industrial proletariat, was a socialist idea. The state was defined by its marginals; hence their improvement was necessary to change in the society as a whole. It is interesting to note this early emphasis and contrast it with a later one in the USSR, in which military purposes and technology have replaced the former elite role. See the speeches on education, 1926–45 by M. I. Kalinin, *On Communist Education, Selected Speeches and Articles* (Moscow: Foreign Languages Publishing House, 1950).

The new administrative elite are the skilled architects of complex organization and administration. They are also members of the functional status elite, but their liaison is not with populist patrons. Rather it is with other stratification groups, particularly the old industrial and professional elites (the American Medical Association, for example). Unlike these old elites, members of the new administrative elite recognize the value of the theory group, may utilize its expertise, and, indeed, are often part of it by virtue of specialized educational background (in electronics, for example). They may follow a similar style of life. They, too, maintain close contact with universities and other research centers. What distinguishes this group from the theory class is that its members are not creators but consumers of information. They are structural innovators who can perform in any of the corporate structures of industrial society—as corporation heads, generals, government officials, and foundation or university administrators, for example. Comprising a much larger group than the theorists, they perform in more than one of these capacities during the course of their functional lifetimes, generally moving between industry and the administrative areas of public service.

Unlike the theorists of the functional status elite, they are less likely to publicly identify their interests with those of the marginals, even though they may head social welfare programs and (in nonsocialist countries) contribute time and money to philanthropic causes. They have a bureaucratic style and are committed to organization qua organization. Philosophically, they are torn between the new norms of creativity and change represented by the entire functional status elite and the old norms of the bourgeois industrialists. In terms of prestige, they are the new leaders of industrial society, knowingly dependent on the functional status elite for the information that will determine the direction of leadership, and therefore regarding the theorists with a mixture of fear and respect.

The antithesis of the new industrial elite is a new group—the *bourgeois radicals*—that rejects the functional status groups along with all other utilitarian sectors of the social system. It, too, identifies closely with the functionally superfluous. The bourgeois radicals are bright, well educated, and often from the comfortable upper sectors of the differentiated stratification system.[16] Out of contempt for the new establishment—or a more permanent anger—they refuse to participate in society (except, perhaps, on behalf of the functionally superfluous). Quite often their anger takes the form of deliberate anti-intellectualism. Although bourgeois radicals

16. In the USSR this group was called the "gilded generation" and came from the families of the new administrative elite.

share in the culture of the functional status groups, they will also identify
with the morality of the marginals to whom they offer devotion, personal courage, and the articulation of wider meaning. They create their own
subculture as well. This subculture, more than any other in industrial
society, is the source of new consummatory values and the revival of
older ones. Not necessarily counter-elites, the angry young men often re-
produce some of the conditions of intellectual radicalism of the nineteenth
century, although perhaps on a much larger scale. Even arguments over
spontaneity versus organization, economism versus scientific Marxism,
freedom versus bureaucracy—all of which formed the substance of nine-
teenth- or early-twentieth-century radicalism—have been revived. In the
West, this group's folk heroes include Trotsky, Mao, and Castro (the
full range from Bakunin to Kautsky, from Rosa Luxembourg to Lenin,
are represented). In socialist countries the heroes are poets, writers of the
past, and the members of the radical group itself who have been per-
secuted by the regime. Che Guevara would be the prototypical folk hero
of this group.

The bourgeois radicals are caught between the new functional status
and administrative elites, on the one hand, and the interest and other
bourgeois groups, on the other. Although they may attack the former, they
are vulnerable to the latter. Characteristically, the bourgeois radicals are
objects of contempt for the ordinary utilitarian sectors of society, including
the residual fused bourgeoisie as a class and the multibonded bourgeoisie
that makes the broad internally competitive differentiated system. Such
contempt is mutual. The bourgeois radicals have a particular hatred for
those associated with distribution of goods or services, whether shop-
keeper, insurance agent, advertising executive, college-educated sales-
man, government bureaucrat, plant manager, party official, or professional
educator—in fact, a large proportion of the differentiated system. They
also reject their family backgrounds. The bourgeois radicals, thus alienated
from the social environment that has created them, use it merely as a
springboard for attack.

Since the functionally superfluous marginals present a moral predicament, the bourgeois radicals may seek to ally with them to transform the
system, by creating new meaning and new functional arrangements. The
administrative elite, on the other hand, will attempt to incorporate them
into the system by using available knowledge created by the theory class.
(Populist reactionaries either pretend they do not exist or see in them a
special group to be brought into marching legions, conservation corps,
or other suitable patriotic and functionally useful bodies.) Whatever the
solution, it will involve the incorporation of new marginals in the differ-

entiated middle class, increasing the demand for material rewards and thus increasing not only the consumption that is the basis of individual society but also the loss of self-respect that follows from such narrow objectives. These groups will try to avoid downward mobility with better education, in the process creating a fused middle or lower middle class.

The members of these groups will still be different from the functionally superfluous, who lack consummatory values, except primordial ones like pariah solidarity and negative caste-ethnic identification. Whereas the multi-bonded groups suffer from excessive instrumentalization accompanied by the ritualization, or worse, sentimentalization, of consummatory values, the marginals suffer from an inadequacy of both.

The bourgeois radicals assume that the functionally superfluous are the group most accessible to new consummatory values. But history shows that this is not the case. Given the opportunity, they are more likely to respond to instrumental values than to consummatory ones. After they have gained some access to allocation, they are more likely to identify with the older consummatory values than with the new. That is to say, they desire embourgeoisement and are likely to respond to nationalist, fascist, and other "backward-looking" ideologies. We do not rule out a possible identification with revolutionary ideologies in the future, but for the time being, our assumption is that the functionally superfluous are most likely to opt for embourgeoisement and to avoid ideological formulas altogether.

This description of industrial society has been a bit unconventional, for it has not relied on capital goods production, the size of the industrial labor force, per capita income, or even in general terms, on self-sustained growth. As a function of all these, but transcending them in importance, we have stressed the capacity of an industrialized system to generate new information that can be translated into output in the form of industrial exports. This capacity implies an infrastructure that combines research, administration, and entrepreneurship in a different mixture from that of the usual view of class stratification.

THE NEW PLURALISM

On the basis of the foregoing observations, several general hypotheses about each of the groups that comprise industrial society may be offered.

1. The functionally superfluous have minimum access to resources and standing outside a normative dialectic are normatively apathetic and therefore difficult to organize.

2. The segmentary caste-ethnic and residual fused groupings, particularly the old bourgeoisie whose functional roles are decreasing in significance, attach themselves to primordial normative values, reactionary

values (derived from a real or mythical past) or conservative values (designed to conserve their functional significance) as a normative compensation for functional loss.

3. The multibonded class groupings at the lower end of the scale are concerned with embourgeoisement, maximizing their functional significance, and engaging in highly instrumental bargaining for short-term gains.

4. The bourgeois radicals, who reject functionalism and instrumentalization, occupy roles of lesser functional significance and adopt utopian progressive or other radical innovative ideologies.

5. The administrative elite creates and recreates structures to justify the instrumental norms of the system but increasingly looks toward the theory class within the functional status elites for direction and salvation.

6. The functional status elites represent maximum functional significance and, by virtue of the dynamic quality of the new information and knowledge they create, are continuously defining functionality. Their ideologies tend to be associated with opportunities for creativity itself.

Thus there is a conflict between residual groups that are susceptible to consummatory values and multibonded groups that stress the instrumental. Coalitions are likely between the bourgeois radicals and the functionally superfluous, and between the new technocrats and the multibonded groupings. The latter coalition would opt for a progressive, highly instrumentalized, corporatist society, whereas the former would demand a drastic reevaluation of norms relevant to equity and allocation. Other coalitions are possible, for example between the residual-populist groupings and the functionally superfluous, and between the bourgeois radicals and the technocrats.

We have called the postindustrial stratification pyramid "emergent." It has by no means replaced the older pyramid described by Warner and others, but it is the juxtaposition of two systems, which makes possible complex coalitions. The older system involves power and prestige rankings of a fused type, rankings based on class (lower, lower middle, middle, upper middle, upper) or on descriptive characteristics (subproletariat, proletariat, bourgeoisie, haute bourgeoisie, aristocracy). In our theory the lower occupants of the fused pyramid move, in a late-industrial setting, not simply into higher ranks of the same hierarchy, but into the differentiated system. It is this crossing over from one stratification system to another that is the essence of the embourgeoisement phenomenon.

Comparisons of the sort we have been making are possible in all industrial societies including socialist ones. The categories themselves are descriptive in order to enable us to determine the relative significance of the groups described, those whose power is based on aggregative populism, those whose power is based on coalitions of interests, and those whose power is based on their functional relevance. From this pattern of comparison we can analyze the specific forms of pluralistic competition that result. This notion of pluralism in industrial societies goes well beyond the normal use of the term in representative government.

If our analysis is correct, industrial society is more likely to contain the conditions for revolution from above than from below. Revolution from above involves conflict between elites that occupy in varying degrees central and relevant roles in the society. Industrial society has two types of highly educated elites: the first type is the functional status groups, which include a theory class that creates new information and an administrative class that consumes it in order to create new structures to uphold old norms; the second type consists of bourgeois radicals, many of whom want to change the meaning of the society and break through its increasing reliance on instrumental goals. All compete for links with the functionally superfluous.

At the same time, norms associated with embourgeoisement dominate the modernizing part of industrial society. These are primordial, reactionary, and conservative and frequently not relevant to the creative and innovative parts of the industrial society. The functionally superfluous, the fused residuals, and the downwardly mobile differentiated groups have little patience with what they accurately regard as the subversive attitudes of the intellectuals. Those for whom embourgeoisement is a recent reality are grateful to the state. They see the anti-utilitarianism of the intellectuals as dangerous. The factors that allow both groups to occupy the same space are industrial society's need for structural differentiation and the separation of corporate groupings according to distributed interests. The more pyramidal the authority and the more instrumental the values, the greater the crisis of meaning at the top and the less dangerous the society at the bottom. Embourgeoisement within industrial society is thus a real substitute for tolerance and compromise.

The horizontal spread of industrial groups, as they compete, form coalitions, and break apart, gives rise to what is known as "group theory," which is an assessment of the coalitions of power generated by numbers, interests, and knowledge—the three main claims to power. Industrial society also has a vertical set of linkages, however; thus it is more than a collection of the coalitions prevailing at any given time. Any individual may be a professional specialist, a member of an interest group, and a member of the community at large. The division of society into multibonded minigroups and the telescoping of all three levels of affiliation into one create a structural problem that parallels the normative problem of excessive instrumentalism. Moreover, insofar as the widest group affiliation involves the least functionality and the strongest attachment to shared consummatory values, the vertical relationship is obviously based on more than self-interest. (See Figure 3.2.)

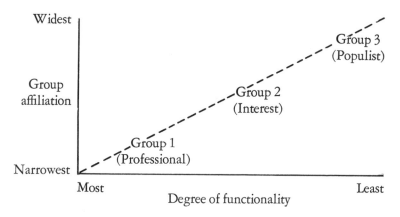

Figure 3.2. A vertical model of industrial groupings

What, then, can we say about the differentiated stratification pattern that occurs in industrial society? First, it creates a corporate structure of social life in which corporate interests compete. Second, it restricts populist and primordial attachments to the downwardly mobile, the functionally superfluous, or the residual fused groupings in society (like the old middle class). Third, it permits a pattern of social commitment in which the functional status groups form alliances with those at the bottom, if possible. The greater the degree of utilitarianism manifested in instrumental values based on work, the more intense the crisis at the top. The greater the degree of industrialization, the more severe the crisis of meaning. If our theory is correct, *despite the coalitional possibilities already described, there is greater pluralistic competition and more polarization in industrial society than in modernizing society.*

Such are the contradictory tendencies in industrial societies: on the one hand, increasing coalitional pluralism in day-to-day activities based on interests and, on the other, polarization of the antifunctional and functional. Specific normative ideologies mirror these contradictions. The least functionally relevant marginal groupings tend toward primordial norms,[17]

17. For example, in Britain today there is a tendency toward rightwing radicalism among workers, lower middle class groups, and the less functionally relevant that is

but these groups themselves are subject to rapid change, as the industrial society exchanges one group of marginals for another.

The normative aspects of the meritocracy create two severe crises of meaning in the functional hierarchy. The functionally superfluous pose the first problem—the need for more egalitarian entry into the utilitarian sectors of industrial society. If it is correct that the functionally superfluous must be admitted to the utilitarian sectors, then they will have to develop a basis for representation. But they are unincorporated and consequently have no means of representation. One way to organize them, is to revive populist and primordial affiliations; once solidarity is established, the second step is to widen access in a more generalized way, through voting, for example. A third step is to foster entry into the utilitarian hierarchy by representation of interests, usually organized around ethnic affiliations, as with Pakistani and Indian pressure groups in England and black power associations in the United States. The problem of access to the utilitarian sectors of society is great, for conflicts between segmentary and fused groups may arise, as may the more tension-producing conflicts between the functionally superfluous and differentiated utilitarian groups. The first type of conflict is normally reflected in a fundamental social cleavage; the second is more subtle.

Interest protection is the second critical problem of the meritocracy. There is little conflict between the creation of new knowledge and its translation into use by the differentiated utilitarians. However, there is a struggle to influence policy-making. The theory class tends to be disengaged from contemporary events and thus to embody long-term social purposes. Interest groups, on the contrary, are immediately affected by changes. In a differentiated system, the overlapping role sets, the smallness of the interest groups, the internal and external problems of competition, create a highly complex pattern of cross pressures. In other words, it is difficult to find a consistent line of activity either in pursuit of some common interest or in organizing coalitions. What is most important structurally for affecting decision-making is the multiplicity of relationships between interests and professions. Awareness of this multiplicity is the basis for social learning in highly industrial systems. Patterns of mutual intelligibility, accommodation, and payoff become keys to the system at the top. Results of negotiation are likely to depend in some measure on how bargaining occurs, whether accommodation of interests and profes-

---

shared with downwardly mobile upper middle class groups of the residual fused type, such as the old middle class. This radicalism takes the form of populist, primordial, and nationalistic consummatory values.

sional expertise is possible, and which pattern of bargaining is employed
(for example, the hard bargain to establish a norm of multiple concessions
as part of the rules of the game). Moreover, the greater the proliferation
of differentiated groups and functional status elites, the larger the bureaucracy needed as a mechanism of control. At the same time, individualized
patterns of creativity are greatly increased by the increase in differentiated
and functional status roles. A person may compare his abilities and his
rewards with others and thereby have a basis for self-esteem. Self-reward-
ing identification depends on nonbureaucratic relationships like friendship. Cliques are likely to form, based on mutual self-esteem and trust,
reinforcing the relationships between individuals and defining outsiders
and insiders. Hence, bureaucracy and personalized relationships are antagonistic social forces, but the one "breeds" the other.

Thus, superimposed on the multiple coalitions and relationships between roles on the structural level (determined in very general terms by
populist, interest, and professional claims to representation in decision-
making) are quite complicated networks of cliques and friendships, some
of which may be interlocking, some of which may be polarized, and some
of which may be simple.[18] The complexity of industrial society magnifies
individual pressures. Multiple access implies multiple opportunities, but
also multiple tensions at the behavioral level. For most of its citizens, the
industrial society is no paradise, and social unrest is reflected in political
action.

CHOICE AND EQUITY

In industrial society the expansion of choice occurs at the top of the
stratification system. Those near the top of the differentiated system, including the functional status elites, gain the most, but not without cost.
Pressure to perform is applied earlier and earlier in the educational system, beginning at the primary level and reaching its peak at the post-
graduate level. Indeed, this pressure becomes so great that the very advantages of a system based on merit—real alternatives for individuals—
become almost restrictions, the absence of choice. It is not surprising that
those engaged in the process become angry, exhausted, and bitter about
the system.

The behavioral consequence of this situation is a loss of confidence;
members of the society begin to feel that freedom of choice is an illusion.

18. See the extremely stimulating discussion by James A. Davis, "Structural
Balance, Mechanical Solidarity, and Interpersonal Relations," in Joseph Berger,
Morris Zelditch and Bo Anderson, eds., *Sociological Theories in Progress* (Boston:
Houghton Mifflin Co., 1966), p. 88.

Success at the social level brings failure at the individual level, which in turn precipitates a normative crisis of meaning. The more complex the status hierarchy, the greater the number of interlocking relationships and the wider the range of structural opportunities for mobility in an increasingly egalitarian system, the more intense the behavioral predicaments created by choice. In the last analysis, how to live in a universe of choice is a question no ideology has been able to resolve. It is the special problem of meritocracies in highly industrial societies.

The greatest difficulties facing industrial societies still lie ahead, namely, when anti-utilitarianism begins to spread more rapidly. The various competitive groupings in society will then be pulled in one of two directions. One pull will be toward a different kind of populist-corporate society—a kind of neofascism in which hierarchical authority and primordial values will be elevated as a mandate for rule. The other pull will be toward a secular theocratic system, in which shared but highly internalized ultimate beliefs will allow individual diversity and egalitarianism to flourish. It will be interesting to see in which direction industrial societies will go, regardless of the labels attached to the new systems.

The functionally superfluous and the bourgeois radicals share an attitude of aggravation toward the system, although the causes of their grievances differ. They both want a system in which they may participate; in this sense the bourgeois radicals are as marginal as the functionally superfluous. Yet their vaunted identity of purpose and condition is only superficial. The bourgeois radicals may use the functionally superfluous to validate revolutionary aims, to create new norms, and to support counternorms, even though, on the whole, the functionally superfluous themselves rarely support such norms. The latter may also be radical, but not the way the bourgeois radicals want them to be. (Marx was much more aware of this problem than are today's militants.) As a consequence, the bourgeois radical is in a paradoxical position. He, too, is functionally superfluous, but he has chosen that role. He is regarded as marginal, but he has been trained by the system. How can he make himself heard in an environment where complexity is itself an obstacle and where the solutions to the problems of the marginals are largely the work of technocrats and experts? By narrowing the gap between professionals and technocrats (the administrative elite) and the more creative and generally intellectual bourgeois radicals, although it can never be closed. We are talking about co-operation, not about the two-cultures argument of C. P. Snow. How can this co-operation be brought about? First, there is a need to stress in the social and behavioral sciences the role of intellectuals as participant-observers and the ways learning and understanding occur in this type of analysis. Second, the administrative elite must involve intellectuals at the planning level. Finally, both need to perceive the obstacles to reform and organize accordingly. In terms of our model, intellectuals must combine professional claims to representation and interest claims (both expressed in terms of populist needs) in order to compete with other interest and populist groups for access to government, where they can help formulate goals for society and increase the institutional coherence of the system.

To summarize, we may say that the chief characteristic of industrial society in its upper echelons is the continuous competition for knowledge and skills that will assure mobility in a highly differentiated system. This competition is personalized in that the competitors have no sense of solidarity with a class. Rather, the chief organizational unit to which they belong, with a hierarchy composed of accessible minute increments of gain, instrumentalizes all other aspects of life. For the bulk of the middle class population, the result is a ferocious productivity, a feverish round of activity, and in the end, a sense of having been used up, spent, and thrown away. Meaning is doing. To stop doing is to face an abyss.[19]

This rather dramatic picture suggests a predicament that emerges to some degree in all highly industrialized systems, not simply the United States, where the tendencies described are perhaps most apparent. Less industrial societies show greater sensitivity to the aged, less ruthlessness in the differentiated sector, and more traditionalism. This is true, for example, of Great Britain and the Soviet Union. In the USSR efforts are made by the state and party to prevent individuals from being or feeling superfluous.[20]

The competing strains of an egalitarian meritocracy have produced conditions to which public policy must respond. As fused systems of allocation give way to differentiated and functional status systems, and as consummatory values are instrumentalized, no simple answer to the basic imbalances of the variables is possible. The progressive increase of choice

19. Within these groups, there is an intense fear of aging. (Indeed, the retired are viewed as somehow embarrassing, shameful, and often grotesque). Intense activity and rejection of its consequences by the new generation compounds the fear of death, for one can no longer look to the young for earthly immortality.

20. The problems are only a little different in advanced socialist countries. There, creative intellectuals are the marginals and are regarded as dangers to the utilitarian foundations of socialism. The crisis of meaning, similar but not the same, is localized, at the moment, in a small group of writers, a larger group of students, and some creative artists looking for some exemption—the extension of academic freedom, in the widest sense—from an otherwise bureaucratized universe.

only intensifies the problem, as does the weakening of authority. What is required is a major attack on all four variables of the structural theory more or less simultaneously. But that is never attempted in practice, even though various types of reformers would like to stop the world and recreate it according to their own images.

Meanwhile, we remain stuck in an age of somewhat backward political ideologies, each of which purports to supply a solution. Those who want to return to a simpler day support various nationalist or fascist ideologies. Others, more or less revolutionary, support forms of communism, socialism, or liberal democracy. Each has its plan for structural reform and the revival or stimulation of consummatory values. But the problems, as we see them, reside precisely in the new hierarchies that are established alongside the old.[21]

As opportunities for choice expand with increasing knowledge and the application of that knowledge in industry, roles relevant to information and processing increase; the result is growing conflict between representatives of the various stratification groups, both between interest groups and professional elites. Such competition poses an organizational problem that affects the quality of industrial society itself. Overorganization, either through the incorporation of too many elites in decision-making or the too narrow restriction of their participation, is one part of the problem. Another part is the attempt to compensate for short-term competition (a "gambler's choice" situation) by means of long-term centralized planning, because when the "hiding hand" no longer operates, as A. O. Hirschman puts it, creativity declines. This suggests that a high level of information can be generated only with a certain structural openness and normative ambiguity. Among the system types we have discussed, the reconciliation system supplies this structural condition. Not too much information and not too much control is needed, for as Hirschman says, "Creativity always comes as a surprise to us; therefore we can never count on it, and we dare not believe in it until it has happened."[22] Decision-makers do not consciously begin with the intention of applying creativity to their tasks. Hence, the only way we

21. Such a double hierarchy exists in all contemporary industrial societies, although it is more significant in nonsocialist industrial societies than in socialist ones. But even in the latter, the older hierarchy persists, more openly at the bottom, to be sure, since socialism favors the working class, at least in theory, and more subtly at the top. To some extent these residual upper class and middle class groups, which retain and cultivate an outmoded style of life, have mingled with the functional status elites to emerge briefly when the political situation allows, as it did during the Polish, Hungarian, and Czechoslovakian crises.

22. A. O. Hirschman, "The Principles of the Hiding Hand," Reprint no. 130 (Washington, D.C.: Brookings Institution, 1967), p. 13.

can bring our creative resources fully into play is by misjudging the nature of the tasks, by presenting them to ourselves as more routine, simple, and undemanding of genuine creativity than they will turn out to be. The innovations that come as a surprise, bridging the narrow gaps in information, are the key to a solution of the problems of industrial society. The special skills of the knowledge-generating professional elites should provide ideal soil from which innovations can spring. Hirschman's point is extremely important. In terms of order, it means that an industrial society needs a high degree of accountability, providing a high degree of information, but not too much predictability, and a highly rationalized decision-making framework that appears to reduce all problems to a routine level. Extensive information-processing devices that are adequate both scientifically and structurally are implied. The information function involves certain other critical functions, the specification of goals, the identification of institutional conflicts and overlapping jurisdictions, and participation of various groups in the control of general social conduct. To the extent that these manifest themselves in the relationship between elites and government, they define the pattern of authority, the degree of hierarchy and accountability.

But precisely because industrial societies find it difficult to find the correct proportions, the problem of order remains unsolved. In the reconciliation system, if there is too much participation, the government will be glutted with information and become so accountable to its elites that it can hardly act independently. In a bureaucratic or mobilization system, if there is too little participation, governments may lose information (although a daring and creative honeymoon period may occur before that happens). These are continuous and insoluble problems for any government, and attempts to solve them result in many regime changes. We shall try to show that if there is an appropriate political system for industrial society, it is the reconciliation system operating within the limitations described.

4. Elites and Political Participation, Information, and Coercion

Development occurs as the number of differentiated groupings able to enter the allocative process increases. As the number of groups increases, the range between poor and rich widens. If opportunities for access are not absolutely foreclosed, however, as they are in a caste-bound system, the embourgeoisement phenomenon will be manifested as a growing competition between classes and class types.[1] This growth in access by differentiated groups has characteristically taken the form of expansion of the middle classes.[2] Whatever the terminology employed, it implies the expansion of choice and of roles guaranteeing access. It says nothing, however, about the actual pattern of choice distribution, which may be determined only by examining each particular stratification cluster.

In industrial societies, the strategic means of access into a fluid role situation are education and training. Collective mobility, which plays an important role in modernizing societies, is replaced by individual mobility. Individual mobility, in fact, serves as a measure of inequality, since it is determined increasingly by unequal capacity and performance. The greater the degree of opportunity for individuals, the greater the burden of inequality—a condition that fosters radicalization, the most important effect of the meritocracy in industrial society.

It should be clear that the embourgeoisement and radicalization phenomena result from specific equity-allocation relationships. They are products of structural changes and normative consequences. Embourgeoisement is a populist phenomenon associated with upward mobility. Radicalization, in contrast, is an elite phenomenon, or a "revolution from above," in which the revolutionary seeks support from below. Embourgeoisement implies not only acceptance of the prevailing principles of equity in a system but attempts to use these principles to achieve

---

1. One might expect a caste-bound system to result in radicalization, but instead there is more likely to be widespread apathy. This is particularly the case with extreme marginals, such as some of the Indians in the highlands of Peru who have not yet entered the "Choloization" process.

2. For a discussion of this, see for example, John J. Johnson, *Political Change in Latin America* (Stanford, Calif.: Stanford University Press, 1958).

reallocation on behalf of social aspirants. Radicalization involves either the rejection of the prevailing notions of equity or a drastic reinterpretation of their terms. If the key problem of modernizing society is a reallocation of roles according to shared notions of equity, the key problem of industrial society is a reinterpretation of norms.

Historically, development has produced a general predisposition toward social egalitarianism. Its normative opposites are monarchy, oligarchy, and the relevant anti-egalitarian ideologies these represented. To put it another way, in the early periods of industrialization, a meritocracy based on function meant democracy as opposed to aristocracy. Today functionality produces different consequences, and the normative dialectic is instead between meritocracy and democracy. Meritocracy, in fact, appears to negate democracy: one of the outcomes of competition based on function, for example, is the creation of a new kind of intellectual aristocracy based on superior knowledge. Such a structural tendency reinforces functional significance as a norm of reallocation. The downwardly mobile become increasingly redundant, and marginality grows. It is this redundancy of function, as we have suggested, that leads to a redefinition of meaning—whether to the left or right in the ideological spectrum—through radicalization. That, in sum, is our argument so far.

Since political life is a part of society such incongruities will find their counterparts in the types of political norms and patterns of political participation that they generate. These relationships and combinations, normative and structural, create a field of information generated by competition between elites for access to decision-making and can be understood by studying elite participation. What we have called "political elites" are the occupants of roles with access to decision-making.[3] Political elites represent conflicting tendencies in the distribution of norms and structures, tendencies whose impacts vary and require continuous changes in governmental policy. The elite constituencies, however, enable government to appraise such tendencies by providing it with knowledge (the adequacy of the appraisal depending on how effectively elites participate in decision-making). The competition between elites to participate exists in

3. We prefer the term *elite* to *leader* or *leadership* because leadership is an attribute of an elite. An elite is composed of leaders. Leadership suggests connection with followers and can best be analyzed behaviorally in terms of the qualities and capacities of the leaders themselves, matters we will not consider despite their obvious importance. The following parallel should clarify our usage: as stratification categories identify groups, so elite categories identify leaders. As Suzanne Keller puts it, "Strategic elites and social classes must therefore be considered as twin-born but not identical." See Suzanne Keller, *Beyond the Ruling Class* (New York: Random House, 1963), p. 34.

all types of political systems, and the way they participate indicates the tendency of the political system.

The tendencies of political systems, determined by the functional and dialectical boundaries may be normatively expressed in terms of conflicts between (1) consummatory and instrumental values; (2) sets of consummatory values; and (3) sets of instrumental values. They may be functionally expressed in terms of competition between (1) functionally less and functionally more significant groups; (2) sets of functionally less significant groups; and (3) sets of functionally more significant groups. These six sources of variation analytically summarize all the types of political inputs with which the concrete system must deal.[4]

These processes, in the context of each type of political system, generate inputs to government by means of elites. Such inputs result concretely in more or less efficacious decisions by government, some of which are designed to strengthen or otherwise protect the entire society, and some to increase, modify, or otherwise affect development. To evaluate how this works, we must measure the prevailing political balance of norms and structures. Elites will be seen as mediating groups between society and government.

To summarize, equity and allocation have been dealt with at the level of society. Society is the most highly generalized concrete unit we employ. Political norms and participation we deal with at the level of government. Government is the most specific concrete unit we employ. The link between the two concrete units is established by elites. Elites are more general than government and less general than society. Government responds to equity-allocation problems in terms of elite access. Society responds to government policy on the basis of elite participation in goal specification and central control. Response itself is determined by political system type, information, coercion, and decisional efficacy.

ELITE COMPETITION AND CLAIMS TO REPRESENTATION

The participation by elites in government is, in our view, active not passive; in the behavioral sense this means that elites have a propensity to manipulate the effectiveness of their access to decision-making. The

4. From the six sources of variation, we derive four main types of information, two normative and two structural. The first normative type concerns instrumentalization (including secularization) of norms. The second involves conflicts over which set of consummatory norms or which set of instrumental norms shall prevail. The two structural types concern conflicts of power (1) between functionally more and functionally less significant groups, and (2) within sets of functionally more and functionally less significant groups.

structural assumption is that development, by defining the characteristics of functionality, creates its own elites and restricts those likely to lose their bases of support.

Elite competition is the result of two main pressures: one arises from claims to legitimate participation based on certain normative principles; the other arises from modes of participation based on function. These two pressures, normative and structural, form a matrix on the basis of which elite representation and effectiveness can be examined. They encompass various modalities of competition between elites (normative competition for access and structural competition for an increase in the share of decision-making). Concretely this means constantly changing relations between elites and government, determined by normative variation in claims to access and by structural changes resulting from functional competition. Implied in this formulation is an information model of the relations between government and society. A change in the type of political system results in an information gain or loss. Such gains or losses influence the efficacy of decision-making, which in turn influences development rates and priorities and the maintenance of the system. This information model translates the organic approach of structural-functional models into a mechanistic one for the examination of information and its outputs.[5]

In all societies today, representation is indirect. How indirect depends on the way the political elite emerges from the main body of citizens— by election, co-optation, appointment, and so on. The degree of representativeness of the elite and its quality of service depend on the nature of the claim to access and the way the representational functions are performed.

In our view, the political elite is not necessarily a prestige group deriving status from the exercise of power.[6] Our idea is of a representational elite serving as a broker between claimants and allocators. Such a concept is intended to be universal, as is the notion of elite competition. A typical and recurring goal of elite competition is to overcome the consequences of favoritism—the awarding of power to particular social groups, classes, and families whose claims to access may be powerful. In competition with each other, elites draw on political, economic, social, or

5. See the discussion of mechanistic (or cybernetic) models in L. Sourrifnal, F. H. George, A. Cuzzer, and G. Tintner, "Etudes sur la Cybernétique et l'Economie, 3," in *Cahiers de L'Institut de Science Economique Appliquée,* no. 98 (Feb. 1960).

6. The power of groups comes from diverse sources—size, special access, or utility—quite independent of prestige. Trade union leaders, for example, have less prestige but more power in contemporary industrial society than doctors.

intellectual resources as claims to access. Their representative functions may be performed in assemblies or based on constituencies; in councils of workers in factories or communes; in tribal councils and tribunals. The idea of selection by a body of peers, with citizenship the universal warrant, lies behind all forms of popular sovereignty.

As our discussion has implied, conflicts arise during the development process over competitive claims to representation. As each group seeks to expand its basis of support (hoping to widen its access to government), it creates an elite that as a representative of the group competes for access to decision-making in government. Each group puts forward certain normatively defined claims to representation that convey particular forms of information: (1) *populist claims,* which are based on a concern about the general well-being and opportunities of citizens and their children and by extension about their general satisfaction with government and society and their loyalty and commitment to it; (2) *interest claims,* which are based on common, corporate, specialized criteria of affiliation such as occupation or education but not necessarily function; and (3) *professional claims,* which are based on function. Populist claims include ethnicity. Professional claims include the ability of technocratic and professional groups to respond to society's need to employ knowledge for prediction and responsible future planning.

Access not only determines the ways elites participate in the concrete actions of government, in decision-making, but generates information inputs that when transmitted to government, represent the elite's share in the responsibility for carrying out the government's decisions.

REPRESENTATIONAL FUNCTIONS OF THE ELITE

To accomplish its role an elite shares in two main structures of government—the structure of authoritative decision-making and the structure of accountability. Participation is by means of two functions, an input function called *goal specification* and an output function called *central control.* If government accountability is low an elite will be employed for central control. If accountability is high, the elite will be employed for goal specification and sharing in decision-making, a situation that occurs when the goals of the society as defined by official government leaders are formed in response to messages transmitted by members of the political elite from the groups they represent. To that extent the elite shares in decision-making with reference to goals. Central control involves the elite in coordinating the work of government and translating governmental decisions into practice. Elite acquiescence of this sort is colloquially known as participation in the establishment, the network of ties binding an elite to government and to various other elites, primarily as administrators and civil servants but also as educators, scientists, and trade union leaders.

These two functions involve both information and coercion. As a mediating group, the elite is always allocated some authority to recommend decisions or to make decisions that will resolve conflicts between two or more concrete groupings in all systems. The greater the degree of elite participation in such decisions, however, the more effectively conflicts can be resolved before they reach the top levels of government.

This formulation suggests that the degree of elite participation in government (that is, political allocation) determines the degree of information and coercion available to government. Mobilization systems are low information systems, and reconciliation systems high information systems. But information involves not only the degree but the spread of elite participation, the way it represents various types of allocation groups defined according to stratification criteria. Since such groups are interwoven in complex ways, the matter of conveying messages by elites involves not mere "aggregation" or conveyance but interpretation and transformation to simplify and sharpen the messages. Hence the elite becomes functional in relation to its informational qualifications.

With these variables in mind, we will now attempt to show the relationship between the model as a whole to the particular variable referred to in the model as participation. Participation affects the type of political system in structural terms, determining the degree of hierarchy. In turn, the degree of hierarchy determines coercion and information. We are particularly interested in government, for it is the surrogate for the political system and is a concrete subgroup of the elite that by its organization affects the relations of the society. Figure 4.1 suggests that where elite

| | Information | | Coercion | |
	High	Low	High	Low
Hierarchical authority (Low participation)		A	A	
Pyramidal authority (High participation)	B			B

Elite participation appears to the left, spanning both rows.

Figure 4.1. Participation and information

participation is low and authority is hierarchical (A), we can expect information to be low and coercion high. Where elite participation occurs in a more pyramidal system of authority (B), information is high and coercion low. Our manner of discussing elite participation suggests that insofar as information defines governmental obligation, participation "triggers" specific political norms. Hence the activation of political norms becomes part of the response to government decision-making on the basis of information received. It also suggests that precisely because the three types of information—populist, interest, and professional—become so complex when they are aggregated and disaggregated, any simple conveyance notion of representation cannot apply.[7]

Populist claims to access require elites to convert highly diffuse and symbolic sights and sounds into evaluated messages. Insofar as these become a part of goal specification or informational inputs, elites translate them into generalized suggestions for remedial action on matters affecting large groups in the population and cutting across class-type boundaries, matters such as welfare, education, and health. Populist elites do this by actively mediating between class-type groups, splintering organized public bodies where necessary, creating mutual and overlapping associations, and in general acting as buffers between ethnic, class, or other nonfunctional large clusters in the population. Central control of a populist nature requires conformity to highly generalized symbols such as the flag and support of patriotic wars. Elites will attempt to carry out governmental policies that affect fundamental normative positions on questions of property, national interest, "loyalty," and so on. Such elites who deal with populist groups are what we mean by the term "politician." Their most common role is that of political broker.

Interest claims to access depend more on the capacity of the elites to serve each interest group and forward its demands purposefully. Central control is exercised by the interest elites to benefit one group at the expense of another. Goal specification not only requires working out legislation that provides special opportunities for each interest group but also includes seeking arbitration, as in conflicts between labor and management. Elites who act on behalf of interest groups are essentially "lobbyists," using that term in a broad sense.

Professional claims to access depend on the nature and importance of information functional to development. Central control may in fact be equivalent to the possession of or special access to specialized information.

7. Indeed, most democratic theories of representation are simply inadequate for contemporary purposes. How elite representation can actually work—through worker-management councils, the breaking up of larger units into smaller information units, and the sometimes bizarre manner in which such alternatives are suggested—is a critical political question not receiving enough direct attention.

In highly industrial societies knowledge with a superior technology may give particular professional groups virtual veto power over the rest of society. Goal specification under such conditions takes the form of competition between experts to establish priorities, a critical function in view of the need for long-term commitments and allocation of resources. Elites who serve the professionals are usually regarded as "advisors."

The functions of the elite are by definition shared with government, which is a strategic part of the elite itself. The extent to which government officials monopolize the functions of goal specification and central control varies from society to society and forms a basis for comparison between political systems.

Combining these elements will enable us to identify a structure of information and coercion somewhat similar to Easton's formulation.[8] Operationally, information is composed of claims translated by elites. Untranslated claims (like unheard sound) do not exist for political purposes. Government action converts informational inputs to outputs. Depending on the type of political system, this action may take the form of orders and threats or consultation and discussion. The end product is the same in any case: compliance by members of the elites' constituencies. Whether or not compliance is forthcoming, it creates new information for government through elites, and so on around the cycle. (See Figure 4.2.) It should be

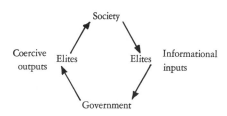

Figure 4.2. The cycle of information and coercion

possible to operationalize the access claims of various groups by representation and to evaluate the significance of the elites' participation in decision-making by their functional significance. The access to decision-making of particular elites, such as landowners, members of the government, civil servants, businessmen and merchants, and trade union officials, can be ranked in terms of the degree to which they perform the functions of goal specification and central control. A businessman or investor in the

8. See David Easton, *A Systems Analysis of Political Life* (New York: John Wiley and Sons, 1965), passim.

United States, whose claims to access are based in interests, may take a great part in goal specification. His access will be limited by the competing popular and functional claims of other elite representatives. In Guinea, the claim to access from the equivalent investor or businessman would be far less acceptable in general and much more restricted in scope.

If we were to assign numerical rankings to the participation of elites, what significant but derivative theories might emerge? Apart from revealing many specific structural relationships within society and between society and government by using regression analysis, we should be able to locate major sources, gains, and losses of information in a system. Our analysis should also be able to forecast the general capacities of different political systems to handle integrative and developmental tasks at different stages of development. The general matrix, then, is comparative. Its object is to find correlations that will test the types of political systems and their capabilities.

Periods of system change can be analyzed internally by using the criteria of access to decision-making and the representational functions of elites. Hence, changes in the principles of access to incorporate greater numbers of groups should coincide with a shift toward a reconciliation system. In such a system, participation in goal specification by broadly populist elites should also intensify measurably.

Samples of the composition of elites may also be compared. We would define the elite sample from counter-elite to functional elite. Each type of political system should show a consistent bias toward one or another combination of claims to representation and type of access. We would expect bureaucratic systems to be least willing to accept populist claims to representation and most willing to allow interest claims, least willing to allow elite access to central control and most willing to allow access to goal specification. Mobilization systems would be least willing to allow claims to representation from populist and interest groups and most willing to allow claims from professional groups. Theocratic systems would be least willing to allow claims to representation on the basis of professionalism and interests and most willing to allow claims on the basis of populism; their most accessible elite function would be central control and the least, goal specification. A reconciliation system would be more receptive to populist claims to representation than to interest and professional claims, but it would give access to elites in both goal specification and central control.

Political systems of similar types at similar levels of development should display correlations that can be standardized. For example, all industrial societies of the reconciliation type should have a predominance of multibonded miniclass groupings, with elite access based on populist, interest, and professional claims. Industrial elites should perform their information-producing function by competing to participate in central control and goal specification, but their coercive functions should be limited. All industrial societies of the mobilization type should show multibonded class situations in which populist and interest elites participate relatively little in goal specification and central control, while professionals score high on all counts; with respect to coercion, populist and interest elites should show correspondingly heavy involvements.

Standardization of responses to industrialization should enable us to formulate hypotheses based on a mixture of qualitative and quantitative measures. By "qualitative measures" we mean judgments of the more-less or plus-minus variety that provide a crude score in contrast to the precise data and techniques of quantitative mathematics.

Qualitative rankings are possible when development is represented by a set of points on a single scale based on the proliferation of industrial roles. A type of stratification can then be correlated with elite access. The type of access resulting from claims put forward (demands, petitions, memorials, and so on) can be measured by normative principles of access such as "one man, one vote," special interests, and expertise. Moreover, such measurements can be correlated with the representational functions of elites. For example, in what decision did those representing landowners, trade unionists, businessmen, special language and religious bodies, or particular regions share (either by goal specification and central control)? This type of question may be asked in the context of different types of political systems. It may be varied by focusing on decisions in areas of major importance, such as land reform, taxation, and education. The timing of participation in decision-making may also be compared. Some elites may participate in both functions before a decision is made; others are more effective afterward in achieving compliance.

These comments suggest several stages of analysis. In the first stages, gross correlations between types of political system and the way in which the descriptive variables cluster should be studied. That is to say, the first concern should be with the accuracy of the generalized political system as a forecasting model, although it is not yet a means of predicting how access and representational functions cluster. Because of the large number of comparative units, the elite categories provide a shorthand method for describing elite participation. Thus patterns of access and elite functions should consistently correlate with appropriate developmental levels and types of political system and consistently differ from other developmental levels and types of political system.

A REPRESENTATIONAL SUBSYSTEM

We have now begun to link equity and allocation with the political system on the basis of elite access and functional variables. Each political systems type tends to grant access to decision-making on the basis of different claims to representation. The mobilization system may be populist in character, but it tends to favor functional claims to representation that may not be restricted to relevance for development but may include significance in the party organization. Bureaucratic systems tend to favor claims to representation based on interest and regulate them according to recognized and institutionalized standards. Theocratic systems (and here we have in mind mainly historical cases) tended to favor populist claims to representation in the area of religious movements or reform, and yet allowed scope for claims based on interest in the instrumental side of social life. In reconciliation systems, all three types of claims to representation—populist, interest, and professional—tend to compete, and considerable conflict arises between the first and third types. (See Figure 4.3.)

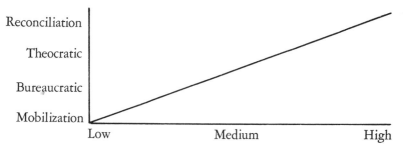

Figure 4.3. Degree of access by type of political system

As it moves from traditionalism to industrialization, development stimulates a proliferation of needs and an instrumentalization of ends. At each stage in the process there is a characteristic response by each type of government to the problems of managing and controlling pluralism and embourgeoisement. *Mobilization systems* respond to pluralism and embourgeoisement by restructuring society along political lines; in the process, popular representation is invoked symbolically to reinforce unity, and interest group representation and professional representation are bureaucratized. *Reconciliation systems* respond to pluralism and embourgeoisement by using an elite oligarchy to manipulate economic advantages and limit the effectiveness of populist representation, while expanding interest-group representation (to which professional representation is subordinate). *Theocratic systems* respond to pluralism and embourgeoisement by insuring a good fit between consummatory religious values and popular beliefs and by allowing populist, interest, and professional representation as long as none threatens the sanctity of religious values. *Bureaucratic systems* respond to pluralism and embourgeoisement by manipulating interest and professional representation and by restricting populist representation. To translate these propositions into operational terms, we can select groups from the various sectors of the stratification system and rank them according to the significance of their access claims. Claims to representation, as we have already suggested, are links between patterns of stratification and alternative types of government. (See Figure 4.4.)

Stage of development	Type of stratification	Type of political system			
		Theocratic	Bureaucratic	Mobilization	Reconciliation
Industrial	Differentiated Functional status Residual fused	Representational claims (populist, interest, and professional)			
Modernizing	Fused Differentiated Segmentary				
Traditional	Segmentary				

Figure 4.4. Differentiation and claims to access

The evolving relationships between stratification patterns resulting from development and types of political systems are linked by representational claims, the precise nature of which and the rights and proprieties they imply form an important part of the normative dimension of politics. Moreover, they define the kind of information government has at its disposal. There have been many political struggles over the degree of access to be granted each type of group in a political system. Development appears to move society away from support of primordial and populist claims and toward interest and functional claims. But the sequence is not smooth and direct. We have already pointed out that even though segmentary or fused groups become functionally obsolete they nevertheless continue to exist. Furthermore, because development proceeds unevenly, the loss of functional significance by these groups intensifies their search for appealing populist or primordial norms.

Although we speak of development as a continuum that moves historically from traditionalism to industrialization, in practice the process is reversed as roles originating in an industrial setting are transferred to a nonindustrial setting. If this concept of development is true for the segmentary, fused, and differentiated clusters with their normative claims and functional roles, is it also true for the functional status groups? To some extent, yes—in the sense that if functional status groups cannot perform their roles in accordance with norms associated with expertise, they may simply become like other opportunistic differentiated groupings bargaining for short-term gains. As modernization proceeds and these groups grow they may become successful interest groups with high-access elites.

However, there is another possibility. There are groups that while maintaining their sense of professionality become radicalized in one sense or another when their claims to access are ignored. This occurred in Norway in the 1920s and 1930s when the civil servants became interested in communism. It is true among many agronomists and engineers in Peru and Chile today. Their aim is to create a revolution from above, establish a wider populist claim to access, and mobilize the other sectors of society to support them. The tendency toward radicalization among functional status groups is not yet a very clear one. But as the role of the technocrat expands in industrial societies (as in the United States, France, and Italy), functional significance becomes better understood and more widely accepted. The effect of this wider acceptance especially on industrial-role counterparts during advanced modernization will be to sustain their professionality. These new technocrats will become political activists in order to create the industrial opportunity that will fulfill their concept of themselves and the society in which they want to live.

All these are of course hypotheses. Correlations involving stage of development, type of political system, and elite functions should confirm or disprove them. The matrix for these correlations is given in Figure 4.4.

To summarize, each of the elites tries to maximize its normative claims to access. As modernization proceeds, these claims shift from the primordial toward the functional, from the populist to the professional. At the same time, stratification types move away from caste toward functional status. The political elites of each of these groups create appropriate information. Segmentary, fused, and differentiated elites produce information about loyalty based on wants or needs. Functional status elites create new utilitarian information that is essential for innovation. The desire of the last type to apply the new information fosters a professional sense of role.

Using a five-point qualitative ranking scale, we should be able to describe a highly industrialized system with a high level of functional status stratification (5), a high level of the differentiated type (5), a low level of the fused type (1), and a moderate level of the segmentary type (3). If it is an industrial reconciliation system, access claims would rank high on populism (5), high on interests (5), and high on professionalism (5), thus setting the stage for conflict and competition between elites for representation. Such competition would be reflected in wide participation in the information functions of goal specification (5), and central control (5), and very little participation in coercion functions (1). Given the same stratification pattern in an industrial mobilization system, we would expect low access claims based on populism (1), moderate claims based on interests (3), and high claims based on professionalism (5). With regard to the informational functions of the elite, the scores would be quite the opposite of those in the reconciliation system (1), (1), (1) for participation in information and (5) for participation in coercion.

Such qualitative predictions serve several purposes, the most important of which is to articulate a standard against which concrete variations may be measured. The original hypothetical statements to be translated into operational terms would concern the location of concrete groups (for example, such functional status groups as technocrats, theorists, and educators), their access claims, and their degrees of participation. Similar assessments could be made of many other groupings: on the differential levels, churchmen, military officers, senior civil servants, clubs, consumer bodies, neighborhood and residential groups, professional organizations; on the fused level, working class, middle class, or upperclass groups; and on the segmentary levels, caste-ethnic groups, such as Negroes in the United States. Discrepancies in size, functional relevance, and representation would all serve as specific derivative hypotheses generated by the theory when applied to the particular case. Shifts in the rankings over time would thus locate developmental change. See Figure 4.5.

REPRESENTATION AND INFORMATION

The range of groups and leaders is obviously very broad. Since it would be impossible to compile a comprehensive checklist, our categories are general and descriptive enough to locate a sample. The descriptive categories include *populist* groups, based on generalized solidaristic affiliations (political parties, political movements, youth organizations, political clubs, cultural associations, tribal associations); *interest* groups, based on specific instrumental ends (trade unions, business organizations, reform and educational associations, language and linguistic groups, religious bodies); and *professional* groups (top administrators, some bureaucrats, most techno-

Predominant type of political system

Stage of development	Type of stratification	Theocratic		Bureaucratic		Mobilization		Reconciliation	
		Functions of elite		Functions of elite		Functions of elite		Functions of elite	
		G.S.	C.C.	G.S.	C.C.	G.S.	C.C.	G.S.	C.C.
Industrial	Differentiated Functional status Residual fused								
Modernizing	Fused Differentiated Residual segmentary								
Traditional	Segmentary								

Figure 4.5. Differentiation and representational functions.
(G.S. = Goal specification. C.C. = Central control)

crats, members of the professions engaged in activities involving the society as a whole).[9] These categories will serve as subjects of our questions about the stratification types of specific groups (segmentary, fused, differentiated, functional status, and the relative proportions of each), the contents of the various claims put forward by leaders of each group (populist, interest, and professional), and the extent to which these reflect loyalty and reward. The revelant sources of information are from populist, interest, and professional claims.

Populist claims to access[10] may be based on a variety of solidaristic, generalized residual rights. By "residual rights," we mean fundamental or inalienable principles that cannot be awarded but may be restricted by government. Among these principles are the consummatory values held by members of a society, based on race, "blood," language, religion, or even more broadly, culture. Mixtures of these values are normally to be found in so-called nationalist ideologies. They may also be present in class ideologies, such as socialism.

9. Members of medical research teams would be professional in this sense; but the American Medical Association would be an interest group, not a professional body.

10. By *populist* we mean the widest body of ideologically defined norms that identifies a common solidaristic bond and defines the widest possible membership. Hence, the emphasis is on inclusiveness. But there is also a sharp (and symbolic) exclusiveness, with boundaries expressed in primordial terms, that is, race, language, religion, ethnicity. Populism can, of course, take many forms: it can include an entire population, select a mixture of primordial ideologies, be more or less rural, and so on. See the point made (p. 172) by Donald MacRae in the discussion of populism held at the London School of Economics, May 1967, the proceedings of which are printed in *Government and Opposition,* Spring 1968.

Concrete groups serving as the carriers of populism can be found in all stratification categories. Nevertheless, one would expect populist claims to be strongest among the caste-ethnic and fused groups, although coalitions of differentiated groups also advance such claims on the basis of sheer numbers.

Sample surveys or polls of public opinions and attitudes are the most obvious means of ascertaining populist claims. Periodic elections are another device, with negative public judgment being indicated by defeat. Similarly useful are referendums on public issues. Public criticisms and commentary in the press provide another significant expression of populist information, as do private journals of advocacy. Public assemblies are another source of populist information: rallies of political parties, patriotic celebrations, memorial ceremonies and services (including those for the war dead), military formations, and even huge calisthenics displays performed under huge banners proclaiming solidarity and the tasks that lie ahead. Populist information will be fairly explicit—statements of approval or disapproval of governmental activities, for example. But there will also be populist "resonance," information that is nonverbal, visceral, or kinesthetic and that may be generalized, blurred, or even percussive—the pounding of drums or barrels, the playing of happy music embodying motion, color, vitality. This kind of information is not random even though it is not explicit. It is prompted by public uncertainty—the beating of drums when a chief dies, a dance when a young boy approaches manhood, and similar expressions of feelings when a society must change leaders, engage in war, or alter in other ways a given set of social conditions.[11]

Elites aid governments by scanning public expression and noise in order to assess the response to various government acts and judge the mood and state of well-being. In effect, they draw up a sort of normative ledger in which credits reflect loyalty and debits anger and possible dissaffiliation.

Information derived from *interest claims* has a much narrower base than populist information, is much more specific in quality, and is dependent on acts of persuasion, personal relationships, and at times, corruption. Insofar as information from interest groups is functional, it is selective.

---

11. This idea was suggested by Rodney Needham, whose interesting theory connects "percussion" with "transition," as when shamanistic behavior such as drum-beating accompanies rites of passage. See "Percussion and Transition," *Man* 2, no. 4 (Dec. 1967). The term "resonance" was suggested to me by Dušan Lukač of the University of Belgrade.

It need not be based on function, but may take the form of precise demands for certain kinds of recognition.[12]

Interest groups create information that can be used to measure the gains made by one group at the expense of others. The competitive range of information, functional or not, is wide, from benefits or special exemptions for industry and agriculture to the demand for rectification of particular grievances. Characteristic activities include the organization of pressure groups and lobbies, such as tribal associations, cultural bodies, and occupational, educational, and professional groups. The normative claims of interest groups are generally instrumental and narrowly relevant, although failure to deal with the persistent demands of a particular group may widen the significance of its claims until they become populist. If such a transformation takes places, the resulting situation is likely to become explosive, as with the claims of racial minorities in the United States, India, and Nigeria, and the claims of linguistic divisions in Ceylon and Belgium, where lack of interest rewards have been exacerbated by failures to provide dual language facilities in schools and to take sufficiently active steps in breaking down discriminatory barriers.

Professional information is the opposite of populist information. Its creation involves the least "noise" and the most predigestion, care, and discrimination. Whereas populist information is associated with a certain degree of flamboyance and declamatory style, professional information is associated with neutrality, as colorless a style as possible, in keeping with the universe of the laboratory and the norms of rationality. The environment in which such information is developed is virtually indistinguishable from that in which it is created—universities, research institutes, special study groups, conferences, and the new gracious conference sites (Ditchley in England, Arden House in New York, the Villa Serbelloni in Italy). The manner in which professional information is formulated is more and more in keeping with its eventual custodial use, itself part of the justification of the professional claim to representation. Such information is organized in such a manner as to drive out populist noises if they should appear.

The three quite different claims to representation suggest the normative

12. It is quite possible for reservoirs of complaints to spill over, as it were, and be transformed into populist claims; for example, the demands for equal language rights in educational institutions by Flemish-speaking groups in Belgium and for the acceptance of French in Canada. In the first case, the demand has shaken the political structure of Belgium, and in the second, the secession of French-speaking Canada has become a possibility.

emphases of the information derived from each. First of all, the information differs in rationality. Populist information is not necessarily irrational, but a good bit of it is nonrational in the sense that consummatory values are nonrational (embodying nonempirical ends). This would hold whether it were expressed in primordial terms or as self-validating beliefs. Resonance generated by normative changes signals the existence of hostile relationships between individuals, collectivities, and individuals and collectivities. It is a language of friction, virtually contentless but capable of arousing great passion. (The term "Americanism" may serve as an example.) More general than political norms, such catchwords are not easy to translate into informational terms. However, if they defy sorting, coding, or transmitting, they are useful in the crude sense of registering negative or positive noise, normative credits or debits. Interest groups, since their ends are for the most part instrumental, bargain for specific gains, even when the root cause of their dissatisfaction may lie in nonempirical values. Hence, their information is rationalistic, narrow, and hard in the sense of being of value in the marketplace. When their goals are sufficiently articulated, information arises in terms of cause and effect, proposal and result, demand and action. Since the claims of professional groups are based on superior knowledge in special fields, their information is even more narrowly rational, with the additional requirement of functional significance. Such information must be explicit, capable of affecting policy, and useful in making predictions. The possession of superior knowledge must be recognized publicly even though it must also be disguised by a public posture of professional modesty. Thus, rationality is one criterion of comparison between the three types of information. Style is another. So is particularity. All three display what might be called "sustained effectiveness" or the ability to put forward information in the act of claiming representation.

We have implied that the developmental tendency favors the functionally precise and relevant over the resonant and less functional forms of information. Populist groups are likely to be momentarily effective, passing from troughs of passivity to peaks of excitement. Their activities may be organized and periodic, as in election campaigns; they may be temporary manifestations of indignation, as in spontaneous rallies, marches, and strikes; or they may be the signs of more deepseated dissatisfactions as in underground organizations, guerilla bands, and other "subversive" groups. But they can lead to a change in the political system. Interest groups tend to sustain their effectiveness more quietly and persistently, although they, too, wax and wane over time. Professionals, since they work all the time to create functionally relevant information, are the most persistent.

It was suggested that each kind of information has a style. This characteristic is more complex than it might appear at first glance. Populist information, the least specific, is most likely to be received with dignity in great halls and legislatures, and to be expressed in elaborately decorated monuments proclaiming the worth of the common man. Although populist debates may generate resonance in the marketplace, they may also be translated into ritualistic performances of great importance for legitimacy, for creating the illusion of participation. Interest groups are more informal. Meetings occur in small chambers and private rooms, at dinners or quiet gatherings. Often a certain surreptitiousness surrounds these meetings. Often, too, interest information is disguised as populist information, as in corporate societies, when populist noise is used as a screen to hide other purposes and interests. However interest information is presented it is received with less dignity than populist information. Paradoxically, the more directly functional the information of professional groups, the less dignity granted them. Their messages are received in the context of the workplace, the map room, the computer station, the laboratory, and the bureaucrat's office, where, in the main, a spartan environment prevails. (Money is always short and must be spent on the information itself.) Dignity lies in the institutional context of the role: the norm of inquiry, symbolized by academic degrees and, in the last analysis, by buildings, programs, new organizations, better weapons, better plans. The three general claims to representation each embody a loyalty factor, certain rewards, and the possibility of elevation to custodial roles. All members of a system extend their support on the basis of one or more of these claims.[13]

13. Different types of political systems have different information preferences. For example, government in the Soviet Union attaches most importance to information of the instrumental type, information relating to interest and professional activities. The relevant elites are members of research institutes, cooperative or collective economic enterprises and trusts, and various ministries, departments, and planning bodies. Functional and professional claims ranked according to value compete not so much for rewards as for access to planning and related activities. See the extremely valuable breakdown given in Ghiţa Ionescu, *The Politics of the European Communist States* (London: Wiedenfeld & Nicholson, 1967), pp. 55–64.

That interest groups play a large role in the USSR should not surprise us, since they are an important part of industrial life everywhere. They include members of the intelligentsia, administrators of all kinds, heads of rural enterprises (sovkhozes, kolkhozes, machine-tractor stations, and so on), scientific workers, teachers, physicians, planning and accountancy personnel, and the judiciary. The social structure of socialist countries is increasingly organized according to explicit criteria of professionality. Each cluster of professionals works as a collective interest group, as when plant managers compete for personnel and resources by bargaining with government. See the discussion by Milton Lodge, "Soviet Elite Participation Attitudes in the Post-Stalin Period," *American Political Science Review* 62, no. 3 (Sept. 1968). His general dis-

REPRESENTATION AND COERCION

Just as it was possible to see information as a series of normative and structural inputs, so coercion can be examined as a set of normative and structural outputs. The consequences of the exercise of executive authority in accordance with normative proprieties can be defined in symbolic terms.

By *coercion* we mean compulsion, or the implied threat of compulsion, in order to obtain compliance. Any relationship based on authority implies coercion. (This is why there can be no purely voluntary society unless all members are equal in every way.) Coercion can range from physical violence to the stimulation of anxiety or fear. All societies apply some coercion. Our main concern is with political coercion, which we define as acts of violence performed by the state, by the government itself, or by elites with government approval. This is not to say that political coercion is the only important type found in a society. Anyone who has lived in a small town will have been aware of a variety of indirect coercive pressures applied structurally through the network of schools and churches, neighborhood clubs and businesses, voluntary associations, and even banks. Private forms of coercion may be translated into official ones. Ostracism by clubs, schools, and churches, for example, may be made mandatory by governmental decree, requiring not only the acquiescence but the participation of the appropriate elites in coercive measures such as blacklisting for jobs and expulsion from professional organizations. In this discussion, however, we refer to forms of direct government coercion such as the banning of newspapers, censorship, violence against persons (such as putting them in jail or in concentration camps)—the broad range of punishments for serious offenses falling within the definition of treasonable activities. These offenses and punishments are, in fact, the indicators of a polarized consummatory dialectic. Action by a government against

---

cussion of the growing power of functional elites is consistent with the general propositions suggested here.

Such interest-group activity and professionality in a framework of bargaining creates a substitute for a market. These comments suggest that the creation of information itself may exert pressure to shift the USSR, a predominantly bureaucratic system, in the direction of a reconciliation system. In other bureaucratic systems, elites may represent much less functionally significant groups, such as caste groups with populist access claims. The resonance of these claims may overshadow the professional or interest claims the elites also represent or, more likely, combine with them to make populist access more acceptable to government and to help translate it into interests. In other words, to obtain popular support, interest groups may appeal to primordial loyalties, as in the case of the fascist party in Italy or the National Socialists in Germany.

counter-norms that threaten legitimacy will be partly symbolic and partly instrumental; indeed, it will be punitive.[14] A comprehensive evaluation of coercion would include an enumeration of categories of crimes and punishments, how they take place, and what punitive actions follow. More crudely, our assessment follows Durkheim's distinction between "repressive" and "restitutive" law. The employment of consummatory values to justify official violence is an indication of the first, and compensatory actions characterize the second.

In this context, how do claims to elite access and information functions relate to coercion? Where elite access is minimal and hierarchy most highly developed, the elite most closely associated with government has an important official or semiofficial role to play in the application of coercion. Such elites aid governments to specify goals for the groups they represent, exercise a measure of central control to insure that government decisions are carried out, and eliminate sources of ambiguity and overlapping jurisdiction to achieve institutional integration. In other words, in systems where there is a high degree of coercion, elites have narrow access to government, and that access consists mainly of the application of coercion.[15] It could be argued that it is rather old-fashioned, if not foolhardy, to employ Durkheim's distinction to explain why actions regarded

14. Attempts have already been made to establish an index of coercion involving several different categories of punishable actions. Some of the categories associated with consummatory values are felonious crimes against society, publication or distribution of forbidden literature or ideas, and antisocial activities. The more complete the list of proscribed actions that threaten existing consummatory values, the more coercive the system. Punishment may occur arbitrarily, that is, in the absence of an explicit prohibition (as when certain writers in the USSR received sentences for writing unacceptable things, while in principle there were guarantees of free speech). Or there may be a wide range of punishable offences listed, but because of laxity or the passage of time little punitive action may in fact be taken. Since there may be numerous discrepancies between categories of offences and the punishments carried out, a second test would be needed to assess coercion.

An attempt to examine, conceptualize, and measure some of these terms has been undertaken by the Politics of Modernization Project at the University of California at Berkeley and particularly by Mario Barrera; see his *Modernization and Coercion* (Berkeley, Calif.: Institute of International Studies, Politics of Modernization Project, 1969). See also Ivo and Rosalind Feierabend, "Aggressive Behavior within Politics, 1948–62: A Cross-National Study," *Journal of Conflict Resolution,* Sept. 1966, pp. 249–71.

15. However, if elite access is maximal, and there is an emphasis on consummatory values in a system, there will be a low degree of coercion. Of course, unofficial coercion may be applied in the form of social pressures. This would be particularly true of theocratic systems, which have a low degree of coercion but depend on a high degree of public consensus.

as highly symbolic crimes in one society are viewed as ordinary acts in others. Such a use implies an objective measure of the distribution of norms in a system. But we wish to use Durkheim's two types of law as a parallel, not to consummatory and instrumental values, but to the kinds of coercion applied in their names. For high-coercion mobilization systems, for example, our matrix would show populist norms as dialectically congruent, or unitary with populist claims to representation, thereby defining the corporate character of society; deviation from these norms would constitute a negative form of conduct directly punishable by the government. Interest norms would show a high degree of instrumental integration with populist ones, as would professional norms, except under conditions of advanced industrialization.

Accordingly, when a system is predominantly of the mobilization type and dialectical congruence obtains, one would expect populist goals to be corporatist, with punishment for deviation of a highly symbolic sort, while interest and professional claims to representation would be tolerated only insofar as they served wider purposes of the corporation. As populist norms completely internalized, universalized repressive law would presumably decline, coercion would lessen, and the system would change to another type. This system change should correlate with a corresponding increase in restitutive law. An extreme case like China, for example, has tended toward three very different systems—mobilization, bureaucratic, and theocratic (to the extent that Maoism is a system of beliefs calling forth a high degree of popular voluntarism). If the dominant tendency is in the theocratic direction, then not only should coercion be increasingly less necessary, but the government should be able to apply restitutive law employing ordinary correctives to wide areas of behavior that is now considered deviant. A dominant tendency toward a bureaucratic system, on the contrary, would indicate the growing significance of the military and the technocrats, also expressed in the use of restitutive laws, and their interest in the instrumentalization of norms at the expense both of consummatory values and of the theocratic voluntarism based on such values. To the extent that there is a tendency toward a theocratic system, there is pressure for a low degree of coercion and voluntarism, expressed through a pyramidal structure of political participation. To the extent that there is a mobilization system, the structure is hierarchical, punitive, and coercive. In a bureaucratic system, the norms are largely perfunctory and ritualized; interest and professional claims are self-justifying and need only hierarchical authority to carry them out. To reconcile the role of technocrats is difficult, for they rely on the party to apply coercion so that they may carry forward modernization goals. The party relies on the technocrats to further instrumental goals, but it sees them as a threat to consummatory values. Conflicts over who shall be the interpreters of such consummatory values go on between the party, the army, and the younger generation, the latter being more devout in their consummatory beliefs than either of the others and requiring less organization, at least for the moment. The technocrats become increasingly important as modernization proceeds, and the party has to redefine its functional role as it comes into competition with the technocrats. With development, the army is likely to become more technocratic and instrumental.[16]

16. Noting changes in the pattern of repressive law is one way of following such conflicts. One writer, considering foreign trade with China, suggests that "the primacy of political considerations, the opposition to economism, the transformation of Chinese enterprises from purely economic units, where economic performance clearly takes priority, into socio-political entities at the service of workers, soldiers and peasants, the growing presence of the army in industry to maintain order in production, the stress upon collective leadership of party committees, the dichotomy in responsibility between Reds and experts, the disregard for all division of labor, work specialization and formal relationships, and the difficulty in distinguishing who is who in Chinese business, make the situation on the domestic scene rather confused, to say the least." See Gabriele Crespi Reghizzi, "Legal Aspects of Trade with China: The Italian Experience," *Harvard International Law Journal* 9, no. 1 (1968). See also Franz Schurmann, *Ideology and Organization in Communist China* (Berkeley and Los Angeles: University of California Press, 1966), passim.

5. Government and the Political System

Three of the relationships embodied in the structural theory were used to describe how information is generated in a society by elites and how coercion is applied by government. These relationships are equity-allocation (information creation), allocation–political norms (classification of information), and political norms–participation (transmittal of messages). Coercion depends on the political norm–relationship (creation of commands), participation-allocation (action on commands), and finally on the relationship of allocation to equity, by which new values (social norms) are defined. With respect to both information and coercion it is easy to see how critical the participation variable becomes in the structural theory and how much depends on the degree of pyramidal or hierarchical authority in a society. The degree of elite participation in a system will result in a greater or less emphasis on coercion; further, since information and coercion are defined as the functional requisites of government, a change in the pattern of participation means a change in the political system.

Conversely, a change in political system would be accompanied by an alteration in the coercion-information balance. Bearing in mind the connections between participation, type of political system, and coercion and information, let us explore the implications of all three relationships for government. We want to know how different political systems respond to changes in coercion-information balances.

We said earlier that our main concrete units are society, elites and government, which are the instrumentalities through which information and coercion are realized. Information and coercion represent the ingredients of what we mean by *power,* which is defined as the degree to which information and coercion can be mobilized by any unit or sub-unit. Taken together the analytical and concrete units of the model represent a total flow of power. So far, we have divided the participation category into categories of access and representation to measure elite performances that taken together would allow us to compare from case to case what really happens when the coercion and information balance is altered. Now we want to carry the analysis one step further and ask how different types of political system respond to such changes. The total flow model enables us to locate multiple sources of power and evaluate the efficacy of different instrumentalities for transmitting information and coercion. The question is how do different governments respond to pressures to change the information-coercion balance.

We have already suggested some of the types of information and coercion that elites transmit to or for government, which has allowed us to hypothesize that the higher the degree of industrialization, the greater the need for information and the more dysfunctional the application of coercion. Since in our structural model information is a function of representation, some interesting questions are raised about long-term tendencies in political systems that are appropriate for development. Is a tendency toward a reconciliation system universal for societies with high degrees of industrialization? Is such pressure—visible, for example, in the USSR today—manifested in the appeals of writers, poets, and artists for the freer application of information, both for instrumental goals and for freedom as a consummatory value? If such pressures do not result in a change in the character of the regime, there will be changes in the rate of innovation. This effect will be particularly obvious in a highly industrial society (although technical knowledge will perhaps be the last to be affected by a slowdown in development). If, for example, a trend toward a reconciliation system is not followed by an increase in information and a decrease in coercion, inhibitions will arise in the productive process. Various social institutions (factories, transportation systems, and so on) will show lags; managers will falsify unpleasant facts. Shoddy workmanship, misallocation of resources, and the disguise of losses will be among the results affecting development. Such distortions, when sufficiently numerous, can be called *collective corruption,* that is, corruption in which even those in the most technologically important sectors of the society participate in order to delude the government. If the result is increasing reliance on coercion as a policy, then populist information will virtually disappear or go underground and loyalties will become suspect. A new system trend will emerge based on provocative norms that establish a counter-legitimacy. Such a trend may be embodied in a theocratic system—a utopia—that, though never realizable concretely, will be visualized as the only possible alternative to all the other types.[1]

Our suggestion, then, is that changes in the type of political system should correlate with major shifts in the coercion-information relationship, and that in general an industrial society will need high information

1. Of course, such utopias can be very creative. If it is true that the failure of theocratic systems is inevitable, so is their periodic revival. (Nor is this merely a pastime for intellectuals; theocratic revivalism can take many forms, both intellectual and anti-intellectual.)

and a government of the reconciliation type. Although the relations between coercion, information, and type of political system may not be determinate, neither are they random. Structural limitations limit the options
of government. Within such boundaries lie all the important considerations of policy-making, and the governmental abilities to solve problems,
a condition we will call *political efficacy.* The opposite of political efficacy,
failure of efficacy, will describe the condition of a nonviable regime. That
this notion contains a bias in favor of stability of regimes is not so, if it is
accepted that the political ceilings confronted by governments, especially
during modernization, are relatively quickly reached. Indeed, system
change is a way of altering those ceilings; in fact, under some circumstances, it is the most useful way of rearranging the social conditions of
the political elites. In other words, coups d'état, counter-coups, and the
common alteration of regimes through a set sequence (parliamentary governments, personalistic or junta government that attempts socialist one-
party rule, and military takeover), though deplorable insofar as individuals are hurt, killed, or abused in some manner, may be the primary
means of rearranging elite access and participation in decision-making
and incorporating progressively greater numbers of populist groupings
into society as functioning political members.

GOVERNMENT AS A CONCRETE UNIT

Concrete, standardized variations in arrangements and mechanisms of
government are called *regimes.* They involve the links between government and elites and are usually differentiated on the basis of executive,
judicial, legislative, and administrative functions. The role of each function is contingent upon those of the others, so a particular regime can be
examined in terms of the internal workings of its mechanisms (such as
parliament, cabinet, legislative and executive committees, courts, and administrative tribunals). Although inadequate for many purposes, this approach draws attention to the many ways governments can be organized,
members recruited, and relations of politicians and constituents evaluated.
One difficulty with this traditional approach is that it makes excessive
analytical demands upon the concrete mechanism. It makes what is in
reality complex appear simple. Form may follow function, but in ways that
are general so that the conditions under which a concrete mechanism will
have certain consequences are very difficult to specify, especially when
the mechanism is studied in a different political setting. Parliamentary government in England's democratic regime may turn into cabinet dictatorship in Ghana under an autocratic regime. One-party government may be
democratic as it evolves in Tanzania and autocratic in China or the

USSR. Thus, the traditional approach tends to elevate concrete units to the level of analytical ones and consequently fails to define any standardized relationships between regimes and stages of development. We prefer a narrower definition of government, one that accords more fully with our notion of the total flow of power between society, elites, and government. The links between these units should be evaluated in terms of analytical categories that do not prejudge the characteristics of specific regimes.

Government is a unit that is more narrowly defined than regime and is more manageable from an operational point of view. Hence, we agree with the traditional approach in at least one respect: government is the heart of the matter. When we speak concretely of government by men or by laws, it is as an entelechy, the embodiment of a capacity for applying public intelligence to specific problems within society.[2] In our present analysis, then, government is the strategic concrete unit for the analysis of both the structural theory and the coercion-information relationship. Certain well-worn constitutional distinctions, valid though they may be, will not be used (for example, the common separation between the "rule of law" and the "rule of men"). Indeed, if we refer to more usual typologies of government (totalitarian, democratic), it will be only in a common-sense or nontechnical manner. Nor will we distinguish here between the exercise of power as compulsion and as a responsibility of office,[3] preferring to incorporate such ideas in the context of the types of political systems. Given various relationships of government to elites and society, government is viewed as the recipient of the larger units' inputs, which it converts into a set of outputs in the form of decisions. For example, when we describe the behavioral problem of industrial society as the "radicalization problem" and that of modernizing society as the "embourgeoisement problem," we also are describing certain functional and dialectical demands that confront governments at various development stages. Our system types (whether or not a government of law exists) show a variable capacity to deal with these problems by increasing efficiency through authoritative decision-making. To assess their effectiveness we pursue the present formulation.[4]

2. See the discussion in Sheldon Wolin, *Politics and Vision* (Boston: Little, Brown & Co., 1960), pp. 56–57.

3. This is embodied in Weber's distinction between *Macht* and *Herrschaft*, between an individual's will or might and powers that are legally given. See the useful discussion in Alexander Passerin d'Entreves, *The Notion of the State* (Oxford: Clarendon Press, 1967), pp. 1–81.

4. For a discussion of typologies of government, see Bernard Crick, "The Elementary Types of Government," in *Government and Opposition* 3, no. 1.

Despite its central role in political studies (and the lengthy descriptive literature that deals with the subject), the term *government* has an elusive quality; that is, we are never quite certain who actually governs or why. Even if we know the various devices by which citizens delegate authority to their representatives, the boundaries of government remain ambiguous. For example, what comprises the government of the United States? Is the Congress part of it, or does the term refer primarily to the executive branch? Do we include the judiciary? In Great Britain does the government consist entirely of members' of the cabinet with the rank of minister, or does it include the Queen in Council or Parliament? The boundaries of government shift continuously, depending on the perspective of the observer. There are no absolute boundaries. Even with the most restrictive monolithic regime, government is never truly one-man rule; there is always some sharing of power and some consultation. This vagueness surrounding government can be reduced somewhat through the application of a definition. For our purposes, therefore, government will mean the concrete unit with the responsibility for maintaining or adapting the most generalized unit of which it is a part, namely, society. The essence of our approach to government is to think of it as the minimal unit, in contrast to society, the maximal unit. In short, we restrict government to the group of leaders most narrowly engaged in decision-making. Or, to put it a bit differently, *government refers to the smallest number of individuals responsible for wielding executive authority on a consistent basis,* the smallest group with a defined responsibility for maintaining the balance between allocation and equity, development and order.[5] The rights and responsibilities of its members are legally or customarily defined; thus a relevant relationship between law and executive authority is established. This formulation allows us to analyze the relationship between political elites and government. Parliaments, bureaucracies, judiciaries, all constitute a special part of the relevant elite because of their proximity to government. A high degree of proximity means membership in the political elite.

Since government is a subsystem of society's elites, the structures of information and coercion formed by the elites can be treated as the func-

5. Our concept of government is restricted to the executive body itself. In Great Britain this body would consist of the cabinet; in the United States, the office of president; in France, the offices of both president and prime minister; and in the USSR, the chairman of the central committee of the Communist party and the offices of chairman of the presidium and of the Supreme Soviet. In speaking of government as the minimal unit, we are concerned with the roles and offices embodying legitimate power and the individuals who occupy those roles.

tional requisites of government. No government can function without applying some coercion. Both are necessary if a government is to sustain society without reaching its political ceiling. Since governments all need to rid themselves of as much uncertainty as possible, they screen information obtained from elites, eliminating random factors, in order to make decisions that will have predictable results. Since they also need to insure compliance, they depend on the coercive sanctions and power available to them. In addition to the functional requisites of government, information and coercion, it is possible to identify two structural requisites: *authoritative decision-making* and *accountability and consent.* Here the relationship between the government and the political elite is of utmost importance. Thus, in our formulation government not only completes the system of relationship between society and elites, the concrete units, but also locks them into the analytical system. To summarize, the actual boundaries of government are established by its defined responsibilities for the maintenance and adaptation of society and its practical monopoly of coercive powers. It is the unit from which the public expects action in the form of policies. To locate this group in actuality, however, will require further criteria, since different governments vary considerably in practices and methods.

With reference to the structure of accountability and consent, we can ask whether accountability by government is high or low. With reference to the structure of authoritative decision-making, we can ask whether decision-making is centralized and concentrated or decentralized and diffused. Answers to these questions will enable us to identify hierarchical or pyramidal systems of authority.

STRATEGIC POLITICAL ELITES

Turning now to the political elite, we can describe three sets of groups. The first, or primary set, which includes legislative bodies, judicial bodies, and administrative systems, contains the concrete mechanisms by which government employs elites in decision-making. *Legislative bodies* (councils, boards, commissions, and so on) are recruited on the basis of various principles of representation—populism, interest, and profession—and may be appointive, elective, co-optive, or hereditary. *Judicial bodies,* whether chosen by warrant, election, age, or kinship, must resolve conflicts between contending parties; thus they have a special responsibility for institutional coherence. Judicial functions may be kept within government, as when chiefs and kings or their agents dispense justice directly, or they may be kept separate from government in an independent body with power to review the decisions of government itself, as in the Supreme

Court of the United States. *Administrative systems*[6] have always been an integral part of government. In recent years, however, they have shown a great increase in access to and participation in authoritative decision-making, partly because of their growing functional significance in industrial societies. Even with norms restricting access (such as the ruling that the civil service may recommend but not decide policy), this trend has not slowed down. Indeed, it would be difficult to reestablish a concrete boundary between government and bureaucracy because of the specialized functions, including ministerial responsibility, of some administrators.

These three political elite groups occupy a special place between government, which is the unit with defined responsibility for maintaining the system, and other elite groupings. Their methods of recruitment, organization, influence, and so on, each have a literature of long and involved elaborations.[7] So significant are these groups in converting inputs into messages for government, and so close to government, that we can call them *primary organs of access;* that is, they are the official instruments of goal specification, and central control. They include parliaments and committees, councils of chiefs, courts of kings, administrative cadres, civil servants, corps of specialists, magistrates, and judges, which screen inputs and resolve differences before they become public crises. They attempt to channel inputs into laws and precedents, whether the inputs arise from public disorders or crimes, the misallocation of resources, or technological innovation. As primary organs, they help government balance development and tradition. When there is little need for tradition and much need for development, their roles will change and so will their special influence on the performance of the society's elites.

Another set of access organs, referring to secondary access, include the following, by no means exclusive, list: political parties, factions, movements, and groups; military cadres, police, and intelligence agencies; press, radio, and television: research centers, institutes, and experiment stations. Each of these groups is likely to have special access to decision-making by virtue of some claim to legitimacy—populist, interest, or professional. For example, the military claim is based on the contribution it can make

6. We can define "bureaucracy" in functional terms, not as a civil service, but as a particular highly organized and integrated cluster of elites carrying out certain political mandates in a disciplined way through the exercise of the two information functions: goal specification and central control. See the discussion of bureaucracy in J. P. Nettl, *Political Mobilization* (London: Faber & Faber, 1967), pp. 337–80.

7. We regard such matters as most important. At the level of generality on which our concrete units have been gathered, however, such subsystemic properties would have to be the subject of empirical rather than theoretical treatment.

to the maintenance of the system in case of war or rebellion; political parties base their claim on populist support; and so on. Primary organs of access are at times confused with government itself by secondary groups and others, since they share so heavily in making policy.

In a system where there is high accountability, decentralized decision-making, high information, and low coercion both primary and secondary organs of access have different characteristics from those they have in a system where government shows low accountability, is highly centralized, and employs a high degree of coercion.

The existence of such instrumentalities of access does not of itself imply a particular structure of power. Each of the organs of access may serve merely to transmit—or possibly hasten or delay—messages without affecting them in any meaningful manner. For example, judges who have been instructed how to interpret the law in certain cases, although thereby abdicating their power of judgment, may nevertheless use the courts in this way. A powerful military officer or group wielding exceptional power through the ministry of war or defense may diminish the capacity of the ministry's administration as a subsystem to screen his actions.

The tertiary set of access groups are interest groups, which have the most variable access of all, based more or less on functional relevance. They are institutional groups (health, welfare, and education); functional interest groups (management, labor, and other occupations); and nonfunctional interest groups (racial, ethnic, and religious).

These three sets of access groups form the basis for an evaluation of the structures and functions of government. For each set, we can identify specific concrete groupings and screen them in terms of their access roles and their claims to representation. With these results, we can proceed to evaluate the balance of information and coercion in any given political system.

THE FUNCTIONAL AND STRUCTURAL REQUISITES OF GOVERNMENT

The functions of the elite—goal specification and central control may be used to indicate the degree of access by particular elites to government. The kinds of access form two structures of the elite: the structure of information, the pattern of message conversion; and the structure of coercion, the pattern of decision conversion. The analysis of the functions of the elite and the structures of the elite form one matrix. (See Figure 5.1). Since government is a subsystem of the political elite, these two structures can also be identified as the functional requisites of government. They are requisites because without information, government cannot make decisions, and without coercion, government cannot carry out decisions.

Functions	Structures	
	Coercion	Information
Goal specification	r	r
Central Control	r	r

Figure 5.1. Functions and structures of the elite

Hence the functional heart of government is created by the structures of the elite. Carrying the argument one step further, we can say that the structural heart of government lies in its structural requisites: *accountability and consent* and *authoritative decision-making*. (See Figure 5.2.)

Structures of government

Functions	Accountability and consent	Authoritative decision-making
Coercion	r	r
Information	r	r

Figure 5.2. Requisite functions and structures of government

By the structure of accountability and consent, we mean the pattern through which government is responsible to elites, and, in turn, to groups organized in terms of various systems of stratification; by the structure of authoritative decision-making, we refer to the part taken by government itself in decisions.

Let us summarize the analysis in terms of the total flow theory of power. From one standpoint of our analysis, the treatment of the concrete units of society, elites and government, implies that each larger unit sets the limits of action for each smaller unit, and on a cumulative basis. That is, government is bounded by elites and, more generally, by allocation variables, and elites are bounded by allocation variables. Government is both a dependent unit (when it responds to inputs generated outside its immediate boundaries) and an independent one (when industrialization, modernization, characteristics of stratification, and patterns of elites are all evaluated as results of governmental decisions).

It should be clear from Figure 5.3 that although the structures of the elite and the functions of government refer to the same phenomena, their

	Structure	Function
Society	Access	Populist claims Functional claims Professional claims
Elites	Participation through coercion and information	Goal specification Central control
Government	Accountability and consent Authoritative decision-making	Coercion Information

Figure 5.3. The total flow relationship of power

respective structures do not overlap.[8] The information structure of the elite consists of the ways in which it elicits and passes on information to government. The information structure of government is the organization of information for decision-making. The method of organization will vary from government to government, but it is the resulting pattern that we have called the structure of authoritative decision-making.

Similarly, the coercive structures of elites and governments differ. Elites, when dealing with the groups they represent, are not simply instruments of those groups. Precisely because they have a special relationship with government and share in its activities, elites are both representative of their groups and subordinate to government. If they are more representative, their groups' interests impinge upon those of the wider body of collectivities. If they are more subordinate, they are instruments of the will of government. It is the resulting pattern, varying from government to government, that we have called the structure of accountability and consent. When consultation is high and consent for decisions is regularly sought from widely dispersed groups, it is not possible for government to be arbitrary and it is more difficult to apply coercion. Conversely, when it is possible to be coercive, and elites are used for this purpose, it is not likely that there will be high accountability and consent. These extremes define the two types of authority we have mentioned, hierarchical and pyramidal.

8. More specifically, the two structures are results of the operation of elite functions: (1) the structure of information results from the conversion of messages into knowledge by elites; and (2) the structure of coercion results from the conversion of actions taken by governments into outputs that then affect the society as a whole.

If the degree of coercion is high, accountability and consent are low. If information is high, accountability and consent are high. In neither case does the balance determine the quality of authoritative decision-making, a point on which the analytical system remains open. But with a high degree of coercion, this quality can be maintained only by government leaders able to utilize past information with great imagination (usually accompanied by kicks and blows) to carry forward policies of an essential nature that drastically change the quality of development and by liberating untapped human and physical resources achieve a previously established set of priorities. In general, if the degree of coercion is low and accountability and consent are high, government leaders who have inspired confidence may, by means of coalitions and careful bargaining, utilize information to make decisions that reinforce voluntary support.[9] Whatever the relationship between government and society (that is, regardless of which is the dependent or independent variable) elites remain the mediating units.[10]

Turning now to political systems, we can treat coercion and information as independent variables. How they change should correlate with shifts toward one or the other of our four types of political system.

INFORMATION AS INPUT AND COERCION AS OUTPUT

The immediate empirical task is to identify changes in the relationship between information and coercion and to project the effect on particular regimes by following these principles.

1. If information and coercion are functional requisites of government, no viable government is possible without some performance of both functions.

2. If information and coercion vary inversely to each other, neither a pure information system nor a pure coercion system is possible.

3. If there is an increase in the amount of coercion, the degree of hierarchy in a political system will also increase, as will the centralization of decision-making.

4. If there is an increase in the amount of information, the degree of pyramidal authority will also increase, as will the decentralization of decision-making.

9. This is often what is meant by the term *leadership*. In both cases, performance and ability are nonsystemic factors—not random, to be sure, but always empirical.

10. From a purely analytical point of view, the choice of a unit as independent is quite arbitrary. It is possible to link the concrete units as first described, that is, society-elites-government, and then turn them around with quite useful results. Or elites can be considered independent and the others dependent or intervening.

5. If the predominant tendency in a society is toward a mobilization system or a bureaucratic system, policy will depend less on information and more on coercion.

6. If a society moves along a continuum from a traditional system to an industrial one, the polarization of the functionally relevant and functionally superfluous segments of the community will be more pronounced.

7. The larger the number of segments in a system congregating around opposite poles of functionality, the larger the amount of elite competition and the greater the generation of all types of information—populist, interest, and professional.

8. The greater the degree of polarization between types of information in a system, the greater the polarization of consummatory and instrumental norms and of sets of consummatory norms.

9. If the application of coercion becomes so great that there is a notable increase in misleading information from the segments of the system, the likelihood that the system will change is greatly increased.

10. If there is an increase in information of all types, failure to screen and code it properly will lead to an information overload, with uncertainty the result for decision-making.[11]

Although this formulation derives from the use of coercion and information as intervening variables, it should be clear that the relevance of information varies. As we have suggested, there are basically three types of information, ranging from the least functional to the most. By least functional, we mean that which depends least on new technology and which is generated by the broadest units (coterminous with society) with the least instrumental norms—in a word, populist. Populist information conveys the amount of loyalty or support granted a government, as well as claims to access and representation of the most generalized groupings in society. Next in terms of functionality is the type of information linked to the formation of interest groups as intermediate groupings between populist and professional or technocratic ones. Here the specific interests reflect the needs of certain groups. Some of these groups will be less functional and others more (for example, neighborhood groups as compared with businessmen's associations), but all have specific objectives on which they base their claims to access and representation. The third and most functional type of information, professional information, is associated with the evolution of theory and technology. The groups creating this type of

11. The principles of forecasting employed here are in several key respects similar to the formulations of Anthony Downs. See, in particular, "Communications in Bureaus," chap. 10 in *Inside Bureaucracy* (Boston: Little, Brown & Co., 1967), pp. 112–31.

information base their claims to representation and access on functional relevance.

The foregoing propositions about information and coercion apply to all types of information—populist, interest, and professional—each of which is presumed to reflect a mobilizable power based on a normative claim within the system. This brings us to the point in our analysis where we can begin to make use of the concept of efficacy in evaluating change in political systems.

WHY POLITICAL SYSTEMS CHANGE

When does a government reach a ceiling in its ability to take effective action? First, when normative and functional changes cause a shift in the type of political system (this is the result of functional and dialectical changes in society); and second, when either the structure of accountability and consent or the structure of authoritative decision-making is no longer able to support its functions. Specifically, we mean that the structure fails either to obtain adequate information or to successfully apply coercion. In short, failures in the structural requisites result in failures in the functional requisites. When information and coercion no longer function for government, they also fail as structures of the elite. In turn, when the structures of the elite collapse, so do the functions of the elite: goal specification and central control. The result is the randomization of relationships between rulers and ruled, a condition that is the opposite of order. Competition between various sets of values follows, thus undermining the system of equity.

The point at which political systems change, or the political ceiling, is when a regime can no longer vary the relationships between coercion and information or act efficaciously within a given balance. But we have seen that the sources of variation are continuous. They arise from changing degrees of development during modernization and industrialization and from pressures for alterations in allocation, resulting in both different notions of equity and changes in the existing structural relationships of order. Since equity and political norms both have self-generating impulses to change dialectically even if development did not occur, a flexible relationship between coercion and information would be necessary in order to protect the prevailing consummatory and instrumental values and the particular structural relationships.

When reconciliation and theocratic systems attempt to maintain the structures of accountability and consent and of authoritative decision-making by increasing coercion, they tend toward predominantly mobilization or bureaucratic systems; and when mobilization and bureaucratic systems attempt to maintain their structural requisites by increasing information, they tend toward predominantly reconciliation or theocratic systems. Hence the response of government to uncertainty, whether by increasing coercion or information, is the key to why political systems change.[12]

To summarize, we may enumerate the points made so far. The greater the degree of development, the wider the range of choice. The wider the range of choice in a system, the greater the degree of normative and structural imbalance. The greater the degree of normative and structural imbalance, the greater the likelihood of alterations in the equity-allocation relationship and the legitimate authority of government. The greater the disruption in the equity-allocation relationship and the reduction of the government's legitimate authority, the weaker the flow of information or the greater the need to apply coercion, the ultimate result being greater uncertainty. The way each political system responds to uncertainty, reaches its ceiling and alters, is our present concern.

Let us now look at governments in two types of political systems, the mobilization and reconciliation systems, to see how they handle these problems. Confronted with uncertainty, these governments would seek to maximize the information at their disposal in order to promote the efficacy of decision-making. This response presumes an attachment to the political elites of populist, interest, and professional groups. Remembering that at any time the total amount of information available in a system derives from these elites, with proportionately greater amounts from the instrumental and technical spheres as development increases, we can suggest the following propositions:

1. The lower the degree of hierarchy, the greater the difficulty government has in acting on information, unless there is a high degree of consensus.

2. The greater the degree of hierarchy, the easier it is for government to act upon the information at its disposal.

3. Technical information is easier to obtain than any other form.

4. In mobilization, governments tend to maximize technical information and employ coercion to reduce uncertainty in the spheres where information is lacking.

5. In reconciliation systems, government attempts to maximize populist, interest, and professional information and to find an acceptable rationaliza-

---

12. We have stressed the predilection of mobilization systems for coercion and reconciliation systems for information. But there is a limit beyond which increasing coercion fails to create certainty, just as there is a limit beyond which increasing information fails to create certainty.

tion for increasing coercion in order to acquire authority for decision-making.

In order words, to some extent all governments will endeavor to increase their effectiveness through the application of coercion. In mobilization systems, coercion takes the form of governmental control of the elites, and the government acts on the basis of information already available. It is particularly coercive in the sphere of consummatory values; that is, it restricts political values to a highly symbolic set of consummatory "templates" and creates a special language or code. A high degree of symbolic coercion is prepared for violators of this code. They may be cast out of the community or put to death for violations of symbol. Political witches are publicly "burned," especially those representing counter-consummatory values. Instrumental values are more easily contained by a police force or a political party (the so-called single-party system being one device employed), since they tend to be concentrated in areas of economic and political interests, but they, too, reflect interests of the community as a whole rather than of particular subgroups.

In reconciliation systems, political leaders also desire to use centralized coercion, but their power is limited by the pyramidal structure of authority imposed by the diversity and strength of accountability groups. Nevertheless, the need to apply coercion exists for many reasons. In the absence of coercion, there is likely to be considerable private corruption. Resentment of the government is common, since it constitutes perhaps the greatest threat to the rampant individualism characteristic of the system. Competition between the many interests may weaken rather than strengthen the system; interest conflicts may prepare the ground for a shift to a mobilization system or a takeover by groups with high coercion potential and instrumental values (best represented by the military). Cases in point are Burma, Pakistan, the Sudan, and Nigeria. In each case—whether a mobilization or a reconciliation system—the key to political change is a change in the coercion-information balance or the inability to change enough.

When increasing coercion results in information losses, such losses are not necessarily direct and immediate; nor are they all of the same type. They are likely to be highest in the sphere of counter-consummatory values and lowest in the sphere of technical information resulting from the industrialization process itself. Conflict between sets of instrumental values is likely to be disguised and increasingly converted from interest conflict to value conflict. In other words, a two-step process takes place: first, the loss of information about counter-norms, and then an increase in the political significance of interest claims. This effect of increasing coercion is peculiar to mobilization systems. Information loss does not always result in immediate difficulties. If high coercion follows directly after high information (for example, when there is rapid transition from a reconciliation system to a mobilization system), certain priority information about public wants, the demands of interest groups, and technical facilities will continue to be available to the government for some time afterward. The new regime can then direct coercion toward specific priorities by harnessing the social and resource infrastructure. If losses in information produce severe difficulties, reasonably effective crisis management may prevent them from pushing the regime toward its political ceiling, at least for some time. Of course, critical technical information relating to developmental priorities may not be forthcoming. Civil servants responsible for certain kinds of planning or expenditures may fail to contribute honest and appropriate information. But then development will be affected, not order.

In reconciliation systems, the problem is the reverse. That is, information about instrumental conflict is likely to be very high, so high, indeed, that it cannot be screened and evaluated, and government finds it difficult to decide how to act upon it. With its sphere of action limited by diverse accountability groups, government is likely to try compromise as a means of resolving conflict. Moreover, to effect compromise, faced with a bewildering array of information, it is likely to rely on sources that have proved satisfactory in the past, the result more often being stagnation than progress. Ineffectual policy-making then leads to the rise of groups based on populist consummatory values that repudiate government or act as a regenerative movement toward bettering government. If coercion is applied against these representatives of a new moral force, it only reinforces their claims and gives them wider legitimacy. (See Figure 5.4.)

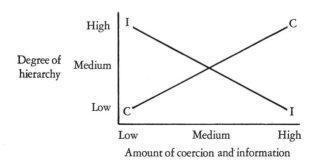

Figure 5.4. The relationship between degree of hierarchy and information and coercion

Our assumptions now can be restated in several hypothetical propositions:

1. All governments involved in modernization show a tendency to increase coercion in order to maximize the efficiency of decision-making.

2. The point at which this tendency terminates is where coercion causes such losses in information that effectiveness in decision-making is reduced; as a result, development is restricted or disorder occurs.

3. Changes in the relationship between coercion and information produce changes in the type of political system; the change may be broad and sweeping (as from mobilization to reconciliation system, and vice versa) or it may involve a lesser shift to one of two other types, to a combination of either hierarchical authority and instrumental values or pyramidal authority and consummatory values (the later changes occurring much less frequently than the former).

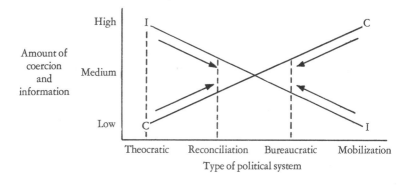

Figure 5.5. The relationship between type of political system and information and coercion

Quite aside from their theoretical interest, these tendencies (illustrated in Figure 5.5) have practical significance, particularly for countries in the early stages of modernization. Former mobilization systems such as Ghana or Mali, which have shown a higher degree of hierarchy through the mechanism of the single-party state, did not apply much coercion in the first stages of their regimes. Moreover, having replaced colonially sponsored reconciliation systems (at least in the final stages of colonialism), they fell heir to highly developed information systems. However, as the pressure to modernize rapidly created problems of organization and discipline, coercion increased causing a decline in information, which manifested itself in "bureaucratic formalism," policy failures, and eventually coups d'etat. The main difficulty with the reconciliation system is too much information inadequately screened. For example, the failure of the federal government of Nigeria to act on information it received was in large measure the result of the excessive degree of regional accountability.

The rationale underlying the theory (and our evaluations of concrete cases) can be deduced from the foregoing discussion and presented in the following propositions:

1. Increasing the degree of hierarchy narrows the circle of decision-makers and enlarges the excluded range of elites.

2. The greater the degree of hierarchy, the more concentrated the power of the decision-makers.

3. To maintain this position, decision-makers employ coercion.

4. To the extent that political elites are eliminated, competition for power between the remaining decision-makers becomes greater, as does the need for manipulative skills on the part of the central leadership.

5. The greater the loss of political elite participation and the greater the competition between the remaining decision-makers, the greater the loss of reliable information.

6. The greater the loss of information, the greater the need for a coercive force, such as an army or police unit.

7. The greater the reliance on coercion, the more significant the role of the army and police and the greater the need to control them.

The information-coercion relationship is more complicated when we analyze it in industrial societies. If it is true that highly industrial societies generate and utilize new information at a rapid rate, then there is an affinity built into industrialization for a reconciliation system. But, as we have suggested, the production of information in a reconciliation system easily gets out of control, eventually resulting in the instrumentalization of consummatory values and the increasing power of functionally relevant groups at the expense of functionally superfluous ones. The paradox here is that the type of system most suitable for industrial life cannot maintain a stable balance between the structural and normative variables. It is this paradox that confronts all industrial societies.

The functionally superfluous elites may generate a new set of political norms, or they may establish a set of counter-consummatory values based on opposition to the instrumental ones held by the functionally relevant elites. If the functionally superfluous respond in this way, the resulting conflict may take the form of numbers against knowledge, or of the functional status elite against the mass, and the information thus made available is likely to overwhelm a reconciliation government. It will be transmitted as sheer noise and percussion, nonspecific and highly charged. Such information can no longer be screened or coded in a manner that allows remedial action. It should be clear, then, that under certain conditions populist information inhibits effective decision-making. What we are referring to is the problem of "information glut," in which noise and overload prevent knowledge and communication. At first in industrial societies, there is an interval or range in which information grows at a constant level of hierarchy. (See Figure 5.6.) Beyond a certain point, the system begins to change

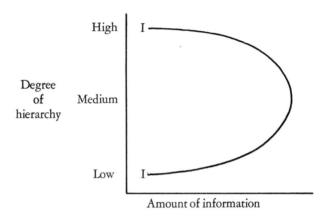

Figure 5.6. Information curve in highly industrialized societies

in terms of hierarchy, whereas the amount of information continues to grow. A limit to the growth of information is reached at a medium degree of hierarchy. Successive elaborations of the hierarchy only produce a rapid decrease in information.

The amount of information per se, however, does not tell us anything about the capacity of the system to screen and use such information for decision-making. In other words, it does not allow us to visualize at what point information overload occurs. By implication, however, it seems likely that participatory democracy, for example, has very definite limits, because information prevents effective decision-making, just as a high degree of coercion does.

This brings us to a variance of the theory. We suggested earlier that a space exists in any reconciliation system for the discretionary application of coercion without an immediate loss of information. Figure 5.7 is a diagram of this situation. This formulation suggests that the reconciliation system has particular advantages in flexibility. It creates conditions in which capable leaders can employ existing knowledge, and thus increase the viability of the type of system.

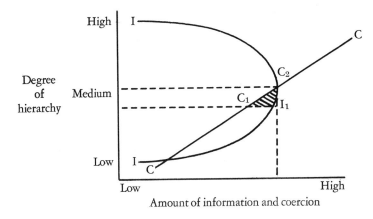

Figure 5.7. Discretionary space in a reconciliation system.
(The triangle $C_1 C_2 I_1$ indicates the area within which coercion can be
increased from C_1 to C_2 at the constant level of I_1.)

In ideological terms, insofar as there is a limit to the degree of accountability a government can survive, there is also in common-sense terms a limit to the amount of democracy a society can survive. In reconciliation systems, where consummatory values decline to a danger point, there are too many interests. Government is unable to reallocate sufficient resources quickly, with the result that offended interest groups are thrown into alliance with populist groups. Information is increasingly resonant, and no policies have the intended effect. The public desire for total solutions grows, as does the inability of government to deal with the situation. But no matter how difficult, it is the task of government to translate populist information or noise, into interests. For this task, an effective political leader is needed.

The discretionary space in a reconciliation system, shown in Figure 5.7, is precisely the characteristic that allows a government to apply police power without producing a basic change in the system. Though the use of police or other coercive power may prevent the system from being completely undermined, however, it does not help in the screening or processing of information. For this reason, a breathing spell will only be useful if it is used for information transformation, which will lead in turn to more effective decision-making. Let us remind ourselves of the types of information that arise and the nature of the overload problem. Populist information is resonant, and by virtue of sheer volume requires attention. It is important as an indicator of public anger or loyalty and is usually expressed in some kind of mass action. One way to handle it is to expand the use of professional skills—in other words, to apply professional information in greater proportions. Policy-making becomes more effective. Priorities are established among populist and interest groupings that eliminate coalitions of noise by transforming them into coalitions of participation on the structural side. This is attempted by all modern governments, particularly those in highly industrial societies. Hence the space for an increase in coercion, if combined with an increase in professional information, is one means by which reconciliation systems can cope with the overload situation. This is what translating populist information or values into interests means.

But professional gains in both access and degree of participation, at the expense of interest and populist information, create a new problem. If populist values are further instrumentalized, leaving even more of a meaning gap in the society as a whole, then counter-norms are likely to arise, particularly in the populist sectors. Meritocracy through the professionalization of information may therefore solve some of the immediate difficulties posed by information overload, only to increase long-run normative problems. In contrast, mobilization systems react to information loss by retaining only the functionally most important types of information and allowing the functionally less relevant, or populist, to remain hidden or latent. Except for the visible arrest and trial of poets and intellectuals in the USSR, there are no populist groups capable of putting forward claims to representation and capable of withholding loyalty if such claims remain unrecognized by government. The case of Czechoslovakia is particularly interesting in this regard because there, for a time, populist information became accessible when coercion was reduced. That a change in the system was imminent was evident not only in the statements and concrete decisions in favor of reform put forward by the Dubček government but also in the speed and thoroughness of the Soviet invasion.[13]

GOVERNMENT, INFORMATION, AND DECISION-MAKING

At the point at which a regime can no longer make political decisions that render political threats harmless for the survival of the social unit of which it is a part, a change in regime (as distinct from a change in the incumbents of public office) is manifested analytically in the shift from one type of political system to another and concretely in a shift in the in-

---

13. See the interesting effort to evaluate populist information in the USSR by Jerome M. Gilison, "Soviet Elections as a Measure of Dissent: The Missing One Percent," *American Political Science Review* 62, no. 3 (Sept. 1968). Gilison distinguishes between an "individual dissent index" and a "group dissent index," finding markedly different types of negative response, particularly at local levels.

formation-coercion balance. Each of these shifts is independently measurable.

The first is the result of both normative and structural variations, a change in the equity-order relationship and a change in the degree of participation by elites. Equity changes occur when new or counter-ideologies become powerful and displace older ones and, in the process, change the content of legitimacy, or alter the consummatory-instrumental balance. Structural changes occur when different coalitions of elites are formed and acquire markedly altered roles to play in decision-making, causing the pattern of authority to move from hierarchical to pyramidal, or vice versa.

Changes in the balance of coercion and information are partly measurable in terms of the types of information deemed relevant to decision-making and the degree to which such information is operative in the decision-making process. But the use of information in decision-making is more complicated than gathering together the three types of information. There is a whole here that is different from the sum of the parts. Different regimes have different "rationality potentials." By this we mean that a regime's preference for one type or another of rationality is linked both with the society's place in the developmental sequence and with the type of system itself. The characteristic political conditions of each of our types of political systems define different types of rationality at different stages of development. The extent to which regimes use rationality in decision-making varies. High-information systems with very high degrees of development, for example, have not only an information-glut problem but an organizational problem, so that extremely important decisions are often made in a semirandom fashion (an example is the Kennedy administration's decision to intervene in Cuba). Decisions made in less random fashion, but without a rational end point and with only partial information, may also bring about events no one intended. Such a system of decision-making resulted in the United States' involvement in a full-scale campaign against North Vietnam. Counterparts may be found in the intervention in Hungary by the USSR and the invasion of Czechoslovakia by Warsaw pact troops, which were based not on information glut but on inadequate information. Both the ideological left and the ideological right provide governments with a more highly developed and capable decision-making intelligence than they themselves may have at any moment. Failure to apply intelligence may result from too much information or too little, but it may also result from a change in the criteria by which the government judges the relevance of information. For example, the USSR as a mobilization system in a hostile universe, organizing its resources, evaluating its decisional costs, and trying to maximize particular internal and external revolutionary goals, is a far cry from the USSR as a bureaucratic system moving toward a reconciliation system in which its goal is likely to be stability in a protected environment rather than revolution. In other words, governments or regimes in societies where the developmental momentum has slowed down are liable to exhibit a type of rationality different from that exhibited by regimes in societies that are proceeding at full tilt, where the totality of the goals and their specificity demand a rationality involving the entire system and its resources. In societies where development has slowed, rationalities are dispersed, varied, and partial. There is no single scheme or plan. Hence when the decisions of the United States are viewed as products of the military-industrial complex (the modern successor to Wall Street), the overall system is being credited with a rationality it does not possess. In fact, the "mature" developmental system may in this sense be less rational than the system still in the early stages of industrialization. Precisely because of the substitutability of rationalities in industrial societies and their consequent competition, decision-making (even at the juncture of peace and war) may be quixotic and idiosyncratic.

The decline of once powerful states and empires, for example, not only is a matter of political legitimacy, judgment, and economic capability but also involves short-term, expedient decisions based on competitive rationalities, each claiming immediate efficiency and preference but often resulting in long-run predicaments. In other words, the rationality of individual decisions by firms and individuals may be impeccable, but the decisions taken together may result in an uninhabitable environment. The rational growth of separate urban communities may result in a jungle of irrationalities. The rational growth of bureaucratic organization may produce administrative paralysis. The examples could be multiplied. It is the absence of a central evaluative principle, the failure of political judgments to be sufficiently encompassing, that reveals that a political ceiling has been reached. At this point great empires decline, powerful nations become helpless, and intelligent men seem incapable of correct judgments in spite of the knowledge at their disposal.

The views put forward here imply that the *content* of information is a function of preferred rationality as well as the amount of information and the levels of hierarchy. For this reason, specific types of norms that are expressed as claims to representation are also definitions of rationality. Coercion that attempts to diminish or alter the priority of any representational claims, and thereby minimizes access, not only limits information but also alters rationality. Hence, the degree to which information will be distorted will be much greater in a coercive system than in any normal bureaucratic or other noncoercive formal hierarchy, which is mainly subject to mechanical distortions and losses occurring as a result of a winnowing or condensation of information at each level. This kind of information loss is thus a result of screening, a quite different matter from repression.[14]

Where coercion is employed, we are concerned not only with what happens to the screening process but with the representation of deliberate misinformation to government in order to mislead it into a sense of security. Certain officials with special access to government may by-pass regular channels for the object of specific premeditated distortion, as when the secret police in the USSR directly supplied Stalin with misinformation. In contrast, a system producing large amounts of information may have the problem of overload. The differentiation of groups that occurs in highly industrial societies, for example, may be so great that the resulting structural hierarchy, while not necessarily coercive, makes it impossible for the government to understand the full import of the information that is available. Such difficulties arise in evaluation, coding, sorting, retrieving, and otherwise working with the data explosion that in industrial societies the importance of elites in screening data and formulating general knowledge into information inputs pertinent to decision-making cannot be underestimated. Where there is both unreliable information and a high degree of coercion, the result is randomness, that is, decisions that are unrelated to the underlying problems of the society. At a certain point, the need for reliable information becomes so critical that government cannot maintain control without it. This loss of control may be measured by the extension of repressive law and its capricious enforcement.

If our identification of the crisis points of decision-making is valid, we may base a good deal of our theoretical work on the relationship between information and coercion. As it stands, however, this relationship is only partly explicable at the general structural level. Behavioral factors are also important, in the sense that when coercion increases, the members of a collectivity are likely to pass up to their superiors information that will be pleasing to them and to restrict the flow of negative information that may result in punitive action. Information biases are likely to occur, then, for two reasons: first, because of more coercion in complex systems; and second, because elites tend to suppress information damaging to themselves.

It is one of our structural propositions that where there is a high degree of industrialization the need for information is greatest. Thus the society with a capacity to create or generate and apply new information at an

14. See Anthony Downs, *Inside Bureaucracy* (Boston: Little, Brown and Company, 1967), p. 117.

increasingly rapid rate is the one most likely to remain innovative and outstrip its competitors. Its decision-making generates optimal development conditions.

In the case of a reconciliation system operating under conditions of advanced industrialization, the influx of messages requires the establishment of storage and memory systems, retrieval networks, and the organization of many interpretative levels. The expansion of the elite structure involved in information, however, may only compound the problem of information transmittal by enlarging the mechanical difficulties. It may lead to competition for access between screening agencies. Claims to representation may come to be based on the monopoly of a particular kind of information, so that the control of information rather than its dissemination is the basis of power. Competition may thus lead to secrecy, information stockpiling, and monopolistic practices rather than to the generation of new information needed for decision-making. Under the circumstances, government will be inadequately advised and unable to balance priorities between populist, interest, and professional information; professional groups, in fact, will have been converted into interest groups. Excessive discrepancies between decisions and populist demands will lead to a decline in support. The governments of reconciliation systems may attempt to compensate for populist disaffection by increasing coercion, but the same agencies designed to increase information will have to serve as the instruments of coercion, as when a research unit becomes a regulatory force or an information unit a secret service.

Some implications of the functional requisites of government, as we have portrayed them, remain to be reviewed. Several are controversial and bear reflection. If our theoretical conclusions are correct, and if such impressionistic conclusions as the affinity of highly industrialized societies for reconciliation systems are subsequently validated, it would seem that certain policy priorities are unavoidable. If a mobilization system has taken the place of a reconciliation system, for example, it is likely to have a high degree of information at its disposal left over from the previous regime. What it needs to do, then, is determine basic developmental policies and concentrate on their early accomplishment, increasing coercion if necessary. If such policies prove faulty, the system will fail because of poor performance (a matter of the quality and capacity of the leadership) and also because its access groups have been transformed from information processors into instruments of coercion. This transformation implies the centralization of decision-making, the reduction of government accountability, and the application of force against deviation. The government may also employ various normative ideologies to further industrialization, particularly those that combine primordial and millenarian beliefs, such as nationalism and socialism or a combination of the two.

In a highly industrialized society, it is important to expand the flow of information and, by widening access, to provide multiple sources of messages. If no policy can satisfy all groups, at least their claims may be ranked in terms of urgency. The creativity of leadership is displayed in the combinations put forward in the light of competitive needs and demands. In addition to good leadership, industrial societies experience an increasing need to screen, sort, and evaluate information so that policies will not be based on misinformation. The primary organs of access, if they are derived from a reconciliation system, will be inadequate to cope with the volume of information, and the decentralization of decision-making and increasing accountability may reduce the capacity of leaders to act. Consequently, government must seek new types of access through multiple legislatures, houses, and councils, representing populist, interest, and professional claims.

Mobilization systems seem to have a double period of significance. The first coincides with the formation of a revolutionary movement, resulting in a revolutionary government or political independence. This part of their life is likely to be short, however, because of a lack of available means, particularly manpower, to maintain the functional requisites, information and coercion. Rather quickly a shift will take place toward a combination of bureaucratic and reconciliation systems, perhaps with lip service to certain consummatory values. In other words, ceilings for mobilization systems are quickly reached, but the change in system that follows is not necessarily accompanied by a change in government. During late-stage modernization, however, mobilization systems may postpone reaching their ceiling by creating a new motivational synthesis in which consummatory values are understood to be realizable in instrumental goals. They may extend their life by combining well-defined consummatory values with sufficient hierarchical authority and by capitalizing on information left by the previous system. The unity of consummatory and instrumental values creates a powerful motivational system that simultaneously maximizes loyalty, commitment, and discipline. But this synthesis of values is at best temporary; problems begin with the ritualization of consummatory values.

Reconciliation systems show certain endemic problems during early stages of modernization, particularly as a result of the competitive conflict between groups with different claims to representation. Populist, interest, and professional groups are not bound by constraint but by relative degrees of power based on numbers of supporters, economic wealth, and technical utility. The result is a "gambler's choice" situation, producing inequality and weak commitment. The government's role is limited to mediating between power blocs and playing off elites against each other by manipulating their access to decision-making on the basis of function. Reconciliation systems can work best in the early stages of modernization if certain conditions are met: if there has been a previous period of universally high commitment to consummatory values, some form of "new Jerusalem," in which equity was fully institutionalized and internalized in behavior, so that each member continues to act as a silent monitor of instrumental values and goals; and if there is a sufficiently rapid and high rate of payoff, so that the ritualization of consummatory values has few negative consequences in terms of order.

Perhaps the least interesting and the most likely system to evolve during the long middle period of modernization is the bureaucratic system, punctuated by efforts to establish a reconciliation system with some theocratic elements. The difficulties encountered by bureaucratic systems are generally brought on by lack of information and attempts by counter-elites to change the system by establishing new sets of consummatory values. With moderate rates of modernization, however, these counter-elites are likely to fall prey to the embourgeoisement phenomenon, fail to link themselves with marginals, and become willing parts of the bureaucratic regime.

To summarize, mobilization systems are effective for establishing new governments and for making the successful transition from late-stage modernization to industrialization. They make revolutions *for* embourgeoisement. Bureaucratic and reconciliation systems are common during modernization and are continually slipping into each other's skins, so to speak, as development occurs. Theocratic systems remain the ideal of counter-elites and political purists who see in them both the structural and the consummatory conditions for a new society. The question is whether some form of reconciliation system can be found that will serve as well as or better than a mobilization system to promote the change to industrialization.

6. Constitutionalism as a Theoretical Exercise

According to the terms of the structural theory, the dependent variables are development and order. The first depends on expanding choices, the second on their equitable allocation.

We will now try to apply the model to both conditions with a projected set of solutions in the form of a development constitution for modernizing societies and an equity constitution for industrial ones. Let us begin with the assumption that every time a system breaks down there are contending forces with different political system solutions. The harmonious ideal and moral utopia takes the form of the theocratic system in which societal norms and political principles are the same and there is a sharing of allocation and participation on the basis of pyramidal authority. Here the search is for the appropriate belief. The mobilization tendency is to locate some unfolding principle, some ideal of potentiality so that general principles of equity of allocation can be realized in the future, justifying in turn certain norms of political inequity as a means and restricting political participation. The classic statement of this is the distinction between distribution on the basis of work as compared with distribution on the basis of need ("from each according to his ability and to each according to his work" under socialism and "from each according to his ability and to each according to his need" under communism). The transition would be regarded as a system change. Implied in this formulation is that in every mobilization system there lies a theocratic one waiting to be realized; thus mobilization is the means, theocracy is the end. Indeed Marx commented in the 1844 manuscripts that "communism is the necessary form and the energizing principle of the immediate future. But communism, as such, is not the goal of human development, the form of society."

Even with the most profound mobilization revolution then, both the bureaucratic and reconciliation tendencies are likely to occur more quickly than any theocratic ones. Radicalization may create the conditions for embourgeoisement, which in turn in developing societies will require either a bureaucratic pattern of control, or, in the absence of coercion, a tendency toward mutual bargaining necessary for creating unstable coalitions. In neither case is there a moral goal but rather programmatic ones, highly instrumental in character.[1] Given these competitive tendencies in all concrete systems what can serve as useful projective guides for setting up a generalized constitutional formula for modernizing societies and industrial ones?

In industrial society, there is a need to build in a kind of normative "refreshment," which can be done by establishing links between those at the bottom and those at the top of the allocation system; that is, when marginals and functional status elites are deliberately related so that populist information created by the former serves to focus the technical information of the latter on continuing problems generated by the industrial process itself.

The late stage of modernization (just prior to the transition into industrial society) and advanced industrialization (the stage we have called postindustrial) are of particular concern to us. Experience shows it is hard for a society to make the jump from late-stage modernization to industrialization. Many seem to get stuck at this stage. Many of the problems of industrial society are injected into a modernizing society, which lacks the means of resolving them. Even a well-developed organizational infrastructure cannot effect the transition if there is a low level of behavioral commitment.[2] It is this weakness that a mobilization system is most concerned to deal with. Postindustrial society is interesting because it represents the promise that many men in modernizing societies live by. The resolution of its ills and crises is of wide and universal importance, for if it is true that material abundance, greater access, and equality—all the normative and structural arrangements that have in the past been regarded as goals of political life—have latent and unanticipated dysfunctional aspects, then humankind is in a dreadful condition indeed. Moreover, we cannot depend on a stable body of beliefs to be passed down from generation to generation as a nurturing inheritance because the terms of equity continuously change. As a result, uncertainty burdens future generations. The object of our analysis is therefore a reconsideration of industrialization, the problems of equity, and the crises in meaning in terms of political systems.

The type of political system most common to late-stage modernizing and postindustrial societies is the reconciliation system. Although inade-

1. See the vivid account of the Stalinist "turning point" in which the mobilization system moves in a bureaucratic direction in Isaac Deutscher, *The Prophet Unarmed, Trotsky: 1921–1929* (London: Oxford University Press, 1959), pp. 327–89.

2. See David C. McClelland, *The Achieving Society (Princeton:* D. Van Nostrand Co., 1961).

quate for the job of transformation to industrialization, it is the characteristic high payoff system of modernizing societies. For postindustrial societies, it is the best system to satisfy the need for high information. For different reasons, then, we center our concern on the reconciliation system and proceed by asking two specific questions: How can motivation for development be introduced into a late-stage modernizing society with a reconciliation system, so that its transition to industrial status is speeded up? How can conflicts over equity in a postindustrial society become the source both of new meaning for equity and of a better balance of consummatory and instrumental values?

The two strategic groups whose conduct vis-à-vis each other allows us to narrow our constitutional focus to manageable proportions are the marginals (who occupy populist roles) and the technocrats (who occupy functional status roles). Precisely because the points of transition are related to innovation—in industrial society to the creation of new knowledge and in modernizing society to the derivative effects of knowledge created elsewhere—the functional status elites can serve as an indicator set for analysis in both situations.

The marginals are ordinarily the least modernized group in a modernizing society; in an industrial system, they make up the modernizing sector. They are concerned with the very instrumental problem of how to get a better share in the system, a concern that produces embourgeoisement. It is their functional opposites, the technocrats, who begin to act in roles that have radical consequences in a functional sense. These consequences may lead to radicalization in the political sense—whether in socialist, fascist, left wing, or right wing directions.[3] These two groups are worth some further comments. The technocrats represent a small but rapidly growing group, particularly since the industrial sector of societies is continually growing. The marginals are also increasing. In most societies although individuals can avoid marginality, the growth of the group is ensured

3. Professional roles in industrial countries are being increasingly radicalized in the political sense, too, but to a lesser extent than are the roles of the bourgeois radicals. See the discussion of this phenomenon in the USSR by Paul A. Smith, Jr., "Protest in Moscow," *Foreign Affairs* 47, no. 1 (Oct. 1968). In the USSR most of those who protest against state censorship and control are young "university dropouts, expellees, or rejects. Most of them have a record of involvement in unofficial, radical societal groupings." But also, and to an increasing extent, the establishment intellectuals are involved. "Of the four hundred or more signers of protest documents against the Ginsburg trial and the detention of Yesenin-Volpin, virtually all were professionals." Included in Smith's use of the term are mathematicians and physico-mathematicians, civil engineers, geologists, historians, physicists, chemical engineers, architects, biologists, technicians, librarians, and a former major-general.

by the collective downward mobility of the old fused and lower-level differentiated groups.

These changes are due to the maximization of professional power based on information generation and application at the expense of populist forms of power. Hence, the higher the degree of industrialization, the more important the technocrats and the more power associated with new technocratic roles. Radicalization occurs when the occupants of these technocratic roles feel the need for new consummatory values, ones that affirm noninterest and nonprofessional criteria of worth.[4]

The ultimate importance of radicalization is the recognition by those whose professional skills are most in demand that a new set of meanings is required if the full implications of knowledge are to be realized, if excessive instrumentalization is to be countered, and if a new pattern of motivation is to be established. Hence, the radicalization phenomenon leads directly to a behavioral question: What political synthesis can best provide a new motivational base? In modernizing societies three ideological forms, nationalism, socialism, and some combination of the two, are common, and whatever their differences in emphasis, they share the goal of linking individual interest to group interest by means of a sense of collective responsibility. Recurring themes include "socialist emulation," "national identity," and various forms of solidaristic corporatism like Ujaama, "consciencism," and "communaucracy." Their content may seem thin, but they do involve the translation of norms into behavior. Japan, one society that has made the transition from the traditional to the industrial, provides an interesting example. The Japanese show consistently low motivational responses when scored for achievement motivation according to Western criteria. Their responses are high, however, when the questions are phrased in terms of collective mobility and commitment of individuals to the group.[5]

4. See my discussion in "Ideology and Discontent," in *Some Conceptual Approaches to the Study of Modernization,* pp. 257–65. For a discussion of historical cases, see my article "Radicalization and Embourgeoisement: Some Hypotheses for a Comparative Study of History," *Journal of Interdisciplinary History* 1, no. 2.

5. George A. De Vos makes an interesting point: "There is no doubt that McClelland's model well suits American culture, but it is less applicable elsewhere. Even from the limited perspective afforded by projective materials in a culture such as that of Japan, one gains the impression that human psychology as it influences history cannot be so engagingly reduced to a single paramount motivation. . . . The Western idea of personal self-realization apart from family or social group has been foreign to the Japanese system of thought. In Japan, the family rather than the individual has tended to be the traditional unit. Success for oneself only was considered a sign of excessive, immoral egoism. One learned to

This behavioral consequence of a structural variable is important, for if norms remain intransitive, that is, not capable of affecting behavior, they will also not be capable of controlling or limiting choice, as we have specified. Moreover, the system's structure will not be able to sustain itself. The types of political system depend on the content of norms to achieve their objects. The importance of the various types of mobilization systems, for example, rests precisely on their efforts to achieve some sort of Japanese combination—a grafting of some kind of individual achievement motivation onto a corporate ethical ideal of self-realization. In the past, this is what Protestantism achieved. Various forms of socialism attempt it today. The blending of instrumental and consummatory values is thus a framework for a political system and a standard for behavior. How well this blend is achieved is a key factor in development. Theocratic systems are another type that makes utopian, projective efforts to define an ethical system for achievement motivation; they attempt to create new and politically defined consummatory values, a task that preoccupied the classic political thinkers, not to speak of reformers, ecclesiastics, militant divines, political prophets, and their most recent working counterparts, leaders of the third world, spokesmen for black people, and so on.

In our terms, then, the mobilization and theocratic systems capture the imagination because they constitute structural combinations that seek to inspire or change in some manner the motivational basis of social life. They both have transitive norms. One of them sees potentiality as the precious gift that requires discipline and, if necessary, coercion in order to be realized. The other sees belief, overpowering commitment, and intense involvement as the means of creating a self-sustained desire to act for the public good and of obviating the need for coercion. Concrete manifestations of the two systems cannot last very long for various reasons. Some

---

aim at high standards of performance as a quasi-religious act of dedication. One lost one's selfish feelings in the pursuit of goals benefitting the family. The family, not only the self, suffered the consequence of any failure. I have discussed elsewhere . . . how a subjective sense of need to repay the parents for their self-sacrificing care is a very strong moral imperative impelling the individual toward achievement. The sense of dedication of individual Japanese, the nature of group cohesiveness, and group processes within the Japanese community all require one to pay attention to how the need for social belonging is structured in Japanese economic development as well as in the individual need to achieve." G. De Vos, "Achievement and Innovation in Culture and Personality," in Edward Norbeck, Douglass Price-Williams, and William M. McCord, eds., *The Study of Personality: An Interdisciplinary Appraisal* (New York: Holt, Rinehart & Winston, 1968), p. 359. See also Robert A. LeVine, *Dreams and Deeds: Achievement Motivation in Nigeria* (Chicago: University of Chicago Press, 1966).

have to do with the dialectical changes that rob norms of their motivational effectiveness. Others result from the functional needs generated by development that produce normative-structural imbalances. Instead, the most common forms of political systems in development situations are the bureaucratic and reconciliation types. The bureaucratic type is found in various military oligarchies (and in what I have called elsewhere neo-mercantilist systems, like Guinea). The reconciliation type is the more numerous, despite the fact that it usually results in stagnation or very slow development. If the development situation deteriorates sufficiently, a reconciliation system is likely to be punctuated by intermittent periods of bureaucratic takeover in the form of a military coup, a business oriented administrative oligarchy, a protofascist or ecclesiastical party bureaucracy, or any of a great number of possibilities. Such a predicament is endemic to modernizing societies. Because of their emphasis on distribution and the derivative professional character of their elites, modernization induces the spread and growth of interest groups that frustrate the professionals, plunder the populists, and increase their dependence on industrial societies.

In industrial societies, the reconciliation system may also be induced by development. It arises out of the need for high information. If it, too, is in difficulty, the cause is different. The increasing need for information combined with a high degree of instrumentalism results in a spread of meritocratic roles, a situation that creates new marginals and leads to the formation of new consummatory values offered by counter-elites. Two problems —information glut and conflict between counter-norms and existing consummatory norms—combine to frustrate the functional elite and increase the relevance of the new consummatory values. The outcome is a tendency in the direction of a theocratic or mobilization alternative, often resisted by recourse to a bureaucratic system.

Functionality of this sort (which increases the power of technocrats as professionals) is characteristic of industrial societies and is reproduced as well in late-stage modernizing societies. The greater the progress of modernization, the greater the tendency toward functionality, and the greater the power of the technocrats. This crucial role of the technocrats puts them in the category of strategic elites. The greater the degree of industrialization, too, the greater the importance of functionality. The greater the degree of functionality, the less functionally relevant the marginals. A structural gap appears in industrial society that coincides with a normative one; the instrumentalization of marginals (embourgeoisement) and the instrumentalization of function (professionality) drive both the marginals and professionals toward opposite or competing interests.

But if the technocrats adopt consummatory values that prescribe service in the interests of the marginals, then a condition of continuous revolution is possible within the context of a reconciliation system, in which the marginals are transformed by a revolutionary elite. This condition has long been considered most likely to occur in a militant socialist society of the mobilization type, although the expectation has not been borne out empirically. In a society with a high degree of hierarchy, both consummatory values and, with increased coercion, information will probably be lost. By restricting information, the industrial impetus will slow down. Thus we ask: How can a reconciliation system be kept in a continuous constructive revolution without increasing coercion? And, we offer a *radical-liberal* structural solution under an equity constitution.[6]

Toward a Radical-Liberal Structural Solution

We shall now attempt to construct a radical-liberal structural solution to problems of development by creating two imaginary constitutions. The use of the constitutional form in conjunction with our structural theory may come as a surprise, but one of the characteristics of a constitution is that it is a framework for the regulation of the action of citizens; in other words, it is a system of order. The difficulty with most constitutions is that they establish terms of order that fail. Most of the constitutions established after World War II in newly independent countries suffered from this defect. The chief virtue of constitutions drafted according to established normative-structural principles is that they display admirable legal draftsmanship and embody the niceties of liberal terminology. All have a hortatory introduction about the rights of man, which are said to follow inevitably from a "democratic" system of representation. Some constitutions have been purely hortatory documents, as was the 1936 Soviet constitution. So dismal is the constitutional record, in fact, that one would have to admit that constitutions are not very valuable commodities in the political market (except briefly during the period of their formulation, when ordinarily one finds some hard thinking and explanatory ideology expressed by contending factions). Those who lose out in the period of constitutional bickering are silenced only temporarily and in most cases bide their time until they can bring about a change in the political system

6. If the strategic unit for the modernizing society is the technocrat, for the industrial society it is the marginal. In every modernizing society there is some industrial core, and every industrial society retains a derivative modernizing sector. This means that from both a normative and a structural point of view for professional elites to maintain reciprocal relations with marginals requires a mixture of modernizing and industrializing conditions.

and a new constitution. Indeed, this is one reason why constitutional changes can be used as a useful demarcation point for analyzing changes in political system. If the old constitution was federal, the new one will be unitary. If a country began with a regional form of government, the new regime will introduce federalism. Ghana's Nkrumah constitution concentrated powers in the hands of the first president; the constitution offered to replace it decentralizes powers and divides the executive. Independent Uganda began with a federal constitution; the Obote constitution that replaced it concentrated power in the executive. Latin America was for generations caught up in controversies between federalists and unitarians; Argentina is a notable example. Even working politicians who have had some experience with constitutional failures seem incapable of breaking this pattern and ordinarily settle for the old formulas.[7]

As the record of failures grows, constitutions tend to become longer and more explicit, with indigestible codicils, provisos, and specific statutes aimed at reducing ambiguity. But since few new criteria are offered, especially concerning development, the need and consequences of modernizing and industrial societies are not met. All assume that given the right formula, development will unfold in a proper constitutional system of order —an eighteenth-century view. A structural theory of politics should be able to establish different principles for a constitution. Let us therefore consider an imaginary constitution as a challenge to our structural theory. We shall attempt to deal with two developmental levels in the context of two subtypes of the reconciliation system. The specific challenge is to allow for radical action within a liberal framework.

The reconciliation framework imposes certain conditions. It builds in the priority of information over coercion. Considerable voluntarism is necessary for the system to work. The problem inherent in the reconciliation system is information glut, resulting in randomization plus high instrumentalism. Excessively high instrumentalism favors short-term considerations and disaffiliation from norms governing choice. Under such circumstances, the system becomes vulnerable to inadequate decision-making and the rise of counter-norms. The inability to utilize information leads to a desire for coercion. Instrumentalism leaves a normative vacuum. If development is determinate and linear in the sense that it favors the proliferation of functional status roles and the relative growth of professional power, the consequence will be the creation of a meritocracy with marginals at the bottom of the stratification scale, excluded from access and participation and represented by only a small number of elites. The

7. See, for example, the very uninspired treatment by Obafemi Awolowo, *Thoughts on the Nigerian Constitution* (London: Oxford University Press, 1967).

solution is greater utilization of information, the retrieval of marginals, and the balancing of professional power with other forms. Otherwise equitable allocation will not occur. Orderly development will remain impossible. The reconciliation system will fail to work. Regimes will rise and fall.

A mechanism is required to enable popular, interest, and professional groups to share in information-creation by means of participation in central control and goal specification. Elites to represent each of the three types of information sources and to convert the information into messages for government are essential; in fact, the role of the elites is the key to the success or failure of a reconciliation constitution. How can such a diversity of groups, as foreshadowed by increasingly complex patterns of stratification, be incorporated into an effective information-creating body? How can government employ such information efficiently?

A distinction can be made between short- and long-term considerations. Populist and interest information can be identified as mainly short-term, the public and corporate reactions to measures that have been taken. These are most likely to be intense and powerful, and they may lead to immediate pressure on government. In the case of the industrial society, short- and long-term considerations have to be balanced, not only in the context of more development but also in the application of knowledge to the functionally superfluous. Because they have little significance in satisfying needs generated by the development process itself, they become the point of identification for the problems of allocation and equity.

In the two types of constitutions, we will want to elevate long-term considerations for increasing development and making it more equitable as a permanent feature of political life. The formula we seek is one that will link strategic marginals in the society with strategic elites, so that the goal of professional action will become the assumption of wide responsibility for the margin of society. Our first case, the late-stage modernizing society, constitutes a problem in developmental efficiency. The second, the industrial society, is a problem in equity. Accordingly we will attempt to project a *development constitution* for modernizing societies and an *equity constitution* for industrial ones.

Before we deal with these two constitutional situations, we will first need to describe our analytical categories in greater detail. Wanted are criteria for the projected performance capacity of the two subtypes of the reconciliation system that would result from the two constitutional situations. If we assume the high participation of the elites, some institutional arrangements will be more suitable than others for confronting the problem of information overload and randomization. Since a certain coercive space will be needed, especially in the development subtype, we will want to build in a margin of coercive flexibility that permits an increase of coercion without too great a loss of information. We will also use the concepts of functional conversion and dispersion and dialectical congruence and conflict to delineate varying degrees of integration and consensus in the equity subtype. Before we do so, however, it may be useful to recall the basic characteristics of the reconciliation system itself.

In terms of our theory the following ideas pertain to the analysis of modernizing and industrial situations, for it is assumed that all societies will attempt to find the appropriate balance between coercion and information:

1. Development requires considerable coercion that may be inappropriately employed and applied. Wanted is controlled and managed coercion in order to continue to obtain information.

2. Industrial societies require high information. Characteristically they have responded to radicalization by a coercive response. However, when radicalization is viewed as a form of information, it can be rendered useful both normatively and structurally. Wanted is a system for linking radicalization to decision-making as a basis for "normative refreshment" and structural innovation.

3. Industrial societies have by and large responded to embourgeoisement by expanding mobility opportunities. However, if demands for embourgeoisement opportunities are viewed as "radical," this is an erroneous informational input. Wanted is a mechanism for converting embourgeoisement demands into social mobility on the basis of information rather than coercion.

The reconciliation system is a combination of predominantly instrumental norms and a pyramidal structure. Consummatory values are residual or highly internalized rather than manifest and explicit. Its structure of authority is characterized by a great deal of negative power, in the sense that it is easier to prevent decisions from being taken than to make effective ones. The political process is necessarily the business of putting together coalitions or making deals that maximize group or individual self-interest. When there is excessive information, it is difficult to know which coalitions are most suitable. If the leaders do not know, the way is opened for latent dissatisfaction, the revival of old primordial consummatory values, or the acceptance of new values that require a different structure of authority. Since a reconciliation system devotes virtually all of its resources to the maintenance of the system, in the sense that only a high rate of payoff keeps it going, it is unable to undertake development at a very rapid rate. Development is thus limited by the pace at which nondevelopmental needs arise. Although a highly industrialized society can afford this situation because of the technology of information creation and application, the needs and payoffs claims of marginals will not be recognized. Hence, in terms of the criteria of system maintenance and development, what we need to find is an optimum arrangement that will allow a more equitable payoff and will also stimulate development. One type of arrangement, the equity constitution, would balance short-term considerations of allocation (payoff) with long-term principles of equity. The other type, the development constitution, would balance long-term principles of development with short-term considerations of allocation. We can begin to see how the reconciliation system can be used to express the needs and concerns of present-day political life in constitutional terms.

ELITE PERFORMANCE

Certain hypotheses can now be suggested. If a development constitution requires a long-term emphasis on planning for development, then concretely there must be some body, chamber, or lower house that can allow for participation at the populist and interest levels in which the elites can maintain certain roles in goal specification by utilizing existing institutional structures or mediating between them, and can support existing channels of central control. Such a lower house would reflect the needs and anxieties of a population whose social institutions were being altered by the development process itself and who needed a means for rendering such change compatible with their wishes. Hence, the development constitution requires a lower house enabling populist and interest elites to perform their functional roles. In order to foster more rapid modernization, however, an opposite mechanism is required. There must be a mechanism for the special role of functional status elites, whose professionality with respect to development is their warrant of power. These elites need to create new priorities in goal specification, by means of new institutional structures and new methods of central control. A developmental body, chamber, or upper house, concerned with long-term innovative planning in which there is a concentration of talent and abilities is needed. Hence, a development constitution for modernizing societies must provide for popular representation in a lower house, and innovation and long-term planning in an upper house.

For the equity constitution of highly industrial societies, the requirements are just the opposite. There must be improved participation in new types of instrumentalities, including alternative means of representation for populist, interest, and functional status groupings and new ways to contribute to goal specification and central control. The functional status elites are needed to change allocation, incorporating those left out by the changing patterns of participation brought about by industrial development and the explosion of new knowledge. Hence, remedial measures are required for improved participation (of marginals), and to ensure that equity is reestablished during reallocation. For an industrial society, then, the equity constitution must consist of a lower house or some new body in which new forms of participation can occur, and an upper house which provides a basis for protecting equity.

In our formulation the development constitution requires popular participation in a lower house and a functional base in an upper house; the two principles assure that populist and interest groupings will be able to compete through the participation of their elites in representative bodies, without eliminating the possibilities of innovations that may increase the shares for all. In the case of the equity constitution, participation by such groups is assured but is not allowed to disable marginal groups permanently. The negative consequences of development in both modernizing and industrializing societies are thus to be dealt with in a lower house.

In keeping separate and distinct the two developmental stages, modernization and industrialization, we have emphasized the different problems each confronts. Now we need to bring them together. The modernizing sector in any industrial system becomes the place occupied by the strategic marginals. Hence, the functions of the status elites must come to include the application of expertise toward the problems of the marginals. If this is done, functionality may contribute to the reestablishment of equity rather than to the destruction of it through the further instrumentalization of life. In modernizing societies, the functional status elites are a critical grouping for the expansion of opportunities for choice and the continuous modernization of society. It is precisely through the strengthening of their roles that further modernization becomes possible. But it is through this increased importance that they may become narrow, unless their functionality is directed toward humane ends.

For industrial societies, then, we want a constitutional framework that combines elements of both the development and equity types. We want functional status elites to be in permanent juxtaposition to strategic marginals. The upper and lower houses must therefore be combined in a manner that blends short-term populist and interest information with professionality in a context of permanent concern with equity and allocation. The result hopefully would be a society of humane consummatory values that redefine what is important in nonmeritocratic terms and generate a continuous dialectic from within. In modernizing societies, we

want to prevent primordial or antidevelopmental consummatory values
from infringing on development but to render changes brought about by
development compatible with the understanding and interests of the public. The problem is how to enlarge choice without forcing premature allocation. Government in this type of society needs a certain freedom to conserve its resources and plan for the future.[8]

TOWARD A DEVELOPMENT CONSTITUTION

The subtype of the reconciliation system that combines equity and development appropriately will emphasize well-organized corporate bodies
reflecting all sectors of the society. Some of these coalitional groupings
will be based on specific interests. Values reflected in the demands of such
groups, and the criteria of action these imply, will range from primordial
consummatory norms to narrow instrumental norms. The continuous coalition and separation of groups will reinforce the tendency toward short-
term bargaining, creating a consummatory space, which in turn will generate pressure for a change to the mobilization type of system. These
coalitions will not form on the basis of chance or of principle. Rather, the
purpose will be to attain specific advantages, measured by degree of access
to decision-making and type of elite participation in terms of function.
The patterns of such bargains and coalitions can be described as follows:
(1) those resulting from complementarity, that is, the similarity of interests and principles; (2) those that arise out of convenience, that is, the
likelihood that all parties will gain; (3) those that arise out of conflict, that
is, a situation in which one side wins and another is forced to make compromises.

In a late-stage modernizing society, the first pattern needs to be separated from the second and third. Complementarity, based on functionality,
establishes a certain priority for functional status elites. Created by developmental needs, it is related to linearity. Coalitions of convenience and
conflict, arising as a consequence of developmental change, reflect multifunctional adaptations in the public; they are the result of short-term considerations. Complementarity shows long-term interests. By separating the
linear aspect from the multifunctional one, we may suggest the conditions for a compromise based on the differential participation of various
types of elites in different aspects of the goal specification process, particularly in the separation of short-term from long-term interests. What needs
to be avoided is polarization resulting from conflict or the dissolution of

8. Raul Prebisch, "The System and the Social Structure of Latin America," in
I. L. Horowitz, J. deCastro, and J. Gerassi, eds *Latin American Radicalism* (New
York: Random House, Vintage Books, 1969), pp. 29–52.

coalitions of convenience. Differential participation is a necessity if development rather than system maintenance is to take first priority. If conflict based on polarization should become endemic, the likely outcome is a change in the direction of either a mobilization or bureaucratic type.[9]

If these principles of participation are accepted, the broadest corporate representation could be provided by a conciliar body, or a populist lower house. Its tasks would involve short-term considerations in which the functions of the elite would become explicit. In such a body, residual consummatory and new instrumental values should compete, as when tribal groups or strategic marginals (such as culturally alien minorities) seek to protect their consummatory values against highly instrumental attacks over property, location, discrimination, and so on. Here the issues of regionalism and other forms of interest could be aired. The separation of populist and interest issues is not envisaged. A populist lower house should be forced to be an arena for the continuous reevaluation of short-term priorities, no matter how persistent the coalitional groupings are. It should exist for the purpose of juxtaposing what are otherwise incommensurable concerns, such as attachments to language and religion, ownership and property, the siting of schools, the location of industry, and the protection of interests. The separation of regions, tribes, language groups, and institutional groups in different houses would have the opposite effect of what is intended. The object is to create an accurate reflection of the possible coalitions of power. The weaker group, such as the small tribe that lacks an elite with bargaining skills, is the loser, unless it can develop these qualities in its elite. The lower house should be a measure of short-term competitive ruthlessness, the object of which is to politicize without polarizing as many groups as have corporate strength, irrespective of their relevance for development.[10]

Such a body alone would be an open invitation for plundering the poor and weak by the rich and powerful; so, to answer the common concerns of rich and poor we look to a development upper house that would be based on the participation of functional status elites and on long-term developmental considerations, the most important being the expansion of choice—not the reallocation of resources, or the enhancement of equity, or

9. See the discussion by Georg Simmel in *Conflict* (Glencoe, Ill.: The Free Press, 1955), passim.

10. This is not, of course, an argument in favor of survival of the fittest. But it is very difficult to protect those who cannot generate some corporate strength. Constitutional safeguards like bills of rights become useful only after some corporate strength has been established.

the maintenance of order per se, but a check on the process by establishing the priority of choice. Through this combination a balance might be reached between short-term interests of corporate groupings, whether based on function or not, and long-term developmental needs and goals.

We are not just talking about plans: every modernizing country has some sort of plan;[11] most of them are worth little more than constitutions. We are talking about the establishment of certain priorities that not only enlarge the infrastructure but also engage the technical skills of functional status elites and provide the basis for the performance of the elite functions, including coordination and administrative responsibilities and the association with various international technical assistance bodies, such as the United Nations Conference on Trade and Development, as well as other groups such as research agencies and universities.

One difficulty with defining such a role for functional status elites is that they are often incorporated in various bureaucracies, which has the effect of sealing them off from some of the pressure of competitive bargaining and preventing their effective relationship with those on the political side. In other words, the distinction between politics and administration confounds our purposes. Civil servants need to be politicians. Politicians need to recognize long-term issues. The considerations of the one need to provide realism to the deliberations of the other. The separating of types of information—populist and interest in a lower house and professional in an upper house—should help government decide on the right balance. The development constitution thus provides government with a singularly creative role by maximizing its control over information, drawing as many groups into the political process as possible, and at the same time giving long-term developmental considerations special prominence.

The development constitution should establish the conditions for a policy dialogue between two main groups of elites, the combined populist and interest elites, on the one hand (politicians), and the functional status elites, on the other (technocrats). A populist lower house is thus based on broad representation of the corporate structure of social life generally. We have referred to its ruthlessness, but this can be tempered by proportional

---

11. The mystique of such plans has rapidly died away, however. Three years is too short a time to accomplish anything. Seven-year plans become obsolete too soon. Five-year plans have a satisfying sound, but the satisfaction is mainly psychological. People can stand almost anything for five years if they anticipate something different afterward. Hence, most modernizing nations opt for spaced failures in five-year intervals, after which it is possible to begin again.

representation or some electoral device that reflects organizational strength rather than pure numbers.[12] "One man one vote" is thus not necessarily the sole principle to follow because the object is to increase coalitional possibilities while avoiding polarization. The results should be increasing participation, more effective organization, and the aggressive search by elites for followers in order to bring them into political life by whatever means they have at their disposal. The object is politicization.

The functional status elites can be divided into several main commissions that reflect a certain institutional structure and include a civil service, cerain independent agencies, and the military and police, as well as other bodies concerned with public order. Specifically, commissions would encompass the following types of activities. *Fiscal, economic, planning, statistical:* such commissions would include experts whose job it is to produce relevant data about demographic factors, natural resources, income, distribution, investment, and so on. *Educational and manpower:* here we would include planning for higher educational facilities, establishment of priorities among different types of education, development of training programs, including those for teachers, prescription of the broad lines of elementary education, and manpower projections (which are closely related to educational planning).[13] *Welfare and social service:* commissions in these areas would concern themselves with pensions, unemployment compensation, health, and sanitation services. One major problem in modernizing societies is the size of the social services, which are disproportionately large for poor countries, with high recurrent costs and an emphasis on urban over rural areas. A commission composed of professional welfare officers and social service experts would need to compose plans alongside the fiscal economic experts, balancing such needs against those of education and training, for example, and relating them to long-term developmental projections of economic growth. *Security and justice:* experts in these areas would include senior staff officers of the military forces and police and those concerned with legal reform in the context of a developing country. There are several reasons for linking justice and security in a modernizing society. First, there is the internal fragility of order. Second,

12. If there are large, politically passive population groups, their numbers should not be used as the basis for representation. If they are bypassed politically by smaller and better organized groupings, they must organize themselves to compete.

13. A pioneering effort along these lines was the Ashby Commission Report for Nigeria, which combined both educational data and Frederic Harbison's survey material on manpower. See *Investment in Education; the Commission on Post-School Certificate and Higher Education in Nigeria* (Lagos: Government Printer, 1960).

the derivative character of a modernizing society means that without careful legal safeguards, commerce, investment, and other sources of development from outside the country become threats.[14] Furthermore, given the frequency of military coups in modernizing societies, it is important to give military officers a constructive means of access to decision-making—by sharing in some of the functions of elites—without giving them too much power. Moreover, since military budgets are a growing part of the economy of all modernizing societies, there are sound reasons for them to take part in long-term planning alongside representatives of the judicial system and the law.

The commissions would be charged with the task of selecting representatives to sit in the relatively small development upper house, which in effect would be a committee of the commissions occupied with the maximization of information relevant to development and with its application. The idea is to establish a relationship between the practical and the theoretical, the immediate and the remote, the feasible and the utopian. Implied, too, is the merger of consummatory and instrumental values, so that consummatory values associated with the primacy of developmental goals would help provide the rationale for equity.

But how would this work out in organizational terms? In order to initiate legislation for balanced growth, the development upper house would require long-run predictions about developmental change based on information supplied by representatives of the various commissions, who would undertake a continuous review of technical problems, provide information, and above all define priorities of research and evaluation. Below the upper house and its associated commissions, one could envisage research centers in which various developmental priorities are combined, such as a central statistical research body, a manpower survey unit, educational training and development board, and a military and strategic agency. Such research centers have close links to universities and training institutions, both for recruitment of necessary personnel and for the continuous refreshment of technique and analytical skills. The universities, with their links to similar institutions in industrial countries, could serve as a bridge between the main sources of innovation in industrial societies and the elites of their own society. So that the upper house will not be divorced from the working lives of the population the upper and lower houses need to coordinate their formulation of policies. Political parties may serve as a bridge be-

14. Commercial codes in most modernizing societies have developed under a more or less archaic pattern of colonial law, with its favored treatment of expatriate firms. Unless specific steps are taken to reform such codes, the long-term economic drain may outweigh immediate advantages of new development.

tween government and representatives of both houses in order to achieve certain compromises of a political nature. So may other elite bodies, since any set of acts on a legislative docket would require the assent of both houses. Parliamentary standing committees between the two houses are another source of communication (similar to joint committees of the Congress of the United States). Not only would such bridges establish conditions of compromise by means of conflict and convenience, but they would also enable certain principles of equity to grow alongside development itself.[15]

We can outline a constitutional framework on the basis of the following ingredients: high information and high participation; long-term and short-term objectives (corresponding to upper and lower houses with different memberships but similar powers); and compromises arrived at by bridging committees to enable government to select the right policy mixture.

1. The consequences of modernization are instrumentalization and embourgeoisement; hence, requirements for the appropriate reconciliation subtype would be the following:

    a) Development commissions defining planning needs and programs in the areas of fiscal and economic activities, education and manpower, welfare and social services, and justice and security.

    b) Corporate structure of society reflecting the relative strength of segmentary groups, fused groups, differentiated groups, and functional status groups.

2. These groups (the representational base of the system) participate in government through two main sets of elites:

    a) Populist and interest elites.

    b) Functional status elites.

3. These sets correspond to two different legislative houses, which share responsibilities for central control and goal specification:

15. To what extent new equity norms are possible depends entirely on whether all elites, populist, interest, and professional, are able to find common ground in the exercise of the functions of social mediation and goal specification. This would not depend on "bridging committees" alone, of course, although these might be essential if government was to have policy-making flexibility, good screening, and high information.

a) A development upper house, composed of professionals representing the four main development commissions.

b) A populist lower house, composed of populist and interest
leaders who represent corporate structures of power.

4. Several other mechanisms allow policy directives congruent with
existing corporate groupings while rendering points of conflict
compatible:

a) Resolution committees, composed of representatives of both
houses to compromise differences and reconcile long-term
and short-term objectives and to make recommendations to
government about policy alternatives.

b) Joint sittings of both houses, ad hoc committees, and so on.

5. The relationships and functions outlined in the first four items
should result in the application of a high degree of information so
that government may enlarge its area of flexibility and provide
maximum creativity in the expansion of choice. Governmental
efficacy would thus reside in the maximization of developmental
priorities and the minimization of system-maintenance.

Government itself we would envisage in terms of parliamentary party
politics, with its members drawn from the majority party of the lower
house or from a working coalition including co-opted members from the
upper house, depending on the nature of the political priorities that
government intends to pursue. In Figure 6.1 we project these arrangements into a diagram, recalling that the analytical criteria are high information, high access, high participation (through the functions of the elite),
and high accountability. (The object in Figure 6.1 is to emphasize the
two-way flow of communication, needs, and problems between the administrative services and the commissions. The civil service as a body of
experts is downgraded in most modernizing societies because it tends to
be more conservative and cautious than the innovative technocratic elites.
However, one could envisage a continuous conflict between the two
groups, especially when the technocrats are members of the upper house
and therefore have direct access to decision-making. Such conflict already
exists in most modernizing societies, and the point is to emancipate the
functional status elite from the more paralyzing aspects of a civil service
bureaucracy. We can suggest this without denigrating the efficient civil
service in some modernizing societies, in India and Ghana, for example.)

Each house would have the power to initiate legislation. The upper

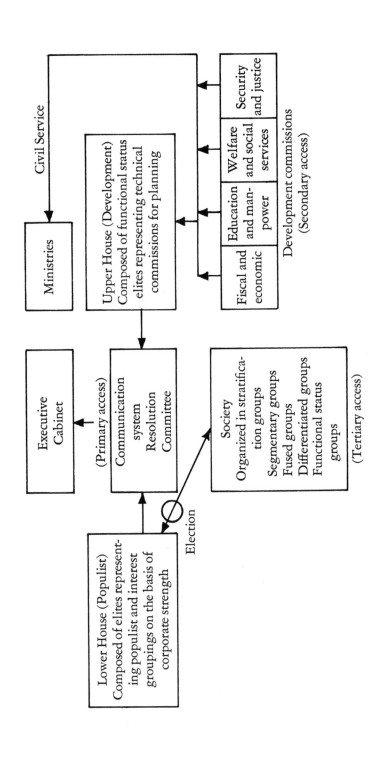

Figure 6.1. Outlines of a development constitution

house would have the power of delay. Depending on the case, it might also be given effective veto power over legislation passed by a certain majority of a lower house. Certainly the burdens on a resolution committee or other joint body would be great, as they would be on government, which would have to select strategies that would both gain its ends and sustain a parliamentary majority. By putting so much stress on participation, both houses of parliament would be able to play a constructive role in collaboration with government rather than a destructive and negative one leading to an emphasis on short-term bargaining and a consummatory vacuum, as is so often the case in reconciliation systems. The effects of such a development constitution should be to increase the speed of embourgeoisement and to pace the way for a transition from a development constitution to an equity constitution, which is appropriate to highly industrial societies.[16]

Toward an Equity Constitution

The equity constitution is an effort to make manifest and explicit what has remained implicit and presumably automatic in the form and style of traditional liberal constitutions, which are still the standard for constitutional draftsmen: that order is a precondition of equity, and equity is a function of law; that allocation of resources is determined by the continuous adjudication of interest, with expansion of choice the automatic result, or conversely that as choices expand, reallocation occurs automatically according to principles of equity, with order the byproduct; that the principles of justice are embodied in the rules of law, with the courts the supreme arbiters; that the natural industry of a population and its basic reasonableness, tempered by legal restraints, combine to solve the problems of everyday life; and that education and information foster a continuous evolution toward more and better choices and greater equity and order.

We have said that the difficulty with this formulation is that the emphasis on functional relevance in highly industrial societies, has the effect of undermining the strategic normative principles of the liberal constitution. If equity becomes an instrumental matter and order is based on power derived from functional significance in industrial life, populist groupings become estranged from liberal principles of equity, which seem only to recognize functional significance. Since allocation is also based on functions, or merit, this estrangement comes to reflect a polarization, a competitive conflict between numbers (the functionally superfluous) and privileges (the functionally significant). Hence, the meritocracy calls into

16. This does not mean that the problems are the same in all respects in socialist and capitalist economies.

question the liberal assumption that harmony is the inevitable result of individualism plus representation in a context of minimum government. The attempts to remedy the effects of the meritocracy through more active government intervention have improved conditions of equity in political terms in the West, and in economic terms in the East, but they have never indicated a realistic grasp of the continuing patterns of conflict in industrial systems. Moreover, when we refer to the traditional liberal ideal, we can include in it not merely the European parliamentary tradition and the American congressional system but also the Soviet system, to the extent that government is regarded primarily as an instrument to eliminate class divisions. When this has been done, in some final stage of communism, the need for all but the most perfunctory governmental activities will have disappeared and men will live in harmony and self-fulfillment. Thus the liberal myth is pervasive, not only in the Western notion of law plus self-interest, but in the communist notion of harmony plus self-fulfillment. The Western liberal myth has at least had a significant record of accomplishment, and it continues to have normative importance, particularly in socialist countries, because it embodies many of the safeguards and liberties that these countries lack. How can these be made explicit, maximized, and transformed into a constitutional framework that will prevent excessive instrumentalism and will establish criteria other than function for political actions? How can the role of government be made more positive, particularly in terms of the continually changing groups that are outside the system? We assume that if we can answer the second question, we can answer the first.

As with the development constitution, we can only sketch in the barest outlines of the equity constitution, since any concrete constitutional document would have to be rooted in time and place, in political culture and political needs. Our objectives are to work out how excessive instrumentalization can be resisted and how the "good" use of information can be ensured.

According to Gabriel Almond, parties and interest groups are supposed to aggregate interests; Easton suggests that they convert interests into inputs that a representative or conciliar system transforms into outputs in the form of decisions. Essentially, the executive, legislative, and judicial organs of government do the job. Regardless of the Western bias involved in this formulation, our analysis suggests that there are differences between populist, interest, and professional inputs, differences in the types of legitimacy involved in each and in the ways the elite of each performs its functions. This view would suggest that the load upon government should be reduced; a relatively small unit with a very general responsibility, government then would issue general enabling acts capable of multiple translation. Participation by elites in decision-making should be increased, and their effective role in accountability should be enhanced by means of a drastic devolution of power to each segment of the pyramid. Just as in the case of the development constitution, there should be a tension between populist and technical claims to access, and therefore a constitution embodying cooperation between the top and the bottom of the pyramid, with greater centralization at the top and greater decentralization at the bottom.

But because of the large number of decisional units working more or less at cross-purposes it may be difficult or impossible for decisions to be made. The sheer number of representative bodies may confuse the political process. As societies grow in size and diversity of roles, the representative capacity of any unit becomes smaller. The response has been to centralize government, freeing it from restrictions imposed by elected groups, which then serve as final checks on the power of the executive. It is precisely at this point that the screening of information becomes extremely difficult in highly industrial societies. As greater role differentiation occurs, based on the functional needs of industrialization, many of the older principles of representation become increasingly irrelevant. The political party then becomes the intermediary between the individual and the decision-making unit, and the region may become an administrative backwater, more or less corrupt and, particularly in rural areas, conservative in the extreme. The result in most Western societies has been that governments are more progressive than their populations, both in furthering development and in balancing functionalist claims to power against populist ones, particularly in economic matters.[17] Governments have also, by and large, been more progressive in identifying problems for solution, as with civil rights in the United States, than elected representatives, who often whittle away at proposals until they ultimately fail to deal with the issues. The opposite situation, where the public is more progressive than the government, would be revolutionary. In fact, a public does not exist, except in a ceremonial sense and as resonance and percussion. The public is fractionalized into competitive groupings whose conciliar bodies allow the coalition of the more powerful populist and interest groups, while the marginal ones are excluded, since they have only a negative rationale for organization.[18]

---

17. Even the disastrous Fourth Republic of France, plagued as it was by an inheritance of war and colonial crises (above all in Algeria), managed to sustain a per capita increase of 4 percent a year between 1949 and 1958, improving, as well, the performance of the agricultural sector. See Philip M. Williams and Martin Harrison, *De Gaulle's Republic* (London: Longmans, 1969), p. 12.

18. Such a negative rationale needs to be very negative indeed—severe repression and hopelessness. Even then there are behavioral reasons for marginal groupings to fail to organize.

On the equity side, then, governments have done rather better than the multiple coalitions gathered in conciliar bodies, although the real redress of inequity has occurred only rarely, when government was forced by violence and other forms of confrontation to act.

The existence of a modernizing sector in every industrial system compounds the difficulty of suggesting the form for an equity constitution, since the two sectors require different provisions. The modernizing sector, with its embourgeoisement and the conservatism of its rural and small-town inhabitants, requires a development constitution along the lines sketched out earlier. We cannot study industrial society as if it had no poor, no marginals, no modernizing population. The industrial society must concern itself not only with technical information but with the loss of consummatory values. The inequality of need between the poor and the rich, which is merely compounded by the continuous redefinition of equity that results from competition for access between groups, must be dealt with. What must a constitutional plan for equity include under these circumstances?

In a highly industrial society, norms based on race, language, religion, and related criteria represent residual consummatory norms. One object would be to convert them into interests. Furthermore, since the instrumentalization of norms is a characteristic of highly industrial societies, we would want to establish conditions in which all types of norms are represented, that is, different consummatory sets as well as instrumental sets. First, a house would be required that would provide a place for the normative dialectic, with the object of a continuing redefinition of equity, particularly in terms of the poor, the helpless, and the weak. This would not be a representative body but a group whose members were selected by virtue of their professional concern with such matters. Second, there would be a house primarily concerned with instrumental values, which would treat certain consummatory values as if they were instrumental, as if they were interests. We can call this loosely a house of interests. Significant groupings and those with specialized or narrow sets of concerns would be represented. The two objects, the reduction of primordial norms to interests and the elevation of normative debate to a priority position, constitute the two originating principles of our plan. However, there are other structural considerations.

The industrial society as a high-information system requires many independent sources of knowledge and favors those that produce information of functional importance for industrial life. This produces a meritocracy in which information creators are at the top and in which the educational system is the key to rank. The differentiation of groups on this basis produces a proliferation of multibonded competitive interest groupings at the expense of class groups and possibly at the expense of caste and ethnic groups, although these ordinarily do not disappear and may increase. For the participants in the industrial system, then, the two main claims to access are interest and expertise. In most industrial societies, there is also an informal pattern of functional participation that ranges from influence to corruption. Finally, the least functional groupings, particularly the least educated persons in society, have been regarded as an obstacle, a herd to be led, heathens to be civilized. This is one reason fascist and technocratic ideologies introduce primordial norms as substitutes for more intellectual ones. Loyalty, not ideas, is required in such a belief—loyalty based on some primordial identification. But populist needs and demands, insofar as they do not conform to either functional or professional access claims, have a primacy of their own. If they are based on modernizing rather than industrial needs, they indicate the degree of assimilation of the modernizing sector into the industrial society. To the degree that modernizing elements remain in the industrial context, there is uneven development and an imbalance between structure and norms that must be dealt with in the political system.

A single political system needs to respond to two basic and different phenomena, radicalization and embourgeoisement; it needs to be able to screen, filter, and synthesize information and must be able to reconcile particular ends. It must also provide for effective government.

(1) We want to renew the conditions of equity through reallocation. (2) In order to accomplish this object, we need to make equity a long-term goal rather than an immediate payoff. (3) We need a means for singling out strategic marginals for special compensatory allocations that will widen their opportunities for choice. (4) Such compensatory allocations must lead to increased participation on the basis of populist, interest, and professional claims. (5) Strategic marginals and the strategic elites must have a closer relationship with each other so that the functions of the strategic elites will include compensatory allocations, and the consummatory values of the system will include a sense of obligation that this be done.

However, the object of the concern with marginality is not merely compensatory action but the redefinition of equity. The relations between the strategic marginals and the functional status elites can be the basis of defining the pattern of equity for the whole of society. As new groups are excluded from the equity-allocation relationship, they become the strategic marginals, identifying new principles of equity by enunciating grievances. With such dialectical and functional transformations, there is a continuous renovation of the system. The decisions concerning system maintenance are thus transformed into developmental decisions. A condition of efficacy is created in which the application of knowledge by functional status groupings to future problems of marginality is the key activity.

What kind of constitutional arrangement is suggested by such a pattern of needs? First and most important is an equity upper house, by which we mean something more than a supreme court, more than an ordinary legislative body, and more than an administrative court. The object of an equity upper house would be to seek out discrepancies between accepted norms of equity and practices, particularly with respect to the functionally superfluous. That would be its mandate. In this respect the United States has quite by accident pointed the direction in its Supreme Court decisions on desegregation in 1954. It has been charged that the court was influenced by sociological factors. (The charge could perhaps be sustained, but one would also have to ask whether such considerations have a place in law.) That is not a job for lawyers but for economists, planners, and urban and education experts who, in the performance of their work, depend on the existence of the problems. The basis of an equity house would be precisely a sociological sense of justice rather than a legal sense. Its task would be the continuous scrutiny of imbalances between equity and allocation with the object of bringing about orderly development, for it is on the principle of orderly development that the reconciliation system depends.

The particular subtype of the reconciliation system that would be appropriate for the equity constitution would be one that would concentrate on making marginal groupings institutionally relevant (by removing their impairments and deficiencies, whether these are religious, linguistic, racial, or class based), and by making possible the participation of their elites in political life. This would be the main object of an equity upper house. Meanwhile, the dispersion of new knowledge and innovation through the system would become the object of the lower house, since the application of knowledge is the generating power of the industrial system. This object emphasizes broad changes, with continuous consequences at the social level and requirements for action at the equity level to prevent injustices. In these terms, developmental decisions would come to serve as system-maintenance decisions. With regard to the development constitution we wanted to maximize coalitions in the lower house and targets for achievement in the upper. Here we want to turn the emphasis around. In an equity constitution, the representational lower house needs to specify targets for achievement, particularly because of the innovations being dispersed through society, whereas the upper house must respond to conflict, on the polarization of consummatory and instrumental values that give meaning to the terms of equity in the first instance and may threaten legitimacy in the second. This, then, is the general program for the equity constitution.

1. The identification of the changing conditions of norms, consummatory and instrumental, arising from development.

2. The location of the carriers of such norms with a view toward continuous review and articulation of the norms.

3. The evaluation of the groups holding such norms, with emphasis on populist versus interest groups and, more particularly, primordial versus nonprimordial groups.

4. The evaluation of the functional relevance of the carriers of such norms.

5. The redefinition of the equity problem in terms of the need for reallocation, compensatory programs, and greater participation.

We have suggested that the more bureaucratic and organized a society, the easier it is to effect changes from the top, and that, although governments are more conservative than the most dynamic groups in society, they are generally more progressive than the entire society, except during revolutionary situations.[19] What is wanted, then, is a government that is more responsive to the dynamic elements of society and dynamic elements that are more closely associated with the strategic elites and the strategic marginals. But industrial society with its modernizing sectors presents a complicated situation in which a conflict between consummatory values of a primordial sort and consummatory values of a utopian sort may occur. Since the marginals defined as functionally superfluous are also prone to consummatory values of a primordial type, we now have dynamic groupings: marginals for whom allocation works least well and who are testimonials to the failure of equity, members of the modernizing sector who are oriented toward interests and embourgeoisement, the downwardly mobile fused middle class with orientations toward primordial norms of the right, and the alienated bourgeois radicals. A fifth group, the functional status elites, the basis of the meritocracy and the generators of new knowledge, comes to preempt a greater and greater share of the elite functions

19. We refer, of course, to the willingness to support change and innovation, not to the political coloration of the results. For example, today literary intellectuals and many academics are strategic marginals. Government, by concentrating on the group most closely associated with embourgeoisement (the workers), becomes conservative, resists change, and contributes to one pattern of inequity.

of goal specification and central control at the expense of the elites of the other four groupings. Such conditions are primed for chaos. No agreement is possible about equity; little can be done to rearrange allocation except by force; choices are randomized and disorder endemic. Can a constitution be devised that can handle such conditions?

The honest answer is no. The only reason for trying is to see if the application of our principles could help change the patterns of conflict. To do this, let us make certain assumptions.

1. Competition between bourgeois radicals and functional status elites for support from marginals is necessary and desirable. Either the functional status elites will apply principles of equity and techniques of reallocation so as to expand the choices of the marginals and bring them into the modernizing sector and the process of embourgeoisement, or the bourgeois radicals will urge alternative principles of equity and a different political system on the basis of new consummatory values. It seems that if an industrial society cannot use its skill and information to help the helpless created by industrialization itself, then it does not deserve to continue in its present form. This should clarify the challenge at present to industrial countries: either there will be a continuous revolution from above, or there will be uprisings from below.

2. Competition for the adoption of new consummatory values will be between the bourgeois radicals, on the one hand, and the downwardly mobile fused middle class, with its growing attachment to primordial consummatory values and the functionally superfluous marginals, on the other. Here, then, is the source of growing polarization. Meanwhile, the instrumentalized groupings, the modernizing and functional status groups, may join either side. Some technocrats may attach themselves to the right, others to the left, some to the "solid citizens," others to the "radicals." Once the dialectic between sets of consummatory values is polarized between concrete groupings, the results are conflict and disorder followed by revolution.

3. The functional status groups and the marginals must be linked to bring about the greater functional participation and instrumentalization of the marginals. It is easiest to deal with the most extreme marginals and to bring about amelioration of their conditions of life. Hence, the most extreme marginals become strategic for the functional status elites, just as the skills of the status elites become strategic for the marginals. Two principles are implied by this relationship: first, the division of marginals into those most urgently in need of vast amounts of "unequal" treatment and other less desperate groups; second, the division of functional status elites into those most useful for social development and others not directly

concerned. Identification of these strategic groupings means, in terms of an equity constitution, that greater importance is given to the sociological side of equity than before, and—since it is impossible to do the whole job at once, that different groups of strategic marginals will be handled in succession as problems are solved for the preceding group. Hence, functionality and sequence are to be built into the equity constitution.

The group to suffer most, for a time, is the downwardly mobile fused bourgeoisie, whose continually increasing marginality is built into the character of industrialization. When their turn comes as strategic marginals, they, too, can be brought into the functional life of industrial society once again.

Our discussion implies that government makes continuous policy decisions to eliminate segmentary and fused groupings in society. By doing so, it also intensifies the conflicts over values, which take the form of continuous argument and debate over equity. Hence, in this formulation, the functional adaptation of the population to industrial life occurs in a context of dialectical tension that, by promoting a continuous reevaluation of the relations between consummatory and instrumental values, prevents a normative vacuum.

Although our suggestion is called an equity constitution, it combines features of the development and the equity types.[20] The specific ingredients of the constitution are as follows: (1) consummatory and instrumental dialectical pulls; (2) short-term versus long-term policy priorities; and (3) populist and interest elites versus technical and functional (sociological) status elites. Figure 6.2 is a diagram of these competing tendencies. The four commissions of the development constitution are retained but linked into a greater complex of research organizations, professional associations, and so on. The two houses may initiate legislation, but now the developmental function has been separated from equity, with the latter put in a position of central importance in recognition of the continuous need for reallocation. A special planning commission has been set between the two houses in which cross-pressures for resources meet. Flexibility and creativity are provided by the differing types of information and the pattern of communications afforded by this arrangement. The power of government is based on consent; hence, maximum participation is facilitated by universal suffrage and proportional representation or some variant of it. The kind of representation needed is opposite to that which is based on an assessment of the relative power of various organizational groupings

20. Indeed, built into our design is the recognition that when a modernizing society reaches the point of transition to industrial society, the development constitution will have to be converted into an equity constitution.

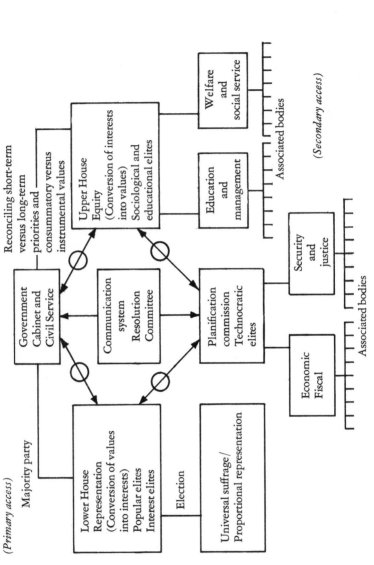

Figure 6.2. Outlines of an equity constitution

irrespective of their type. Here we want maximum participation of interests, even if they have little power in organizational terms. In Figure 6.2 the place of a high court is left out, although such a body is essential. In essence, the type required is a "political" high court, whose task would be reconciliation of the normative dialectic. But the most important change involves the role of government in the information system. The civil service would be enlarged so that it might undertake information screening, processing, and evaluation. The lines tracing the information system would be punctuated by committees of consultation, including resolution committees and joint ad hoc committees. Extraordinary sessions of both houses would also be possible, as well as hearings in which members of the planning commissions could present proposals.

Our purpose in this chapter has been to introduce principles and criteria of constitutionalism not normally treated as a fundamental obligation of government. It turns our attention away from the liberal framework which would create a reconciliation constitution in the form of a political marketplace, one which, by registering social attitudes, allows for governmental response as a plurality of politicians deems it necessary. In modernizing societies, this condemns the vast majority to political silence, except in the form of relatively sporadic acts of disorder. In industrial societies, such a political system responds to those with manipulable sources of power, particularly the most durable and bureaucratic organizations.

Precisely in this latter case the new role of information, the anonymous position of "experts" working in bureaucracies which serve particular interests and exert increasing power, and the momentum which often can be established when instrumental aims are translated into populist issues of national prestige or other primordial norms, requires a more responsible political framework. There is no reason why technocrats will be more disinterested in their service to the community, for example, than lawyers, whose activities in this regard are not consistently distinguished. But the role of the Supreme Court justice in the United States, or the legal members of the House of Lords or the Privy Council in England, as with similar bodies elsewhere, can, when suitably provided for, bring out the wider commitment of the calling, the obligation of the role to its relevant public, and in a context of equity. We can not design a precise form for that or state the method of selection. Obviously the instrumentalities suitable for such purposes would need to vary with time and place. What we want to do here is locate the general problem and define that aspect of the role of a specialist which makes obligation a norm and translates that obligation into a criterion for public performance.

A second concern is the politicization of primordial norms in the form of interests. Here the problem is the proliferation of conflicts which arise from parochial demands. An accumulation of such demands may produce a condition in which high information results in governmental paralysis. That is always a danger, of course. In the case of highly industrial societies, however, if our analysis of the emergent stratification systems is correct, the expansion of possible coalitional opportunities for instrumental rewards should prevent such a situation by, in effect, emphasizing alternative consummatory values and compensating with greater choice those likely to pursue the more primordial.

The object of the equity constitution is to increase participation and thus facilitate adaptation to the needs and changes induced by conditions of high choice. It is designed to reduce immobility and the creeping paralysis that characterize present forms of legislative activity. Its arrangements suggest how increasing development can be used to maximize equity and maintain order as long as a process of continuous reallocation is also established.

A development constitution builds in conflict and complementarity around the goal of expansion of choice, utilizing developmental results to help maintain the system. An equity constitution does this and much more: it must resolve the crisis in meaning that is endemic to postindustrial society. It requires the life-renewing goals that are based on consummatory values. Without these, industrialization will become the instrument of human destruction rather than the point of transition to a richer more creative life for all. By describing the constitutional outlines that the structural theory suggests, we have attempted to solve that political problem.

7. Toward a Socialist-Liberal Solution

We now want to draw our theory more tightly together in order to show the relationship of norms to structures—a relationship which, in the present view, will determine behavior. Let us go back to the formulation discussed in chapter 1, where it was said that norms change dialectically and structures change functionally. We tried to show some of these changes in the character of social and class structures and the multiple claims to power and participation these generated. We suggested how dialectical change helped to alter both legitimacy and the character of the political system, as well as the implications of such changes in the form of typical systems problems. What we did not do is discuss the character of dialectical change itself, which is from a theoretical point of view left hanging. By clearing up this omission now, we can proceed to some normative considerations.

As we see it, the pattern of dialectical change is partly a function of language, of how signs and symbols change in their tone, weight, relevance, and connotations. Some of this is denotational and formal, as with the construction of precise meanings and their references. Some is esthetic, as suggested by Susanne K. Langer and others.[1] Analysis of both these aspects would be one important theoretical job. To do it properly would involve political theory with linguistics and the analysis of symbols more generally. We cannot do that here, nor do we have the competence to undertake such a task.

More important for immediate purposes is that if norms change dialectically, it should be clear that what we mean by this dialectic is a process of "objectification," bringing to a public level those principles of equity that have weight, that is, have publicly recognized authority and form the basis of legitimacy. But it should also be recognized that bringing to a public level such normative changes will change the character of functions. In other words, in our theory, norms and structures relate by means of the interconnections between dialectical and functional relations.

Of course functions do not exist in outer space. They are connected to

1. See Susanne K. Langer, *Feeling and Form* (New York: Charles Scribner, 1953), passim. See also William Empson, *Seven Types of Ambiguity* (New York: New Directions Paperback, n.d.), passim.

mechanisms like the function of price vis-à-vis the firm, or communication vis-à-vis a bureaucracy, or other concrete groupings. But the depth of such functional concerns, and the possible range of nonreducible significant functions germane to societal units, is a matter of what an observer regards logically and empirically as relevant to the maintenance of that unit. Quite clearly then, dialectical change, which is a form of objectification, and functional change constitute a reciprocal process. In this regard our theory is closest to Marx. Indeed, one could say that this reciprocity is the inner kernel of neo-Marxism in the present structural theory. Function is affected by the dialectic, because the latter is the means by which people come to rank their role priorities. For example, dialectical changes generate new norms that allow the creation of new forms of class and status affiliation as already described. Similarly function affects dialectical change. It generates that which is to be objectified and creates the structural conditions out of which dialectical meanings arise. This dyadic basis of the normative and structural relationship is perhaps the most essential element in the structural theory.

It is possible to put content into these terms. Such content may be normative without being hortatory when it is based on functional and dialectical changes brought about in a context of development. This is one reason why development is so important. It is a source and a standard for both dialectical and functional relations. Here too the theory does not depart from Marx except insofar as it extends his analysis of capitalism into the broader realm of development itself.[2] With development the dynamic element in the theory, functional content, will arise from the process itself, while the terms of any normative dialectic will be based on principles of equity, that is, how best to allocate the consequences of development.

In discussing principles of equity relevant to development we can now project some specific normative and structural principles. What has emerged within the terms of contemporary norms of equity is what perhaps can best be described as a demand for *social liberalism*. Social liberalism as a principle of equity is different from individual liberalism, that is, the liberalism of an early day that was associated in particular with capitalism as a structural system. Social liberalism is a statement of equity in terms of mutual obligation—the obligation not of a class or an ethnic group for itself but rather for the society as a whole. The terms of that

2. See the discussion of this point in D. E. Apter, "Political Studies and the Search for a Framework," in Christopher Allen and R. W. Johnson, eds., *African Perspectives* (Cambridge: Cambridge University Press, 1970). See also my "Commentary on Pasquino's Appraisal," *Comparative Political Studies,* October 1970.

social obligation are precisely the dialectical issues which now confront us in all industrial societies, but those societies in which individual notions of liberalism have remained strongly entrenched have not been quick to opt for the social alternative. One of the more remarkable dialectical differences between Great Britain and the United States is precisely the former's capacity to make such a normative shift.

In structural terms, we indicated that an increasingly competitive fractionalization of groups, each with increasingly differential access to different types of power, occurs as industrialization takes place. Such a structural situation is not likely to produce a condition under which principles of social obligation can become binding forms of equity, that is, political norms. Quite the contrary. In our view it is the highly industrial societies that show a structural tendency to create functions which, although not necessarily antithetical to norms of social obligation, at least no longer promote them. This is particularly the case in industrial systems, where there is private control over the main sources of power. This is the case under capitalism, such as prevails in the United States, Brazil, and other societies where public control of the private sectors has not been extended sufficiently to realize normative obligations. It is also true of the USSR when a small group of power holders treats the entire economic structure as a private preserve. It is precisely where this discrepancy exists that violence, conflict, and repression become endemic.

What we would suggest as a structural solution might be called the socialism of the strategic sectors. By socialism of the strategic sectors we mean that both the private use of "public" property, that is, socially valued property in terms of current principles of equity, and the public use of private property need to be subject to public control under conditions of high participation in that decision-making. For example, the setting aside of large land areas as military reservations rather than public parks or the buying up of seashore property for private purposes may be equally reprehensible with regard to norms delimiting equity in terms of environmental considerations. What is necessary to consider subject to socialism are those sectors which, defined functionally, become relevant in terms of a newly stated form of the public interest. Such sectors are not only economic but include all the main institutional promontories of society: education, welfare, property, recreation, health, etc.

Finally, and in more direct political terms, the implications of our model clearly include the notion that increasing participation by increasingly competitive minigroups, while it does not render obsolete the more usual mechanisms of party and parliamentary politics, nevertheless requires further consideration of means and models to give more people a share in various levels of decision-making without, at the same time, making the political task impossible because of an information glut. This is more easily said than done.

It is with these expanding possibilities that the structural theory must come to grips. Indeed that was the main purpose of the exercise in the preceding chapter, which was designed to illustrate some of the ways structural principles might be applied to society to maximize development and order. The approach emphasizes the continuously changing relationship of norms to structures as principles of equity and allocation of roles vary over time. Like other theories, ours leads to certain preferred principles of equity and methods of allocation that, in the case of industrial societies, would maximize the effective use of information and minimize the reliance on coercion. The preferences are toward socialist structural forms of allocation and a dialectic between social and individualistic liberal principles of equity.

As originally stated the theory employed six variables: norms and structures were independent; development and order were dependent; and political norms and participation were intervening. The content of the independent variables was left open and was designated simply by the terms *equity of allocation* and *allocation*. These two variables employed throughout the analysis can now be described in terms of socialist liberalism.

	Norms	Structures
Norms	Equity	Order
Structures	Development	Allocation

Figure 7.1. A normative equilibrium model

What we are suggesting can perhaps be clarified by the use of a diagram. In Figure 7.1 a continuous alteration in the relationship of the variables is implied. As a static equilibrium model, the structural theory depends on the perfect responsiveness of its parts. Any change in equity or allocation would affect the rate of development and the degree of order. Any change in order or development would be reflected in a change in the relations of equity and allocation.

We cannot claim for this structural theory the importance of the pure competition model in economics. It is designed to perform a political purpose. It is an equilibrium statement with radical consequences as implied by the proposition that *equity of allocation is equal to orderly development;* for any change in one variable there must be a compensating change in the others. If equity is considered to change more or less continuously, then consensus needs to be based on principles that reflect such change and remain responsive to information about its causes. If allocation is subject to alteration on the basis of new functions and dysfunctions of roles in relation to industrial and modernizing societies, then what is needed is a means to prevent the dysfunctional consequences from outweighing the functional ones. Stickiness in either of these independent variables will inhibit development and maximize disorder. We argue that a liberal ideology would promote receptivity to changes in equity and a socialist system of allocation would provide the means to continuously reallocate within the context of the equity constitution.

In terms of industrial societies this suggests that the political form that would maximize information is a reconciliation system in which decentralized, pyramidal authority is combined with highly participatory decision-making; it also implies a socialist form of allocation and multiple access to power. It is necessary to eliminate not only the condition in which capitalist control of allocation makes principles of equity fatuous but also the condition where coercive and hierarchical decision-making in effect produces the same result (as in the Soviet Union and other socialist countries).

Why, then, do we opt for a liberal principle of equity rather than for a socialist one under an equity constitution? And why do we prefer a socialist system of allocation rather than a liberal one? We have implied the answers to both these questions, but because they are so central to our analysis they require further elaboration.

The political norm that expresses social liberalism is democracy. The political norm that expresses individualism is anarchism, which as a doctrine is long on principles and short on structures. Liberalism as a general principle of equity seems best able to live and prosper as a result of the continuous form of normative conflict, between both. That is the importance of the dialectic. A liberal system of equity can handle the terms of the dialectic and indeed profit from it. It is normatively open. A socialist principle of equity assumes a final solution to the problem of equity of allocation. It is normatively closed. If our notion of the normative dialectic is correct, such a final solution is in the nature of the case impossible on a long-term basis.

However, a socialist structure of allocation means that as function changes a more immediate reallocation of roles is possible. Socialism as a structural basis of allocation makes it possible to distribute roles on the basis of developmental need, with structural arrangements generated by developmental functions. But not all social needs are derived from the expansion of developmental opportunities. Some arise because of the dysfunctionalities of such expansion, including the need to compensate by political means for the consequences of development itself. Hence political allocation when it is balanced with democracy as a political norm implies a highly participatory structure of rule, with social responsibility as the expression of access by multiple elites the most practical and egalitarian form of liberalism.

We have suggested that an equity constitution, if it is to work, requires a system in which the distribution of functional roles is independent of ownership and pyramidally arranged and in which planning and social ownership of the main means of production have replaced autonomous entrepreneurship. Normatively, socialist liberalism implies highly egalitarian political norms combined with structurally diverse and highly participatory forms of decision-making. Actual normative-structural balance would depend on combining highly decentralized methods of decision-making with political responsiveness, itself a principle of equity. Such a system would require a high degree of planning under circumstances that would maximize information and minimize coercion, and it would remain responsive to both radicalism for embourgeoisement, the kind that occurs in modernizing societies and in the modernizing sector of industrial societies as well as the radicalism that embodies a genuinely new normative-structural synthesis.

	Norms	Structures
Norms	Liberal	Order
Structures	Development	Socialist

Figure 7.2. A radical equilibrium model. In this usage liberalism is a purely normative variable and socialism is purely structural.

By providing doctrinal content to the model and using the equity constitution as its organizational form, we should be able to compare and
evaluate the workings of real societies in terms not only of the degree to
which they approximate this ideal but of their capacity to move toward
it. Empirically, the most difficult structural change in societies where private
ownership of the means of production prevails is the shift to social
ownership. In societies where social ownership already obtains, the reallocation of political roles is necessary for a structural change from hierarchical
to decentralized and pyramidal authority. To be radical in a socialist society
is to emphasize the liberal aspect of socialism and change the political
infrastructure accordingly. It should be clear that we are excluding precisely that aspect of socialism most attractive to contemporary socialists,
its normative side. In this respect our view is closest to orthodox Marxism,
which treats socialism as a structural phenomenon and not as a superstructure.

BEHAVIORAL IMPLICATIONS

Socialist ideologies in general show a greater concern with the social
consequences of the functional allocation of roles in industrial society
than do most others. There is a considerable body of socialist literature
devoted to the problem of how individuals can be made to feel more competent in an organized social setting. We prefer to treat these matters as
behavioral consequences of functional roles except where individual dysfunctionalities can be reduced by realizing systems of equity that stress
compensatory public action. The behavioral consequences of a socialist
reconciliation system in an industrial society should be to increase an
individual's capacity to make choices that enlarge his sense of competence
and efficacy. This may seem too simple a behavioral assumption. It raises
the question of the relationship between personal competence and the
consequences of functionality. This is an important matter, if we assume
that if an individual feels competent in one area of significant social
activity he will be likely to gain confidence in his capacity to perform in
other aspects of social life—family relations, attitude to learning, and the
capacity to adapt to changing conditions. An assumption is that a socialist-
liberal synthesis brings about a greater sense of competence than may be
found in any industrial capitalist society. For example, the behavioral response to continued development in the United States is increasingly a
demoralization that weakens the capacity of the society to continue developing. Initiative is destroyed. Public confidence in the ability of government to solve pressing social problems declines. The condition of life in
American society is an eloquent testimony to the need for socialist liberal-

ism both as a system of equity and as a representational system. Given the particular features of functional problems of industrial life, it is time for a change in the direction of a socialist reconciliation system, which would substantially improve the behavioral responses of large significant parts of the population that are now marginal or alienated from the system and from themselves.

Our model is a "frictionless" equilibrium in which we assume that in concrete societies the greater the degree of responsiveness among the variables of the model, the greater the likelihood of individual feelings of competence. Efficacy, the opposite of inadequacy and alienation, is a positive rather than a negative behavioral response to increasing choice, and this is what we want to maximize. The relation between the structural options of choice and the behavioral responses might be clearer with the following analogy. Suppose the degree of development in a given system was suddenly increased; other things being equal, would it follow that behavioral efficacy would also increase? Probably not. The consequences of suddenly increased choice, like the flooding of a carburetor, may have a negative effect. But we would argue that in a highly responsive situation feelings of efficacy would be increased. This is why we examine development controls according to different types of systems. We emphasize the structural aspects of industrial development. Modernization is a function of roles germane to an industrial setting being established in a nonindustrial one and generating their own infrastructure. Create the role of teacher and the occupant of that role will create a school. Create the role of administrator and the occupant of that role will create a bureaucracy. Such roles breed institutions, and it is this breeding process that we are calling modernization. This does not mean that behavior will automatically fit the role. Indeed, one expects that there will be greater ambiguity in modernizing societies than in industrial ones between role prescription and role performance. Such behavioral variation in role prescription and role practice will change the institutional character of a modernizing society so that it will not be a mirror image of industrial societies. It is in this way that modernization produces diversity rather than similarity among societies. In short, for them we could not prescribe a socialist-liberal solution. Ambiguity of role performance has too many diverse effects. It may help make innovation easier to accept and to cope with. It may increase individual creativity, or it may make people feel that they are not doing their jobs properly, which may have the effect of increasing corruption. Such behavioral effects are as diverse as the devices people use to gain a feeling of self-respect and a semblance of achievement—reason, perhaps, for the exaggerated life styles and the search for opulence common among elites in modernizing societies. For modernizing societies socialism is a better norm than a structure.

If improving the management of choice and increasing individual feelings of efficacy are two of the aims of the development constitution, and if a drastically increased rate of development is the primary goal, then the policy-maker should not try to maximize the responsiveness of the variables of the formal model. Rather, it would be essential to limit the responsiveness of the variables. The political system most suitable for this is mixed —a reconciliation type with socialist norms and bureaucratic structural characteristics. We suggest that such a mix is more realistic than the alternative—a mobilization system, which is more efficient for most societies in the late-modernization stage.

THE STRUCTURE OF SOCIALISM

In our original statement of the model the independent variables were equity and allocation. To maximize order and development, equity of allocation is imperative. The pattern in the West has been to increase the possibility of political equity by means of representative government but at the expense of economic equity. The socialist pattern has been to increase the possibility of economic equity but at the expense of political equity. To closely approximate the equilibrium statement of the pure theory, what is necessary is some combination of both.

Despite the work of such theorists as Anthony Downs, and the classical liberal doctrines of earlier theorists, the pure competition model of economics cannot serve as a normative model for politics. Our model specifies a different set of mutually responsive variables that would seem to work best in a socialist-liberal framework. Socialism as a structural system makes reallocation easier, by means of public control. The system can thus be made responsive to the growing desire everywhere to narrow the gap between rich and poor in industrial societies, and between modernizing and industrial societies. The term *socialist-liberal* also reflects the growing antagonism to the political inequities that exist in bureaucratically organized socialist systems. We would agree with some of the ideas expressed some time ago by Joseph Schumpeter, that socialism can evolve functionally from development, that the spread of norms of equality in economic and political terms will require continuous structural modification, and finally that a socialist reconciliation model implying high degrees of information and participation and a high degree of obligation leading to a sustained responsiveness among the variables will be an appropriate polity in an industrial system. The point is not very novel. Moreover, from the standpoint of both modernizing and industrial societies, socialism in the context of a reconciliation system is not a necessary economic con-comitant of industrialization. But it is a particularly appropriate norma-tive-structural combination for industrial societies, one whose spill-over effect on modernizing societies would also change the character of their relations with industrial societies.

One of the consequences of unplanned and piecemeal development (es-pecially effected by private entrepreneurs) is the degree to which social dysfunctionalities mount as development proceeds: for example, poverty is a function of wealth; as development proceeds there is rural displace-ment, the growth of marginal populations, and growing inequality rather than less. Though we have grown familiar with all these, we do not like to regard them as somehow intrinsic to capitalism. José Nun, however, does just this when he tries to deal with the phenomenon of marginality.[3] He concludes that the character of capitalism is essentially that it produces these "displaced" populations. Like the economist André Gundar Frank, Nun sees capitalism as the general cause of all normative and structural incongruities because of the way capitalist accumulation occurs. Frank goes further to point out two fundamental contradictions, the concepts of "expropriation-appropriation" and of "metropole-satellite," which keep modernizing societies in a dependent and exploited state in the first in-stance and subservient to an exterior market in the second.[4] Both theorists would accept Marx's concept of primitive capitalist accumulation. Frank concentrates on the international consequences, Nun on the domestic. Whatever one may think of the application of their ideas to modernizing societies or Latin America specifically, their theories raise the question of how latter-day capitalism generates predicaments both by causing uneven development and by ignoring the social consequences of long-term human and material inefficiencies. The emphasis on accumulation leads to a con-cern with the relative impoverishment of some sectors of developing so-cieties. This seems to be a particular problem with capitalism because it is above all a system based on the relative autonomy and freedom of action of entrepreneurs. Capitalism, especially for Marxist critics, is at best a gambler's environment in which planning for the game takes second place to the overall consideration of winning. And the consequences of winning are not small: they bring about great structural changes in the form of wealth and inequality and disrupt ordinary ways of doing things. For example, in Latin America certain serviceable old forms of land tenure

3. See José Nun, "Superpoblación relativa, ejército industrial de reserva y masa marginal," *Revista Latinoamericana de Sociología,* V: 2 (July 1969).

4. See André Gundar Frank, *Capitalism and Underdevelopment in Latin America* (New York: Monthly Review Press, 1969).

based on a patron-client system of land holdings are disintegrating because the old system of agriculture is declining in favor of alternative holdings and investments. The patron-client relationship gives way because with reduced agricultural income even minimum benefits can no longer be provided. The result is a drift to the towns, urban employment, and other attendant problems.[5] Our point is that innovation produced by capitalism is above all designed to generate an investable surplus. It is a private system of forced savings and concentrated developmental strategies in which the immediate social impact is less relevant than the creation of deployable capital funds. Under these circumstances, "valued" patterns of life of a more "traditional" character (i.e., that are not functional or are irrelevant for development) are themselves seen as obstacles to be swept away, without regard for the consequences except as these inhibit the development process by becoming dysfunctional. Thus strikes, work-stoppages, labor inefficiencies, and so on may require attention, but only as they affect production and are measurable dysfunctionalities for development. Such a process in the early days of capitalism in Western Europe was the subject of a liberal ethic that eventually became a source of normative conflict of the most intense kind.

This is not to say that expanding choice as a result of development leads only to dislocation. Existing institutional arrangements may be used. Some may become more important, such as the reliance on personal friendship and association. In a universe of chance, these can be relied upon. Some old institutions will be used for new purposes: social clubs that were once the centers for ease and sport may become important for commercial and political transactions. Hence, if there is an "appropriation" polarization and institutional conflict as a part of the pattern of capitalist development that leads in the direction of political manipulation and uncertainty, there is also a pattern of institutional reliability, persistence, and enforced continuity. For this reason the frangibility of social institutions and their durability can be seen to go hand in hand. But the paradox is political. Groups in the social order most capable of deploying resources try to manipulate political power in order to free themselves from the inhibitions of institutional lags and to have a freer hand to pursue developmental goals and the exploitation of specific investment opportunities. How much they are able to use the government for this purpose varies and is one of the causes of political instability. Such threats to order are endemic during modernization. It is above all capitalist development that introduces extreme dis-

5. Obviously the examples are legion. See T. R. DeGregori and Oriol Pi-Sunyes, *Economic Development: The Cultural Context* (New York: Wiley & Sons, 1969), passim.

locations in social life posing profound threats to political order. If political order, once established, is unable to manipulate and reallocate the total resources of the society toward functional needs that include public welfare, it will be unable to direct and expand development. That is the problem of socialist development.

The point is important because if our assumptions are correct, the specific kinds of inhibitions to development (including inadequate fiscal devices, inadequate legal reform, and high production costs, all of which seem to be the most important obstacles to growth under capitalism) are more manageable under socialism. The liberal economic approach defines obstacles in economic terms, the more narrowly technical the better, and by offering solutions to these assumes that the larger questions will solve themselves.

Clearly, in examining such alternative doctrines and ideas we want to evaluate their normative aspects as a differing set of priorities and concerns. Squaring the circle leads many observers to conclude that capitalism is a transitional mode of production leading to socialism.[6] On the other hand, consumer sovereignty is one of the most marketable norms of a liberal ideology; it so successfully disguises unequal access to economic power that political participation and organization (the counterweight to perceived inequities) can compensate. Hence, the durability of capitalism.

What is clear is that capitalism is not a necessary transition to socialism, but if development remains a goal it will be. How the political system deploys and controls property and makes social decisions has become decidedly more important than the decisions of entrepreneurs. Governments are not mere reciprocals of capitalists, as Marx thought. Socialist governments need to confront the problem of excessive government control, for although it may be helpful in early stages of development in limiting consumption, obtaining forced savings, and meeting the needs of industrial development and society, it may become inhibiting precisely because of the complexity of the total process. Socialist solutions may need to take the form of decentralized decision-making with an organizational pattern not much different from that of capitalism. When ownership and control are separated completely, the argument over private property becomes less significant.

The implications of the pure theory are that matters of equity and its

6. That the political and economic solutions of fascism can also accomplish many of the same objects as socialism has hardly been dealt with by socialist theoreticians who prefer the more comfortable notion that fascism is merely the highest stage of imperialism, which is in turn the highest stage of capitalism.

priorities cannot be adequately handled in the marketplaces of consumer sovereignty and representative government under capitalism. Although in the long run the voting place as a political market and the transactional market may correspond to values, norms, and preferences, it is more likely that long-term choices and short-term needs will confound each other. The short run is likely to take precedence until people are fed up with the system. Their short-term rational preferences may make for long-term irrationalities and outrage. When such situations arise, norms and structures are at odds.

The political lessons of development are that economic changes rarely accomplish their purposes and that the attempt to compensate for growing uncertainty and conflict by increasing coercion is likely to result in coups, sabotage, and the exacerbation of problems. A total restructuring of society —the rearrangement of roles, their accessibility and their relationship to each other—requires exceptionally stringent efforts in which it may be possible to avoid the effects of Stalinism, as Mao seems to have done, but only at the cost of periodic randomization of role relationships, such as during the Great Leap and the time of the emergence of the Red Guards.[7] In Latin America, pre-Castro Cuba is a good illustration of the consequence of long periods of modernization—all the ills of modern urban life and the worst features of a derivative and dependent monocrop economy. It represented the typical pattern of undigested development that occurs when business is left to pursue its "natural" way, protected by a relatively ruthless and corrupt regime. In Cuba now, many of the worst problems of contemporary industrial life have been taken on as direct political obligations. Improved housing, job security, rural redevelopment, expansion of education, elimination of urban marginality, and so on— ordinarily the byproducts of development for which the "developer" will not assume the responsibility become precisely the main objects of policy in a socialist state. Clearly, stringent controls are required to accomplish these tasks.

The elaborate arguments for single factored change, like Alessandro Pizzorno's explanation of why Western Europe developed, are clearly suspect.[8] The Frank theses about appropriation and exploitation and metropole and satellite as an intrinsic characteristic of capitalism explain too much and therefore too little. A host of factors attend the time,

7. After such periods of great upheaval and anxiety, people tend to be more anxious to cooperate if only to get on with their work and a semblance of stability for themselves and their families.

8. See Alessandro Pizzorno, "The Mobilization of Europe," Daedalus, Winter 1964, pp. 199–224.

place, and manner of capitalistic enterprise. The piecemeal approach of Hirschman and others contains a hiding hand, that is, a presumption that developmental techniques can bypass government and that development is its own reward. Weber commented long ago that "Capitalism is present wherever the industrial provision for the needs of a human group is carried out by the method of enterprise, irrespective of what need is involved."[9] In short, the functional rationality of the industrial process and the functional relations of societies as a whole not only are different, but may at times contradict each other when the needs of one have nothing to do with the needs of the other. For Weber, capitalism required rational capital accounting of the means of production, a free market, mechanized technology, and calculable law. In this sense legal and political mechanisms needed to be predictable. When such conditions are met, a "system" can function, but whether or not it meets social needs, including the ones it generates itself, is in a sense irrelevant.

This leads not to the proposition that Marx was right or that Keynes was right in the sense that he provided the impetus for new strategies about capitalism. More appropriate, perhaps, are the ideas of Weber and Schumpeter on the logic of rationality in enterprise with its implications for the terminating of capitalism (or at least the point at which capitalism and socialism become more or less indistinguishable). Capitalism reduces risk and extends rationality. When it does these things the gambler's environment disappears and so does capitalism. Schumpeter suggests that capitalism will come to an end when it atrophies.

> There would be nothing left for entrepreneurs to do. They would find themselves in much the same situation as generals would in a society perfectly sure of permanent peace. Profits and along with profits the rate of interest would converge to zero. The bourgeois state that lives on profits and interest would tend to disappear. The management of industry and trade would become a matter of current administration, and the personnel would unavoidably acquire the characteristics of a bureaucracy. Socialism (or state capitalism) of a very sober type would almost automatically come into being. Human energy would turn away from business. Other than economic pursuits would attract the brains and provide the adventure.[10]

9. See Max Weber, *General Economic History,* trans. Frank H. Knight (Glencoe, Ill.: The Free Press, 1950), p. 275.

10. See Joseph A. Schumpeter, *Capitalism, Socialism, and Democracy* (New York: Harper and Brothers, 1947), p. 131.

Schumpeter did not see this occurring in the calculable future. But certainly there are tendencies at work in this direction in highly industrial societies. The protests against the spread of technology and particularly computers, for example, correspond to a Luddite revolt against the bureaucratic consequences of mass participation. But such revolts offer no solutions. In the past every society could rely on the passiveness of the overwhelming majority of its inhabitants. Not so today. The result is the machine processing of knowledge and preference and the mechanization of choice. This technology requires a new normative—structural synthesis. The suggestion to return to a simpler environment can be discounted as sentimental, similar to the attempt to found simple communes and New Harmonies in the face of an industrial way of life. Instead, as Schumpeter points out, "economic progress tends to become depersonalized and automatized. Bureau and committee work tend to replace individual action. A similar social process . . . undermines the role, and along with the role, the social position of the capitalist entrepreneur."[11] The point made by Schumpeter should be clear: the rationalizing effects of capitalism and its growing burden of unattended byproducts, such as the increase of marginals, the destruction of a class system, and the bureaucratization of mass participation, all lead in the general direction of socialism—not the socialism of the technocrat and bureaucrat. It will be the socialism of high participation by means of a rationalized bureaucracy combined with instrumental values. The future, then, will be a reconciliation system in which the mechanisms of pyramidal authority and the priorities of instrumental values will be different from capitalism and in which decentralized planning rather than entrepreneurship will be characteristic.

Although, as we have said, we will not speculate at length about how such a system might come into being, one possibility derives from the pressures toward greater bureaucratization that are functions of mass participation. The growth of population, the using up of resources, the expansion of higher education, and the reactions against all these under capitalism (which becomes the repugnant purveyor of destructive antihumanism) will pave the way for the transition.[12] The last point forecasts a withdrawal of the political norms but not the principles of equity from present-day capitalist and socialist societies. Indeed, their principles of equity are on a higher moral plane now than ever before. Socialism as a structural system can then be "run under" such norms to be the appropriate infrastructure to replace capitalism. In turn, this infrastructure

11. See Schumpeter, *Capitalism, Socialism, and Democracy,* p. 133.

12. See Martin Trow, "Reflections on the Transition from Mass to Universal Higher Education," *Daedalus,* Winter 1970, pp. 1–42.

will turn about the same features of rationality, bureaucratic participation, and so on, toward a wider social responsibility that for a time at least will represent a new and more satisfactory social balance, a better degree of congruence or fit between the norms and the structures. If this is the prognosis it leads us to a further question, the question confronted by Lenin when presented with the chaos of a successful revolutionary state: does the process of development in Africa and Latin America need to continue through "stages" of capitalism in order to make its "revolution" to the next stage?

Perhaps it is a grim form of humor to point out that the key to this transformation in industrial societies is a highly participatory bureaucracy, for if that is true, socialism in developing countries would be a great leap backward. The already large · bureaucracies, with their provision for participation by friends and relatives, are enervating to all processes of development. Such "premature" socialism would be an argument for capitalism as a necessary transitional phase for the accumulation of manipulable surpluses.

What do we mean by socialism in highly industrialized countries? Certainly our speculation does not include a narrowly defined form. Nor do we consider Schumpeter's approach sufficiently broad. Structurally we have in mind a rationalized system of mixed public and private ownership in which many sources of interest mediated through diverse forms of access to participation will be translated into a stream of messages, the decoding of which will define policy needs and obligations, the objects of decision-making. Decentralization would be necessary with diverse modes of participation using a variety of techniques based on the application of organizational theory, group theory, information theory, sampling techniques, and computer technologies to allow consumer markets without the tyranny of consumer sovereignty, and with the markets themselves a means of reconciling long-term and short-term priorities rather than a standard of value. Already there is a pronounced trend in highly industrial countries toward public ownership in the form of public corporations, in which the managerial and engineering skills of management will predominate in the effort to match social efficiency (i.e., the accounting for the social dysfunctionalities with economic benefits).

We do not envisage a dramatic or revolutionary change from the capitalist reconciliation type of system to the socialist. Nor will the liberalization of bureaucratic socialist regimes occur in some drastic manner. We can expect a continuation and an extension of probing actions, confrontations that are designed to weaken the powerful roles of industrial society, especially those that symbolize its values so that the normative aspects of roles as well as their functions will continue to be altered. It is by functional and dialectical means that a normative-structural change will occur. Revolutionary tactics are most likely to be epiphenomenal. The role of the doctor will be made responsible by means of socialized medicine; social medicine and public preventative treatment will become part of an administrative system with medical administrators as its functionaries. No doubt, too, the academic profession will confront a decline in the autonomy of the role of the professor; university professors will in this sense become more like high school teachers and part of an elaborate administrative apparatus in a university structure in which education is a right, not on the basis of a single chance but on a multiple-chance basis. (In this respect, contemporary radicals who attack the university on the contradictory grounds of making it both more accessible and relevant and more pure and intellectual serve as the instruments of its bureaucratization.) Such a changed role for education will be normatively crucial. In capitalist systems education is at present a screening system of increasingly egalitarian entry and unequal benefit, based on functional criteria. It is a determinant in the hierarchy of social inequality.

The point is that the transition from capitalism to a socialist reconciliation system will not be in terms of revolution seen as some broad watershed event, but in the continuous transformation of the simple into the complex accompanied by individual acts of violence. More and more rules of fair play, more systems of appeal, more diverse channels of access will be the result. Entrepreneurs and others long regarded as the power wielders of the capitalist community will give way. Behind each new increment of socialism will lie a protest, and beyond will occur a newly rationalized administrative unit. However, if the prospect of such administrative socialism is not to be most unappetizing, it must be confronted by a social ethic of choice. Viewed from this standpoint, even the most responsible bureaucracy will require continuous reform, particularly of the kind necessary to increase freedom of choice for persons. Clearly, however, such reforms will be increasingly of a scientific as well as a normative nature. The mechanization of many tasks will be required to speed up the process. Indeed, the new image of the administrator is not the power wielder or obstructive bureaucrat but the technically trained information engineer who can function relatively efficiently, is quick to learn, and can translate needs into appropriate priority categories, resolving these without passing trivia to superiors. For these purposes present patterns of administration are obsolete. If administrative socialism in a liberal context means high degrees of obligation and participation and a high degree of information with access expanding to include ever more diverse elites with growing competition for significance in decision-making, it also implies greater decentralization of decision-making and more diverse mechanisms of participation. That is the ultimate implication of the equity constitution and the socialist-liberal normative-structural synthesis.[13]

Implied in our analysis is that socialism in a modernizing reconciliation system is the structural effect of the embourgeoisement of radicalism. The situation is like that of the trade union movement, which, having embodied consummatory values as part of its organization drives, soon settled down to the practicalities of collective bargaining. Arbitration became a profession. Indeed, today it is difficult to distinguish a trade union official from a business executive. But if our theory is correct, we can expect radicalization to crop up repeatedly, especially in industrial societies. Our assumption is that it will take the form of dialectical responses to the behavioral and normative environment of administrative socialism. We suspect that these will be increasingly "anarchic" based on the need to randomize the universe, to break through the planning. The prospect is for greater behavioral freedom, with fewer personal constraints of the family obligation. We can expect such a dialectic to result in more diverse kinds of marriage, the breaking down of sexual differences—in short, a vastly increased range of personal choices, many of which will result in intolerable individual pressures. The behavioral implications of such widened alternatives under a liberal form of socialism are just beginning to occur. Such freedom of choice will intensify anxiety.

---

13. We have described the relationship between modernizing societies and industrial ones as essentially based on innovation and derivation. This implies a form of imperialism, economic, cultural, and above all, systemic, in the interlocking of roles based on technical infrastructure and exchangeability of knowledge between elites. On this basis exploitation continues to be built into the relationships between industrial capitalist societies and modernizing societies. With a change in industrial societies from a reconciliation system of the capitalist type to the socialist, this relationship should alter not only in form but in content. Neoimperialism would give way to a new form of socialist internationalism in which relationships with overseas modernizing societies would be based on information about need and hence an obligation to incorporate those needs into the planning mechanism. In other words, instead of the hit or miss, private and public pattern of manipulative and exploitative aid as provided now, concern with a modernizing society's overseas debts, balance of payments, and welfare and industrializing needs would be built into the considerations of professionals in the industrial country. Because of the interlocking web of relationships, such decisions would require participation by members in the more professional and interest-group roles in modernizing societies. In this way the relationship between industrial and modernizing societies can help to reduce the derivativeness of the latter by strengthening the roles and institutions favoring more rapid industrialization.

Hence we can expect that a kind of "psychological" marginality will emerge and spread to modernizing societies, particularly to those where roles are most directly linked to those in industrial societies. This psychological marginality will embody new consummatory values pertaining to individualism, privacy, autonomy. Older forms of socialism in the last analysis can accept such values only in some penultimate stage. But there is little doubt that whatever form the transformation takes, it will provide the basis for new confrontations.

A fundamental change in the use of property combined with new methods of political participation will need to be found, more in keeping with the need for high information and its utilization. The fact that this makes social life a scientific problem should not deter us. It is politics that makes science moral. Hopefully such a point of view can turn our attention once again to the question of the mechanisms that will allow us to deal in a more equitable manner with the functional needs and work of people and enable them to participate more effectively in an increasingly complex world. The dialectical consequences will continue to define our humanity.

Index